A WHIFF OF BURNT BOATS

GEOFFREY TREASE

Girls Gone By Publishers

COMPLETE AND UNABRIDGED

Published by

Girls Gone By Publishers
4 Rock Terrace
Coleford
Bath
Somerset
BA3 5NF

First published by Macmillan and Co Ltd 1971
This edition published 2009
Text and photographs © the literary estate of Geoffrey Trease
Preface © Jocelyn Payne 2009
Geoffrey Trease's Early Writings © Sally Dore 2009
Publishing History © Clarissa Cridland 2009
Note on the Text and Illustrations © Sarah Woodall 2009
Design and Layout © Girls Gone By Publishers 2009

Typeset in England by Little Pink Cloud Limited
Printed in England by CPI Antony Rowe

ISBN 978-1-84745-071-5

Geoffrey Trease in 1939

CONTENTS

PREFACE

This first part of my father's autobiography concludes with the early days of the Second World War when I was only three years old, so naturally I cannot claim to share these early memories of his childhood and youth. However, once the war was over and he returned home to settle in our house in Abingdon I was old enough to take an interest in his work. I used to enjoy listening to him exploring ideas for the current story, or future ones, and most days he would read the latest chapter, which would be a treat after my homework was completed. He would also tell me about the schools he had visited to talk about his books and the questions some of the children had asked. I sometimes heard him talk to pupils and students and saw that he was an instinctive teacher, mingling plenty of humour with serious content.

Just as I was leaving school in 1954 we moved to Colwall and the Malvern Hills, where my parents remained until the 1980s when they returned to Bath to live next door to me. During their many happy years in Colwall I was less able to share in his day-to-day preoccupations, as I was thoroughly immersed in my own, having left home to go to university, which was swiftly followed by marriage and motherhood. Our meetings were less frequent and our conversations usually distracted by four small girls who had their own agendas when in the company of their loving and much-loved grandparents. His weekly letters, however, were always a joy, full of interest about the latest book, hopes, and sometimes disappointments, as well as entertaining accounts of proposed holidays, usually for research, and visits from family and friends. Sometimes he would combine a visit to London with an overnight stay, which would enable us to have a more relaxed conversation about his work.

That said, I have no memories of discussions about the writing of *A Whiff of Burnt Boats* in its early stages in the late 1960s. When he told me about its forthcoming publication (in 1971) I remember feeling slightly apprehensive. Over the years I had grown used to the occasional recognition of elements of character or incidents, but so carefully woven into the fiction and transposed in time and place that they caused no embarrassment. I expect many relatives of an autobiographer must feel concern when the writer reveals family history, even though, in our case, there were no exciting skeletons to uncover. Memories may be vivid or hazy but are inevitably subjective, and most people do not expect to find themselves in print as viewed and recollected by one particular member of the clan.

I think my father must have anticipated my hesitation, because he quickly reassured me that his objective was not to provide detailed descriptions and anecdotes about family and friends except in so far as he felt they had contributed to his development as a writer. The influence of inspiring schoolmasters during his schooldays provided the intellectual stimulus he needed to develop an interest in books and writing. His family gave him confidence and the freedom to pursue his own goals even if they were sometimes unconventional ones.

As the wording of this book's dedication to Marian, my mother, makes clear, she never sought the limelight herself, but her sensitive observations enabled him to reflect on the effect some of his anecdotes might have on other members of the family. I believe some of them, as I did, had reservations in anticipation, but I have no record that any individual relative was ultimately unhappy with the family memories he evoked. Many, indeed, seemed greatly diverted by them!

On reading the autobiography myself I was delighted to realise that he had provided us in the early chapters with a wonderful kaleidoscope of family history, including affectionate cameo portraits of grandparents, aunts, uncles and cousins, many now long gone but with an influence that lingers still. Some of the succeeding generations have spread far and wide but many remain in Nottingham, and the family wine business is still owned and run by my cousins, now into the fifth generation. It is still in the same premises, with the cellars cut into the rock that many Trease children remember, and that feature, disguised of course, in his children's story *Flight of Angels* (Macmillan 1990).

Unlike my cousins who were born and lived in Nottingham, I should probably never have understood the family and its traditions had my mother and I not spent the war years living with my grandmother at 142 Portland Road with regular visits to Great Granny and the Aunts in Waterloo Crescent. My father's vivid anecdotes of his childhood in the same settings enrich my own childhood memories in retrospect.

Browsing through some of the many letters that my father received in response to publication has made it clear to me that sharing and comparing personal memories provide an impetus for reading autobiographies. Many of the letters were from friends and fellow writers, often commenting on work in progress and other personal news, but others were from acquaintances, or strangers even, with whom the book had struck a chord of shared memory. One, a neighbour in Portland Road and, I suspect, older than my father, recalled the early 1900s: 'Your mother was so elegant and beautiful and we thought her no end of a lady' and 'Your dog was Jim to us and the words "dog" and "Jim" were synonymous to me. I see every hair of him now, snuffling round our gate.' An old school friend wrote: 'I share a great deal of the experience that is recorded at firsthand and this is most enjoyable in retrospect, as much of it was at the time.' A greatly treasured letter came nearly forty years after his undergraduate days, and was inscribed on the envelope: 'Sir, I should be grateful if this letter could be forwarded to Mr Trease from his old servant when he was at Oxford.' Inside, this affectionately remembered College scout explained: 'I am your redfaced little Welshman Thomas, who, if I may say had the pleasure of looking after you when you first came up to Queen's.'

I think this book encapsulates for me what shaped my father before I knew him. (By the time I was old enough to understand his aspirations he was already becoming established.) I had not realised how single-minded he had needed to be, from his early childhood, to pursue his ambition to be a writer, or how many bitter disappointments and setbacks he had to overcome. There were no dramatic tragedies, as in my mother's early life, but there can surely be nothing so lonely for the aspiring writer as the rejection of one's efforts. He took some enormous risks, in the eyes of many, but this, together with his innate optimism, gave him the drive to prove that he could, and would, eventually succeed.

Jocelyn Payne
2009

GEOFFREY TREASE'S EARLY WRITINGS

Geoffrey's autobiography makes it clear how much he wanted to be a writer from an early age. His first publication was the proverbial 'slim volume of poetry', entitled *The Supreme Prize* (1926), which was privately published at great, and partly unexpected, expense to himself. *A Whiff of Burnt Boats* contains his description of this salutary event (see pp70–4), which he later used in *Black Banner Players*—but there he gave the hero, Bill, unlike his young self, the chance to realise what a rip-off the whole affair was before it was too late to back out.

In 1933, with the support of his new wife, Marian, Geoffrey took the decision to try to make a living as a full-time author. He contrived to do so for the rest of his career, apart from the period of the Second World War and its aftermath. When he began his career as a children's novelist his books were very unusual in the overtly left-wing slant with which they were written, at a time when the vast majority of books for children were very much in favour of maintaining the status quo. In *A Whiff of Burnt Boats* he remarks: 'My becoming a children's writer was an accident, for it was in politics, not children, that I was then mainly interested. I wrote because there was something I wanted to say' (p130). He described the prevailing ethos, particularly in historical fiction, as 'the Henty values—the glories of war, the superiority of the British Empire and a white skin, the inferiority of the female … You sided with the Cavaliers against the Roundheads, the French aristocrats against the howling mob. The working class were tolerated only if faithful retainers' (*Sixty Years On*). It was in reaction to this norm that he began his career.

In rather bizarre contrast to the other early publications of his career, one of Geoffrey's very first pieces, perhaps arising out of a need to pay the bills, was a pretty traditional serial. *The New House at Hardale* is a rather conventional boys' boarding-school story, written as a serial for the *Boy's Own Paper* in 1934 before being published in book form nearly two decades later. The clear politics of Geoffrey's other early writing meant that at first his books were brought out by avowedly left-wing publishers like Martin Lawrence (later Lawrence and Wishart), with one book, *Red Comet* (1936), even appearing first in Moscow. A Lawrence paperback edition of *Bows against the Barons* (1934), Geoffrey's first book for children, has an explanation of the publisher's aims on the back cover: 'Nearly all books written to amuse children take very good care to build up only that point of view which will be acceptable to their employers in later life. This means that parents who hold views inimical to the existing regime are hard put to it to find literature which will not stifle the minds of their children but which will not deprive them of the excitements they naturally demand.' (See p131.)

Bows against the Barons was a re-telling of the famous story local to Geoffrey's home town of Nottingham, that of Robin Hood. In Geoffrey's novel he was a rather more hero-of-the-proletariat Robin than the traditional figure of legend, a difference indicated immediately by the frontispiece of an outlaw's dead body hanging high from a tree in Sherwood Forest (see p137); as the author himself observed several decades later, 'My outlaws talked round their camp-fire like a Communist Party cell' (*Sixty Years On*). His second book, *Comrades for the Charter* (1935), about the Chartist struggle in the 1840s, was a story similarly lending itself to his vision of the heroism of the ordinary people struggling to become freer. *The Call to Arms* (1935) is about three young people frustrating the attempts of Big Business to foment war between two South American countries in order to obtain access to oil supplies, while *Missing from Home* (1937) was a contemporary story where two middle-class children who run away from an uncongenial uncle find themselves sympathising with the working people they encounter who are organising a strike to challenge unfair actions by their bosses.

Geoffrey wrote some short stories which display the same left-wing stance as his children's novels, and, not fitting the prevailing ethos of children's literature, these again found a home in annuals that were known for their left-wing slant, such as *Martin's Annual*, produced by Trease's

" HE'S FOR US, OF COURSE, COMRADES ! "

Frontispiece from The Call to Arms

early publisher, Martin Lawrence. The influence of Russia is visually clear in the illustrations of these annuals, which take their style from the posters of the Bolshevik Revolution. The contents lack subtlety, to say the least (one poem by Gertrude Ring contains the memorable lines: 'The world is still closed to us./ Still we proletarian children learn how things will change,/ How our big Red brothers will conquer the power in the world;/ We also will become fighters'). However, they are very clearly afire with a hatred of injustice and a vision of a better world (usually allied with an admiration for a Russia that seemed, at least from a distance, to be on its way to achieving this), views outside the mainstream in the 1930s but widespread enough to support publishing ventures such as these annuals and the famous Left Book Club, for example. Without the space for characterisation and more complex plotting, Geoffrey's stories in these annuals, although fascinating as period pieces, do not indicate much promise as a writer. They are much cruder than his novels of the same period, since the few hundred words are spent driving a point home with a sledgehammer. 'Men Who March By', for example, contrasts a recruiting parade for the army with the passage of hunger marchers. Tommy's elder brother is about to go to the recruiting office, and Tommy 'didn't want a brother who was a traitor to his class,' so he asks a neighbour, Mr Barnes, to come and have a word with Bob; Mr Barnes tells Bob 'that a fine strapping fellow like himself ought to line up in the working-class

Two illustrations from Geoffrey Trease short stories that appeared in Martin's Annual*:*
'The Man Who Fought for Freedom' (left) and 'Men Who March By' (right)

struggle, not under the Union Jack which stood for war and tyranny.' It is not until Bob sees the hunger marchers themselves, though, that he sees the light. Another story, 'Comrades of the Chelyuskin' (illustrated on the front of the annual, which is reproduced on the back cover of this book), is an account of a Russian expedition to the Arctic; the Chelyuskin is ripped apart by ice, but the expedition members evacuate to the ice floe and calmly continue their scientific work while awaiting rescue because 'Communists do not despair.' 'The Man Who Fought for Freedom', about the Civil War, is an interesting piece of work, since one supposes at the beginning that Geoffrey is going to extol the virtues of Oliver Cromwell; however, the main character ends up being executed as a Leveller in the cause of the freedom of the common man, and 'Oliver Cromwell, the real traitor, rode haughtily away.'

As Geoffrey grew more experienced and more sophisticated as a writer, the overtly political tone of his writing (what he later referred to as the 'crude partisan stand-point') was softened considerably. A major influence must surely also have been the fact that he was trying to be a professional writer, and so needed to turn his hand to writing for various markets in order to make a living. His books became unthreatening enough to be published by mainstream publishers, firstly A & C Black, and then Blackwell, Heinemann and Macmillan, among others. By this stage, A & C Black felt comfortable enough to claim him as 'a pioneer of the new, true-to-life style of fiction for young readers'. (This is from the blurb of *Mystery on the Moors*, 1937.)

Illustrations from Mystery on the Moors—*'"Come on," he yelled, "run for your lives."'*
(above left) and '"Ye've no right to camp here, ye know."' (above right)—and from
Detectives of the Dales—*'The N.W. Yorkshire Dales' (below left) and 'Luckily the man*
with the newspaper showed no sign of settling down.' (below right)

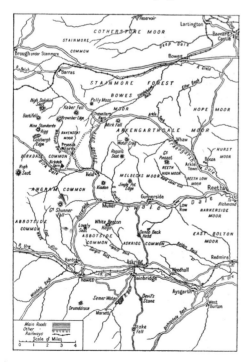

The A & C Black publications in the later 1930s were children's mystery stories, *Mystery on the Moors* and *The Christmas Holiday Mystery* in 1937 and *Detectives of the Dales* in 1938 (*The Christmas Holiday Mystery* was later republished under the title of *The Lakeland Mystery*). In 1935 Geoffrey had published a little book called *Walking in England,* in which he expounded on the glories of the country and the enjoyment of walking in it, and the same enthusiasm for the countryside, its beauty and variety, is evident in these books. Two of them are accompanied by very detailed maps (of the Moors, the area around Buxton and Bakewell in Derbyshire, and of the Dales in Yorkshire), and Geoffrey's introduction to *Mystery on the Moors* says: 'This book can also be used as a game. Every clue except the first can be solved before you read on to the account of its solution by the young detectives. All you

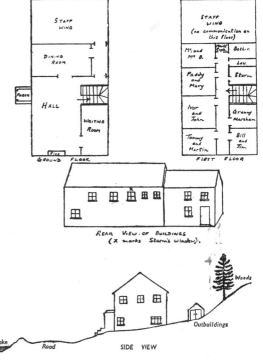

Illustrations from The Lakeland Mystery

need is a good map … and a guide-book … The game can even be played in the actual country, on foot or on bicycle, if someone else is willing to be Uncle Andrew, and lay the clues.' The dedication is 'For Jocelyn and all who love maps, mysteries and mountains.'

With *In the Land of the Mogul* (Blackwell, 1938), however, Geoffrey hit upon the type of excellently researched, highly readable historical novel for children which was to be the cornerstone of his reputation. He later noted: 'I began writing for children in revulsion against the sentimental romanticism then pervading historical fiction.' The sort of authenticity that Geoffrey made de rigueur among historical novelists was in the 1930s a novelty, and in place of the prevailing 'gadzookery' he used ordinary modern English, to convey the idea that those living in each period are modern to themselves. Margery Fisher, remarking that he was not the first historical novelist to present the case for the ordinary man, said: 'Trease's effect upon children, and upon the course of historical writing for children, has all the same been much greater than that of earlier writers, because of his gift for choosing his subject so as to show that past and present are comparable, interacting, interdependent' (*Intent Upon Reading*).

Although best known for his children's books, Geoffrey had always written also for adults, and he continued to hope that he could establish a reputation as an adult novelist. His early book of short stories, *The Unsleeping Sword* (1934—the title is a reference to Blake's poem 'Jerusalem': 'Nor shall my sword sleep in my hand …'), is in the same vein as his early children's books, and published by the same firm, Martin Lawrence. It deals topically with Black Shirts and hunger

This page and opposite: illustrations from In the Land of the Mogul

Illustrations from In the Land of the Mogul

marchers, with unemployment and its impact on young lovers, with the problems of illegitimate babies and botched abortions, and the answer, it says (again with little subtlety), is socialism. But as his writing for children matured, so did that for adults. In 1939 and 1940 he produced two novels, *Such Divinity* and *Only Natural,* both well-received, the second of which earned a very favourable review from George Orwell, among others. He also managed to turn his love of the theatre to good account, writing one-act plays in particular for both adults and children. *The Dragon Who Was Different* (1938) is a collection of plays for children, while one play for adults, *After the Tempest*, was chosen for publication in the 1938 annual volume of *Best One-Act Plays*. It concerns four people who have been marooned on a desert island for twenty years, during which the one-year-old girl among them has grown up and horrifies the other three by consorting with the 'natives' and viewing them as sensible and equal. When a young airwoman lands her aeroplane, however, they discover that the world has suffered a destructive war and pandemic, and that not only is London in ruins, but Eton has gone co-educational! A full-length play, *Colony*, was well reviewed, and was about to transfer to the West End in September 1939. Not only did the war cancel those transfer plans, but bombs completely destroyed the stocks of his two novels held in the publisher's warehouse (hence their present extreme rarity). After the war he continued to write for adults, producing two more novels and some non-fiction, but it was as a children's author that he was becoming pre-eminent.

Sally Dore
2009

PUBLISHING HISTORY

A Whiff of Burnt Boats was published by Macmillan in 1971. As far as we know, no other edition was ever produced.

Clarissa Cridland
2009

NOTE ON THE TEXT AND ILLUSTRATIONS

For this Girls Gone By edition we have used the text of the first edition, which contained very few typographical errors. The only amendments we have made in the text are to italicise '*Wuthering Heights*' on page 76 and to change 'Five Year Plan' to 'Five-year Plan' on page 119 to match the usage elsewhere. We have also corrected the publication date of *Red Comet* in the list on pages 162–3. We hope we have not introduced any new errors.

The capitalisation of *Bows against the Barons* was inconsistent (its first paperback edition, for example, has 'Against' on the front and 'against' on the title page and the back). We have standardised on 'against' for all occurrences of it in this book. *The Call to Arms* had no 'The' on its dustwrapper, though one was present on its title page and running heads. We have used 'The' in all occurrences in new text in this book, and have inserted it in the list on pages 162–3, but have not altered the informal mention of the title on page 141.

The illustrations that appeared in the original are the photographs on pages 26, 82 and 146, the 1939 portrait of Geoffrey Trease that appears on our front cover and as the frontispiece, 'The British Boys' Magazine' (p65) and a late-1940s portrait photograph of Marian Trease, which we have not included in this book because it would be more appropriately used as an illustration for the *second* volume of her husband's autobiography, *Laughter at the Door* (we have substituted the 1920s portrait that appears on p126).

We have added several new illustrations, including family photographs and illustrations from early books by Geoffrey Trease.

We have reproduced the original captions below the illustrations that came from the first edition (with minor amendments to the punctuation), but have used shortened versions of some of them in our List of Illustrations.

The front cover of this edition shows, in the upper row (left to right), the front of the paperback edition of *Bows against the Barons* (1934), the title page of *Red Comet* (1936) and the dustwrapper of *Mystery on the Moors* (1937); and at the bottom (left to right) the dustwrapper of *Detectives of the Dales* (1938), the front cover of *Walking in England* (1935) and the dustwrapper of *In the Land of the Mogul* (1938). The back cover shows (top to bottom) the front board of *The Dragon Who Was Different* (1938); the front cover of *Martin's Annual* (illustrating an incident from one of Trease's short stories, 'Comrades of the Chelyuskin', which appears inside); the dustwrapper of *The Call to Arms* (1935) and that of *The Lakeland Mystery* (the post-war reprint of *The Christmas Holiday Mystery* (1937)).

Sarah Woodall, with thanks to Sarah Mash
2009

A Whiff
of Burnt Boats

GEOFFREY TREASE

FOR MARIAN

at her own insistence

a shadowy figure

in these pages

but in life

not so

Contents

List of Illustrations

Acknowledgements

THE author is indebted to Mr Garry Hogg, the Reverend Professor Robert Leaney, and the representatives of the late H.G. Wells and George Orwell respectively, for permission to quote from their previously unpublished letters to him. He would similarly like to express his thanks to Mr James Lees-Milne and Messrs Hamish Hamilton Ltd for permission to quote from *Another Self* and to the representatives of the late W.B. Yeats and Messrs Macmillan & Co. Ltd for the lines from 'The Scholars' in *Later Poems*.

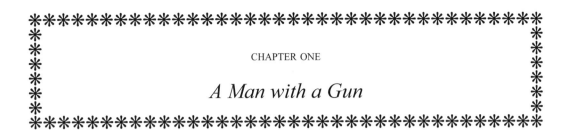

CHAPTER ONE

A Man with a Gun

MY writing began before I knew one letter from another. I sat at a little oblong table, its top chequered for chess, which just fitted the recess between the lace-curtained window and the fireplace with its blaze of best bright coals from the pits on the city boundary. Soft gaslight fell from the globe over the mantelshelf. If I crossed the room, I was still far too small to test that shadow across my father's newspaper which in later years would bring a predictable grunt of irritation.

Before me lay a voluminous and virginal desk-diary which he had brought home for me from the office, a handsome wine-and-spirit-trade production, fat with introductory pages extolling (I now suppose) this shipper's port and that château's sauternes. What mattered was the delectable acreage of plain white pages that followed, unsullied by anything save the printed days of the week. It was for this that the diaries were passed on to me, to scribble in. And scribble I did, the pencil clenched, the small fist moving ceaselessly across the paper, covering line after line and page after page with squiggly 'pretend writing' meaningless to anyone but myself. I was making up stories, muttering the words I did not yet know how to represent, mouthing them silently if an impatient rustle of newspaper reminded me that I was not alone. Somehow I had already acquired the notion that a story did not really exist until it was written down. I could not write in that sense, but I did what I could. I had got the idea. I was infected for life.

Perhaps matters would have developed differently if I had experienced the joys of oral story-telling. But my father was a remote and unintentionally alarming figure, and my mother, who was later to entrance my own daughter with a gift for story-telling that came to me as a revelation, was far too busy to exercise her talent when I was a child. My two elder brothers did not fill the gap, and there were no younger children to provide a captive audience which might have inspired me to perform myself. I can recall only one person who made up and told me stories, and that was the exotic Sleggs, but he came a little later, by which time the printed book was irremovably enthroned at the centre of my world.

I was read to, certainly. Not by my parents but by Grandma Dale. She was, strictly speaking, my mother's stepmother. She lived in a cottage with a brook flowing in front of it, near the River Dove in Staffordshire, and several times a year she would visit us on mysterious business, 'to sign her papers'. This, as I discovered at a precocious age, was merely to collect her allowance from some charitable fund for doctors' widows, which she preferred to do discreetly in Nottingham rather than let her straitened circumstances be suspected in the village. We used to joke about Grandma Dale, her anxiously preserved gentility and the elevated tone in which she alluded to 'the Rectory' as though it were Buckingham Palace, but her patient reading aloud gave me my first taste of books.

Here, again, being the youngest child profoundly influenced that taste. My brothers' preferences dictated her choice. George was my elder by seven years, Bill by four. They wanted Ballantyne, and the earliest stories I remember are *Coral Island*, *Martin Rattler*, and *The Gorilla Hunters*. I have also the most vivid and affectionate memories of the *Chatterbox Annual*, our 1914 Christmas present. I recall not only the cover, with its scarlet-coated soldier and its more topical frontispiece of dreadnoughts and searchlights, but its long serials, scattered in sections throughout the volume, 'Tanglewood Trails' about young emigrants to Canada and a family story called 'The Harum-Scarum Carls'. I was then barely five-and-a-half (I was born on 11 August 1909, so that this memory can be pinpointed) but I do not recollect ever being mystified or bored.

Geoffrey, George and Bill Trease in 1912

A price had to be paid, as I realised only in later life, for this precocious sharing in my elders' pleasures. Those sessions gave no scope for childish fantasy. George and Bill would not have tolerated Beatrix Potter, then at the height of her powers, or *The Wind in the Willows*, published a year before I was born. E. Nesbit was unknown to us. And I was fourteen when my outraged Classics master almost blew me out of my desk with his bellow: 'What, boy, you have never read *Through the Looking Glass*? Go home and read it at once!' The whole rich field of fantasy was unknown to me and had to be discovered from adolescence onwards, with the result that blind spots were to remain for ever in my critical appreciation, and that some highly regarded authors, such as Tolkien, are still to me unreadable, except as a task. Those massive premature injections of Ballantyne, Henty, Kingston, Gordon Stables, *The Swiss Family Robinson*, and the *Boy's Own Paper* made me an addict of the adventure story. I acquired as a reader, or more strictly as a listener, the bias which was to determine my direction long afterwards as a writer.

I must have been bombarded with words and ideas I did not understand, but I seem to have responded to the stimulus. I was attracted by uncomprehended phrases. I was found once with an improvised seesaw, on either end of which I had placed several volumes of the encyclopaedia. Asked what I was doing, I remember answering, 'What Dad does at the office—balancing the books.' I was a somewhat solemn and very literal-minded little boy.

My father ran the family's small wine-and-spirit business in the centre of Nottingham. 'The office' was at No. 1 Castle Gate, the narrow once-fashionable Georgian street leading up to the Castle on its sandstone precipice. Some doors higher up was the surgical-appliance firm at which D.H. Lawrence had recently done his brief stint as a clerk, and Byron's boyhood lodging was not far away. Dad's office had a discreet frontage, the two windows no more blatant than a solicitor's with their GEORGE TREASE AND SON. Inside, however, there was a counter backed by dozens of horizontal bottles. The business was both retail and wholesale— for those who knew of its existence. Behind a frosted-glass partition stood a rolltop desk and a safe, which used to remind me, as I squatted on a stool beside it, sipping soda water and munching cracknel biscuits, of a small black oven that had somehow strayed from a kitchen range. In this inner sanctum I would sometimes be left alone, to watch—apprehensively— the telephone standing upright on the top of the desk. If it woke suddenly to shrill, terrifying life, I must dash in quest of my father, who might be upstairs in the stock-rooms or far down in the cellars. Like most of the cellars in the old part of the town these were man-made caves, supplementing the natural honeycomb of caverns that underlies Nottingham and was remarked upon by Defoe and Celia Fiennes.

The inconspicuous exterior of the Castle Gate establishment reflected both my father's personal horror of self-advertisement in any form and the reluctance of my grandmother and my three maiden aunts to remind the world that their tall house in Waterloo Crescent and their family pew at All Saints' were maintained on the profits of the liquor trade. Castle Gate was acceptable, so long as the place did not look like a wine-shop. But just round the corner in Lister Gate, and connected with the 'office' by a minute backyard, were premises on which the stuff could be not only wholesaled and retailed but visibly and with frank enjoyment consumed. The family connection was disguised by retaining the name of the previous owner for this side of the business and the bar was known as Weaver's Vaults.

To us children, of course, the Vaults were forbidden territory, and my own memories are restricted to the little cubby-hole in the office behind the frosted glass, where I was permitted to dip into the biscuit-tin, squirt my own drink from the siphon, and take the stamps off the violet-inked envelopes from the shippers of Bordeaux. In this narrow space, half-filled with the rolltop desk, my father received special customers, old cronies and honoured visitors—a country parson who shared his passion for shooting, a farmer from over the Leicestershire border, the police superintendent, or the brace of nuns who knew that he was always good for a donation. His own religious views were undefined. He was of that common English type eulogised at their funerals as 'true Christian gentlemen', the clergyman usually looking round the church with a defensive smile as if to add, 'I know as well as you do that he never went to church, but he was a nice kindly man and even I can't pretend he was any the worse for it.' My father's nearest thing to a religious prejudice was an understandable coolness towards 'chapel folk', whom he equated with 'teetotal jokers'.

He was a dapper, some might have said 'perky', little man, with twinkling eyes which could gush tears of laughter, a fresh complexion, a neatly clipped moustache of the kind favoured early in the century, and a broad high brow which did not in fact denote any intellectual tendency. He would have been taller and athletic like his younger brothers, keen oarsmen, bicyclists and golfers, but for a tragic spinal injury when he was four. Grandfather Trease was then managing the Loughborough brewery, with a house on the premises. Playing hide-and-seek, my father crouched in an empty cask in the yard, and a bigger boy, not knowing he was there, jumped in on top of him. As a result, my father's childhood was punctuated with bouts of pain and ill-health, and he grew up a stocky man, erect in carriage and brisk of step, but with something of a hump, if you looked for it, between his shoulderblades.

Debarred from the strenuous games of the grammar school, he turned the more keenly to the outdoor sports he could enjoy, shooting and fishing, and just plain walking on Sundays or in the close season. The fishing he had given up by the time I was born, so that he could concentrate on his first love, the gun. He did not care for summer holidays. The 1914 war offered a convenient excuse for not taking them, and we had just two family holidays in all my childhood, at Bridlington in 1919 and on the Lincolnshire coast a year later. He never quite fancied a meal prepared by any hand except my mother's or his sisters'. Our own maid was not trusted to cut him a slice of bread-and-butter. So, instead of the unwanted fortnight by the sea, he staggered his holiday throughout the shooting season, taking the whole day off each Tuesday and Thursday.

These 'shooting days' opened with the ritual anointment of my father's boots with dubbin, the scent of which threw the dog into controlled ecstasies of anticipation. We always had a large liver and white spaniel, which lived in a kennel in the yard. Spot, Jim and Roy were so similar in appearance that neighbours hardly noticed the replacement of one by another. We never had them as puppies. They came young but trained to the gun by a keeper. Officially they never came into the house, but on those autumn mornings when the boots stood ready in the kitchen and the game-bag with its rich leathery smell was dangling from the hallstand they would sneak in and stretch themselves at the foot of the stairs, ready for the descent of the Master, whimpering with apprehension lest they be left behind.

The Master's descent was seldom early. He worked late, always going back to the Vaults at night to see that they were closed at the legal hour, and in compensation breakfasting about ten the next day. He would come down at about the same time on shooting days and then set off for the railway-station, complete with gun in its tan-coloured cover, game-bag, burberry and brown leggings, and of course the dog at heel. It was a pleasant sight on any day to see that dog's perfect discipline. On many ordinary days it would accompany Dad to Castle Gate, and with never a backward glance (which would have been a professional reflection upon a self-respecting gun-dog) he would stride through the eddying traffic of the biggest market square in England, knowing that the spaniel was never more than a pace behind.

Dad was, as I now understand, a frustrated countryman, never so happy as in the company of working farmers, game-keepers and the like. It was natural enough. His mother was a farmer's daughter and the Loughborough of his schooldays was a little market town with

Charnwood Forest and the Quorn country close at hand. The family's move to Nottingham was a kind of exile. My grandmother continued to take the *Loughborough Monitor* for another half-century and my father rented his shoots on farms near the county boundary, halfway home to his birthplace.

He went alone or with a single companion, at first an old man of eighty, whom I recall as a skeletal Father Time-like figure, with a long gun instead of a scythe, and the alleged habit of pouring whisky into his boots, presumably to harden his feet against blisters. In later years the companion was the parson already mentioned. Careful in all things, my father was particularly fastidious in his choice of company when out with a gun. He was not going to have his head blown off by an excitable sharpshooter or clumsy scrambler over stiles.

He was a fine shot, I am told. He would come home in the wintry dusk, laden with a mere selection of his kill, the spaniel, happy, weary and covered with burrs, still faithful at his heels. 'There's a brace of pheasants,' he might say, 'and this hare for Mother'—his mother, that meant—'and these partridges.' He had shot a leveret, too, but given it to the railway porter at the village station he used. There had been rabbits and woodpigeon: they had been distributed to farm labourers or roadmen or cottage housewives encountered during the day. Sport would have been poor indeed if he had been able to bring everything home. He himself would never eat a bite of anything he had shot. We others enjoyed the pheasants and partridges, but were content to let the hares and rabbits, so soft and pathetic in death, go to Grandma Trease and the aunts. Sometimes he fumbled in his burberry pocket and laid a handful of fresh mushrooms on the kitchen table. 'I found these for the Kipper.' That was the nearest to a pet-name he ever gave me.

The Leicestershire farming connection was all on his mother's side. The Treases believed themselves Cornish, and I know now that until the end of the eighteenth century the family lived in a relatively small area of east Cornwall, occasionally straying into Devon. They spelt their name Trease, Treise, Trees, Treize, Treaze, Trese and half a dozen other ways but never 'Treece', thereby distinguishing two sounds and two names that are sometimes confused. They bore agreeable Christian names like Flower and Thomasine, they married people like John Menheniot, Degory Ruell and Margery Daw, and they lived out their quiet lives as yeomen, carpenters and the like in tiny places remote from England—in St Endelion or Egloskerry or Poundstock, where my great-grandfather John was born in 1797. It was he who, entering the Excise, moved out into the world, first to Plymouth, then Burton-upon-Trent. His son's management of the Loughborough Brewery was a natural sequel. This son, my grandfather George, went to Nottingham about 1890 and set up as a wine merchant on his own account. My father, as eldest son, joined him, whereas Uncle Billy became a stockbroker on the Nottingham Exchange and Uncle Jack an accountant.

By a coincidence fortunate for me my mother's family reached the city about the same time. She was a Yorkshire woman, born at Yarm near the Durham border. Her father, Frederick Dale, was an Edinburgh M.D. His own father and grandfather had been doctors too, riding round a bleak country practice on the banks of the Tees. Thus the two families converged on the city in which I was to be born. Alcohol and medicine came together and, in my veins at least, turned to ink.

CHAPTER TWO

Portland Road

MOTHER'S name was Florence, an obvious choice for a doctor's daughter born in 1874, but nobody ever called her anything but Floss. She was dark with a curled fringe. My father, himself so sanguine of complexion, used to tease her with suggestions of a gipsy strain. She was a pretty girl. He fell in love with her at first sight.

They met on an excursion train to London. Mother was going up to spend the day with one of her current 'admirers', an interesting reminder that respectable late Victorian girls had more freedom to travel alone than is sometimes realised. She always vowed, when she retold the story, that she was surprised by the coincidence when Dad happened to enter her compartment on the return journey that night. Thereafter he laid patient siege. She was not to be won easily, and he always preserved one of her prim little notes, declining an invitation 'because of a prior engagement'. Eventually he mustered courage to propose. 'An unusual name, Trease,' he remarked diffidently. 'Would you like it?' And after seemly hesitation she admitted that she would. The first time he took her home to tea to meet his mother and sisters he instructed his brothers to go out and stay out. At that stage of his courtship he was risking no competition.

Yet in my own recollection it is my father who emerges as the confident, though prudent, character and my mother as the pessimistic distruster of change. One of my earliest datable memories is of the outbreak of war in 1914. Dad marched into the house, brisk and excited. The police and the fire brigade were volunteering, horses were being commandeered. The Germans would try to starve us out, so he had just bought a whole sack of flour and the ironmonger would shortly be delivering a brand-new dustbin in which to store it. He was only acting like a responsible paterfamilias, the conception of the unpatriotic food-hoarder being as yet unborn. The flour (together with a whole ham and a cupboardful of tinned food) merely exemplified his prudence. His usual confidence showed itself in his assurance that the war would be won by Christmas. Mother, by contrast, retained until late in 1918 an uneasy feeling that the Germans would still beat us.

God knows—and I do, now—she had some excuse for her tendency to look on the dark side. Life had not used the Dales as kindly as the Treases up to then. Her father had lost his first wife early and his second while her four children were still small. Grandma Dale, who read us Ballantyne, was his third. He had never been a wealthy or fashionable doctor. Possibly the two bereavements made him restless, or, as I suspect, there was a mercurial element in the Dales which was later to counterbalance the stolid temperament of the Treases. Anyhow, he seems to have moved about during Mother's girlhood, and then finally come to rest in a suburb of Nottingham where his patients were largely factory-workers and their families.

There was no fortune to be made there. One of Mother's brothers went to Saskatchewan, took up a prairie farm, and never recrossed the Atlantic. The other successively tried Africa and Canada, but returned empty-handed. Whether my grandfather was forward-looking for his generation or just unable to support daughters in genteel idleness, he decided that Mother too must be able to fend for herself, and she became one of Mrs Webster's young ladies. Mrs Webster, whom I remember as a formidably furred matriarch who visited our home in my childhood, ran a high-class dress-shop and milliner's, since absorbed into Griffin & Spalding's big department store. Mother used to look back upon her years 'in business' as a golden interlude. Soon the troubles of the Dales began again. Her much-loved sister, married to a wholesale chemist in Liverpool, died young of diabetes, then a fatal disease, and her father, whom I can dimly recall as a kindly man in a sort of light-coloured top-hat, who spun pennies on a polished table for my amusement, died painfully of cancer. Small wonder that Mother, by the time I remember her, had lost the lightness of heart which had captivated my father in that London excursion train in the 1890s.

They had married in 1901 and set up house at 13 Chaucer Street, a mere five-minute uphill walk from the Market Place. My brothers were duly born and christened, appropriately for

The wedding of Geoffrey Trease's parents, 1901
Seated at the front (left to right): Ethel Trease, the bride and two friends. Standing behind them (left to right): an unidentified lady; William Trease (the best man); Minnie Trease; the bridegroom with his father and mother just behind him; the bride's father and stepmother; Jack and Daisy Trease; the bride's brother; two unidentified guests

142 Portland Road, Nottingham

the period, George Edward and Frederick William. When I arrived my mother hankered after a name just faintly more adventurous and pleaded for 'Geoffrey', though I doubt if the association with Chaucer influenced her thinking. My father thought it rather fancy—he himself, born in 1873, was almost inevitably an Albert—but he gave way to her on condition that a solid 'Robert' be placed in front of it.

My own memories start with their third home, 142 Portland Road, a tall semi-detached house close to the Arboretum, in a then quietish residential neighbourhood where Victorian Nottingham had at last burst its banks and flooded over the ancient common lands. In summer the music from the Arboretum band-stand would steal through our open windows and I would run to tell Mother: 'They're playing your favourite—*The Gondoliers*!' It was an area of billowing greenery and steep roads named after famous people, Tennyson, Burns, Addison, Raleigh, Cromwell, or in our case one of the local dukes. On the ridge northwards the High School raised its sandstone tower and battlements, and three times a day its strident bell made itself heard all over that part of the city. George was already wearing the plain black cap with the badge of the three merles, and one day I should too.

It was a three-storey house. At the top were three rooms with slanting ceilings, hot in summer from the closeness of the slates. In the middle one, known as 'the store room', were old trunks and discarded algebra textbooks and copies of *Henry V*. Here, laid out on clean newspaper, were the russets and Blenheim Oranges and Coxes that came in a hamper from a local farm. Here were massively bound volumes of the *Illustrated London News* covering the Crimean and Franco-Prussian Wars, with contemporary accounts of the Charge of the Light Brigade and the Paris Commune, and vigorous line-drawings, all puffs of cannon-smoke, solid blocks of infantry, brandished sabres, rearing chargers, urbane staff-officers with telescopes, and cannon-balls littering the ground like fallen fruit. There was rich food for my imagination in that attic.

At one time or another I slept in each of the other four rooms upstairs—the changes dictated by visitors, childhood illnesses, George's eventual departure to study in London, and whether we had a maid living in—but memory centres in the little back room at the top, with its lofty view of the city skyline and the intervening glimpse of treetops which were only in the General Cemetery down the hill but from my eyrie looked like a continuous woodland. From down there, once in a while, came a volley of rifle-shots and the poignant notes of the Last Post. 'A military funeral,' I was told, 'one of the old veterans.' The 'veterans'—it was my introduction to the word—were men who had served in the Crimea.

As I grew bigger that little room became my private sanctuary. There I learned by heart and acted to myself endless speeches from a small-print, double-column complete Shakespeare, especially the farewell orations of the heroic suicides. Brutus, Cassius, Romeo, Hamlet, Antony—how often I stabbed myself with my school ruler, how often drained an invisible phial, but I do not remember applying an imaginary asp to an equally imaginary bosom.

By that time, of course, I had long been reading fluently. The March of the Ten Thousand, the mutineers of the *Bounty*, Alfred at Athelney, Roland at Roncesvalles, *Gulliver's Travels*, *Captain Cook's Voyages*—these were the books or themes that jostled in my head with the more ephemeral literature such as *Rainbow*, *Chums* and the twopenny issues of the

Buffalo Bill Library. I never bought the famous *Magnet* or the *Gem*, though I was once given a large bundle of those weeklies and became familiar with Billy Bunter and his ageless schoolfellows. Dad ordered the *Children's Newspaper* when it started, which was broad-minded of him for he quickly noticed Arthur Mee's teetotal bias. I have never quite forgotten its opening serial, 'The Secret of the Sargasso Sea'.

Shipwrecks and desert islands fascinated me. They were the commonest theme in those early stories that I scribbled. I was soon writing properly. Penny notebooks must have been almost my first independent purchases. I was shy about my stories and used to hide them, for Bill, four years my elder, was merciless in teasing me. For that reason one sentence at least is engraved for ever on my memory. He fished out my notebook from where I had stuffed it behind the sofa, opened it, and declaimed: 'Chapter One. Crash! The captain's head struck the deck …' Bill then dissolved in mocking laughter and no doubt an unequal struggle began. The rest of that story is mercifully erased from my mind, and I have no idea whether the captain's fall was due to his ship's striking a coral reef or a cannibal's hitting him with a club. At least those first words, immortal for me if for nobody else, indicate that I had already grasped the importance of a compulsive opening sentence.

It is curious that Bill, who grew up to be the gentlest and kindest of men, a brother with whom my adult relationship was entirely happy, loomed in my childish eyes as an incarnate fiend. Physically, he never exceeded the normal roughness provoked by a victim's struggles, but his talent for devising mental torment was considerable. Mother would appear in hat and coat, adjuring us to be good boys while she was out. I would plead not to be left alone with Bill. George, of course, being much older, would be absent on his own affairs, and he does not enter into these memories. Bill would assume an expression of utter benevolence and pained incredulity. Of course he would not tease me. Rather could he be relied upon to 'take care' of me. And so, in a thuggish sense, he certainly did.

Reassured, Mother would kiss us, button her gloves and be gone. As the front gate squealed behind her, Bill would turn upon me in the shadowy hall and go through an instant Jekyll–Hyde transformation, dilating his eyes and purring, '*Alone in the house—with a madman!*' My blood curdles reminiscently as I write the words. I would dive for the stairs. If his clutching hands were very close I had to go through the first door I came to, the lavatory, which had long-term advantages but was a dull refuge. The bathroom was preferable, but if I had sufficient start I would race along the landing and lock myself in the big front bedroom, where I had a comforting prospect of the outside world and occasional passers-by. Best of all, I could rivet my gaze on the street-corner round which deliverance would eventually appear. Yet even behind my locked door I was not safe. There would be an ominous silence, broken only by purposeful footsteps mounting to the bedroom we then shared on the top floor. Down he came again, and a conversational voice would inform me, 'I've got your pets.' These pets were a very small woolly dog and rabbit from the Penny Bazaar, my beloved and inseparable bed-fellows. After allowing me time to contemplate all possibilities Bill would continue amiably, 'I'm taking them down to the kitchen and I'm going to drop them into the range …' That brought me out of my refuge as he knew it would, and I was at his mercy. He never did much, actually. He would spreadeagle me on the floor, and, squeezing together my lips and nostrils, promise me swift suffocation. Then he had had enough of the sport, and by the time Mother's latch-key was heard my tear-stains had long since dried, and all the fear was forgotten—until next time.

One day there was a dramatic variation. Having informed me that I was alone in the house with a madman, and forestalled my dash for the stairs, he announced that he was going to lock me in the cellar. The house was well provided with cellars. A door opened off the hall and a flight of steps went down into the gloom. We had no electricity in those days, but some light filtered in through various gratings. There was first the cellar which later (when the zeppelins began to come over) we furnished with chairs and blankets as our air-raid shelter. Next came an airy cellar with ample shelving used as a larder—a pleasant place of jam tarts, apple-pies, cold joints, and dangling game. Finally, shut off by a door, was the coal-cellar, filled through an oblong grating in the passage-way at the side of the house.

Whether Bill intended to immure me in this Black Hole of Calcutta, or leave me more mercifully among the jam tarts, I never discovered. Over-confidence led him into the fatal and inexplicable error of starting down the steps ahead of me. Surely he *must* have held me by the wrist, and I must have broken free? I cannot remember. I can only remember my exultation as I slammed that door and turned the key on him, and stood there in the hall while he rattled the knob and threatened me with unspeakable revenge. What could he do? Even when his voice gave place to the usual ominous silence I was for once undisturbed. My pets, like myself, were on the safe side of that door. For once the fiend was impotent. I hugged myself with intoxicating joy.

A few moments later came the complete reversal of fortune, the supreme horror. The kitchen door was flung open and in from the back-yard sprang a truly diabolical figure, his face for once suffused with real rather than simulated fury, and streaked, as were his clutching hands, with the blackness of the pit. I reached neither bathroom nor lavatory that time. I doubt if I made the bottom of the stairs.

It is sad, and seems most unfair, that these isolated incidents are remembered for ever, while hours of kindness fade into oblivion. I can—but only vaguely—remember such hours. Bill, who was good at fretwork, made me a model theatre, we played back-yard cricket and football and French cricket—the same old tennis ball, whatever the game—we sparred with the boxing gloves an uncle gave us, and must altogether, despite the age-gap, have shared many activities in reasonable harmony. But it is the moments of terror that leave the scar. It was the same with George. With seven years between us he was a remoter figure and contributed much less to my childhood joys and sorrows. He was a quiet and I am sure exemplary schoolboy, with none of Bill's occasional wildness that could frighten not only me but Mother herself. Nonetheless, the two really vivid memories I retain of George are of terrors I am sure he never meant to inflict—being roughly ducked in the North Sea on my first encounter with salt water, and his taking me into a darkened room where he practised chemical experiments and suddenly throwing sodium into water, with results that gave me an anti-scientific bias for the rest of my life.

These experiments were conducted in the 'play-room', later known as the 'billiard-room' when Dad bought a table for the use of Bill and his friends. This was a separate building, which the original owner of our house had used as an office, and important-looking, though disconnected, telephone wires still ran to it across the yard. Before the arrival of the billiard table it was a splendid place for wet-weather games. There was a period when we 'played shop', a trying period for Mother because she had to open every packet very neatly, and all tins upside down, so that when empty they could be stacked on our counter in seemingly mint condition.

There was no garden at Portland Road, a cause of great regret to Dad, who loved gardening no less than his gun. All he could do at home was to provide splendid window-boxes, but he also rented one of the Corporation gardens on the Hunger Hills, a mile or so away. These gardens, though administered on the familiar allotment system, were quite different in character. They occupied a steeply terraced hillside and each was kept private from its neighbours by tall dense hedges, pierced by a solid wooden door. Our garden, being the last at the end of the lane, seemed a particularly secret place, looking down into a dell of green meadow beneath. There were no dull rows of vegetables but all kinds of apple-trees, a greengage, Victorias with their luscious gummy fruit, William pears and jargonelles, raspberry canes, American blackberry, glistening redcurrants, a rhubarb patch, gooseberry-bushes, a strawberry bed … All this was, as the crow flies, little more than a mile away from the city centre, and our house, though the steep gradients of Nottingham made it seem much further. Dad's particular hobby was roses, for which the red clay soil was ideal, and the other flowers were left to take care of themselves, or so it seemed. Golden montbretia lined the top path, cushions of white alyssum spilled over the retaining walls of the terraces, and there were wallflowers, which he called gillyflowers, and a shady corner of lilies-of-the-valley, which I used to pick for Mother because they were her favourites. There was a swing and a summerhouse, and the bottom hedge was full of pliant willow wands which, when peeled, notched and strung, made ideal bows for Robin Hood games.

Normally, however, my playground was the yard at Portland Road. On one side it was overshadowed by an immensely high brick wall, clothed with Virginia creeper, level with the play-room roof. In one corner was a washhouse with a pump that gushed greenish, fragrant rainwater from an underground cistern. Sometimes we filled jugs of it to wash ourselves, it was so soft. The washhouse often served as a log-cabin to be besieged in cowboy games and the wooden dolly-peg would be brought out to represent the helm of a ship. A heavy square table stood always in the yard—Mother, busy from morning to night, might sit there to take the air while she shelled peas. Turned upside down, this table became a raft. On its side it provided the stage for a Punch-and-Judy show. Draped with rugs, it was a tent or a house. If I wished to shoot Canadian rapids or paddle up the Congo, my canoe was a pair of steps laid flat on the ground. None of these games required expensive cowboy outfits or other equipment—a toy pistol was about all I wanted. Money went on lead soldiers, boxes and boxes of them, and on clockwork railway accessories. Constructional toys like Meccano (of which Bill had a great deal) left me completely cold.

Mine was a narrow little world, almost inconceivable today. There were no car-drives or distant visits, and few holidays. Nor was there any flow of adult society. Mother managed to keep up with two or three women friends of her girlhood, aunts would drop in occasionally, but my father's odd working-routine, added to the shooting and gardening, left him no leisure for entertaining guests at home.

This was as well for Mother, whose existence (I now see) was that of a devoted and uncomplaining galley-slave. God knows what time she got up. *Our* day began with the scrape of a match, the swift golden ripening of the gaslight in the icy bedroom, and her voice, 'Monday morning, boys, school today!' Downstairs, the fire already blazing. Clean collars for my brothers—even the schoolboys wore detachable collars then. Polished boots in the fender—I think I had never cleaned my own boots until I went camping at the age of fourteen. And the air would be savoury with bacon odours.

Thereafter, the cloth was seldom off the table. Dad breakfasted about ten. By one o'clock my brothers were home from school, expecting a hot dinner. All the meals alternated. Dad would be home again at some unpredictable time between three and four o'clock. So it went on, schoolboy tea, another hot meal in the evening for Dad, lemon sole perhaps with a whole plateful of bread-and-butter not to be touched by the maid, sandwiches and cocoa (in later years) for Bill and a whole gang of his friends in the billiard-room—incessant cooking and cutting and table-laying and washing-up until nearly midnight, when my father, if peckish, would content himself with a glass of port and the odd jam tart. The details varied with the years and are jumbled in my recollection, but this general programme continued through my boyhood, and I can remember coming home on dark winter afternoons in my khaki cadet uniform, and finding that she had somehow made time to cut me my favourite marmalade sandwiches and bake me the rockbuns I loved.

Home, husband and sons were Mother's life. She was utterly free from personal ambitions, social or otherwise, and for her own sake it was just as well.

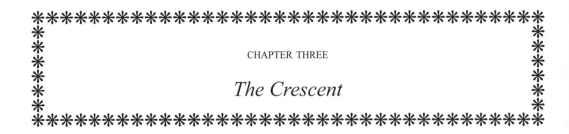

CHAPTER THREE

The Crescent

IN that narrow world of my childhood the other important place was 'the Crescent', Granny Trease's big house that faced one of those secluded grassy enclaves preserved by remorseful Victorian developers when they spread their bricks and mortar over the town's medieval fields. We walked up Burns Street and down Southey Street, then turned between iron posts that shut out vehicles into the asphalt walks of the long Crescent. When I started school I used to visualise those posts, and the similar ones at the entrance of the adjacent Forest recreation-ground, when Miss Rogers besought the Almighty on behalf of 'our gallant soldiers and sailors at their posts'. So many of the soldiers and sailors I actually saw used to be lounging round those posts, especially on a Sunday, though their gallantry may not have been quite the sort Miss Rogers had in mind.

Arrived at the front door of number 85, we would identify ourselves as 'family' by a combined ring of the bell and rattle of the letter-flap. An aunt admitted us. There were three—Ethel, Min and Daisy. Ethel, florid, sweet and gently dithery, had worked for some years as a governess and ranked as faintly bookish. Min was solid, blunt and a shade severe, impressive in her uniform as Captain of the All Saints' Girl Guides. I once disgraced myself by referring to her as 'fat' and had to apologise abjectly for telling the obvious truth, no doubt a useful early warning for an embryo writer. Min was really a much-loved character, especially to the girls she devotedly took camping in Scotland every year. No working-class Guide, however poor, was denied that annual treat, whatever fund-raising efforts and face-saving subterfuges were called for in the preceding eleven months. Daisy, the youngest aunt, had shown artistic leanings and for a time attended the School of Art, where she must have been somewhat junior to Laura Knight. But Daisy did not continue with her art, and by this date, with more and more men called up into the Army, she was helping in the office shared by Uncle Billy and Uncle Jack. The two youngest uncles, Reg and Sydney, were in the Army. Granny's eight children had been spread over a quarter of a century, so that at my father's wedding Uncle Syd was little more than a baby.

'Mother's in the garden,' my aunt would probably say as we passed through into the long dining-room at the back, with its bird's-eye view of built-up valley and dim green ridge beyond. Looking down, we saw the white-haired figure surveying her rock-plants far below. Though we had seemed to enter the house at ground-floor level we were now indubitably at an upper window, so steeply did the hillside fall away. To reach Granny we had to descend to the basement kitchen, spacious, light and itself raised high above the terraced lawns and rockeries of the back garden. A dumb waiter carried dishes up to the dining-room. There was a rocking-chair in the kitchen where one could sway happily, eating one's way through an immense triangle of jam puff or mincepie.

Granny Trease in the back garden at 85 Waterloo Crescent with her eldest son, George Albert, and his sons (left to right) Bill, Geoff and George—about 1912

To a child it was a fascinating house, clinging to the hillside like a cluster of birds' nests. It had its legends too. There was the tale of Uncle Reg's sleep-walking. A rowing man, overexcited by the imminence of the regatta, he had come down in the middle of the night, taken a firm grip of the plush runner on the mantelpiece, and, responding to the imagined voice of some coach on the dreamland towpath, given it a strong steady heave. It was a long, bobble-fringed runner, crowded with knickknacks and photographs. It was not only Uncle Reg who woke up.

The family must have been used to nocturnal alarms. Jack, always labelled in my mind as the 'jolly' uncle, was engaged to a girl who was in danger of losing her sight. One Christmas he had been to London to hear the specialist's verdict, which was reassuring, and he hastened home with the news, reaching the Crescent on Christmas Eve after everyone had gone to bed. A band was playing carols on a street-corner not far away. Explaining his special personal grounds for rejoicing, he led them on tiptoe into the silent house and marshalled them in the dining-room, where at a signal they lifted their instruments and let rip with 'Christians, awake!' Seldom can the instruction have met with a quicker response.

Grandfather Trease I never knew. He was very deaf, and my brothers remembered him chiefly for his ear-trumpet. Granny had always been a dominant figure. It was the Mater, my father used to say, and not the Guv'nor who wielded the cane when they misbehaved. By the time I came upon the scene she had settled into a stately widowhood, consciously or unconsciously modelled on that of Victoria. She wore nothing but black, and scarcely stirred out except to church and to tend her husband's grave. Then she would don a kind of widow's cap, or at least a hat with a veil. But I think of her with her smooth, serene, kindly face and her well-ordered creamy white hair, pottering in her garden or enthroned at her fireside, drawing all the threads of family news together. She was, by universal acclaim, a 'wonderful' old lady. She had made a vocation of it. She cannot have been phenomenally old when I first knew her, though, come to that, she looks well on her way to being a wonderful old lady even in my parents' wedding photograph. She was about ninety-four when I saw her for the last time, during the closing years of the Second World War. Yet in all the thirty-odd years I knew her she seemed virtually changeless. The Granny who offered me the choice of port or sherry from the sideboard was not noticeably different from the one who had offered a glass of milk, fumbled in her purse for sixpences and handed me my Christmas present, the *Boy's Own Annual*.

Christmas and the Crescent are inextricably entwined in my memory.

At home, of course, there was the awakening and the excited exploration of the bulging pillow-slips suspended at the foot of the bed—then downstairs to a cold but substantial breakfast of tongue or pressed beef, an hour or two's play with new toys, and at midday the departure through the foggy, frosty streets, sometimes between ramparts of soiled snow mounded along the gutters, to the main family gathering at Granny's. There, amid the chatter of aunts and uncles, the tearing and crackling of wrappers began all over again and more presents were revealed, paints and puzzles and pistols, long boxes of leaden Lancers and Zouaves and Zulus, goods wagons and guards' vans and passenger coaches in the colours of the Great Northern Central, the Midland or the L.N.W.R.

In the dining-room the table was extended to its last leaf. The lift rumbled up from the kitchen, the turkey and its garland of sausages were set before Uncle Billy, who carved … There was no nonsense then about helping the children first: we had to possess our souls in patience until our cooling plateful at last arrived. The time for indulging the children came with the next course, when the leaping fire was screened, the venetian blinds rattled down to plunge the scene into gloom, and in came the puddings, Dantesque with their girdles of blue spluttering flame. Each pudding was a miniature silver-mine. Threepenny bits, sixpences, whole shillings rewarded the questing spoon and the stomach elastic enough to face a small third helping. I collected one and ninepence, one year. What greedy little devils we must have been! And what powers of metal-divination Granny seemed to possess as she diverted the more profitable portions to the children's plates …

The afternoon was a dim somnolent interlude. The ladies would vanish, the gentlemen draw up to the fire, we boys spread ourselves and our presents about the floor. The air would grow fragrant with Uncle Billy's cigar and my father, normally a non-smoker, might fidget with his annual cigarette. The company varied in numbers. Uncle Jack and Auntie Doll spent Christmas with her family, so there were no young cousins to play with us. Uncle Reg was sometimes there, but only because he had been wounded so often in France: he was an officer in the Royal Horse Artillery, he had won the D.S.O. and M.C. and been recommended for the V.C. and was always being mentioned in dispatches. It was he, I still remember, who gave us the boxing-gloves one year and *The Adventures of Robin Hood* another. His wife Gladys was the youngest of our aunts and she was always there. I looked at her with extra interest because I believed, rightly or wrongly, that she possessed a revolver, given her by Reg when he went off to the war in 1914, to protect herself (for reasons I did not clearly grasp) against the Uhlans should they come galloping into Nottingham. Was Uncle Syd there? Perhaps in the early years. By 1916 he was, I think, a second-lieutenant in the Sherwood Foresters, first in Dublin and then on the Salonika front. Before that he must have been there as a schoolboy. But Syd was by nature self-effacing. While still at school he had saved a man from drowning in the Trent, and Granny might never have heard of it if she had not caught him sneaking upstairs in his wet clothes.

Dusk fell early on those Christmas afternoons and life took an upward curve again. The table resumed its crisp white linen, the crinkly edged china cups were marshalled in front of Granny's place, the Christmas cake appeared, a citadel of ice garrisoned by redcoat cherries and munitioned with silver cannon-balls. With no show of reluctance we drew up our chairs.

Having thus built up our strength, we were ready for strenuous exercise. Tea was cleared, the table contracted to the minimum size and all the furniture was pushed back against the walls. Only Granny kept her chair by the fireside. Everyone else played with abandon— General Post, Nuts in May, I Wrote a Letter to My Love, Turning the Trencher. We went in for the bustling games rather than the imaginative. Charades would have been foreign to the family temperament. But the long room was ideal for the tug-of-war that ends Oranges and Lemons.

After this, in my earliest years, I was taken home and put to bed. Everyone else continued with a miniature whist-drive, and, being a precocious card-player, I was very soon allowed to stay for this too.

Three tables were set up in the drawing-room, we had score-cards and tiny pencils, and moved round as we won our games. Halfway through the programme we returned to the dining-room where the indefatigable aunts had laid out another banquet, with a cold turkey, trifles, mincepies, nuts, raisins, and every kind of dessert. We ate heartily, knowing that we had another two hours or more of whist before us. If Christmas Day fell on a Saturday Granny was punctilious about finishing before midnight, but otherwise we might carry on a little longer. So we did justice to the supper, knowing that we should not get another bite to eat that day except for the constantly circulating bowls of chocolates, toffee, and sugared almonds, the home-made Turkish delight, and the great boxes of crystallised fruit sent us as presents by the French wine-shippers. We did not consider ourselves to be gluttons, but we believed in looking ahead.

My chronology is blurred—could we have got all those delicacies during the war years?— but the scene is vivid. Mother is nodding with the warmth of the room, the weariness of the long day, and her limited interest in the game. Dad, rubicund, life and soul of the party, has as usual forgotten what are trumps, is asking loudly, and being as loudly informed … Uncle Billy, who most evenings plays serious bridge at the Constitutional Club, is studying his hand with weighty concentration … His much younger wife, the gay Auntie Alice, is pretending to flirt a little with my father … Granny, at all other times both the centre of the family and a little remote from it, has joined in the whist and is a benign competitor … And a small short-trousered boy is sitting there, bright-eyed but tired, untroubled by the adult conversations washing over his head, by the stress of involved personal relationships, or by the nagging remembrance of those who were here in past years but are now in Greece or on Vimy Ridge.

Granny lost heart after the war and Christmas was never the same again. I recall coming home with Dad in the dusk of an autumn evening, laden with apples and other produce from the garden on the Hunger Hills. To our surprise Auntie Ethel was waiting at Portland Road—surprise, for it was always we who visited them. Syd was missing on the Salonika front, where the Bulgarians had just surrendered. Two days before firing ceased he had volunteered for some mission or other, and must have been blown to pieces, for nothing but the lining of his steel helmet was ever found. For years Granny refused to give up hope and would not allow his name to appear on the School war memorial. A few weeks later, when the Germans had surrendered too and the war was really over, I lay in bed with the influenza that was raging over Europe and listened to the horse-drawn funerals rumbling and clattering down our cobbled road on their way to the cemetery. Someone came into the room. 'Uncle Reg is dead …' He had died in the officers' hospital at Sidcup, after nineteen operations to patch up his shattered face and body. It seemed to me an awful sell, after winning those medals, to die of flu three weeks after the Armistice. But I was too ill myself to feel anything much. Everyone was ill. Even Mother had taken to her bed. At the Crescent the front door was on the latch so that the doctor could walk straight in.

There was no Christmas festivity at all in 1918, and though family gatherings at the Crescent were resumed thereafter even we youngest ones were made to feel that some of the glory had gone.

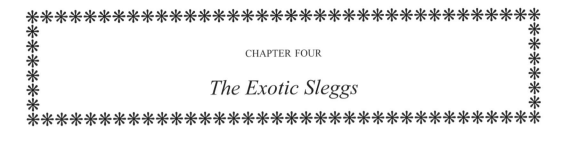

CHAPTER FOUR

The Exotic Sleggs

EMINENTLY worthy, models of public and private morality, my father's family might have seemed dull, I frankly acknowledge, to a critical observer. As a typist once remarked, after working for my uncles at a time when there were about four or five Treases in the office, including Auntie Daisy, 'Oh, they're nice people but there are so many of them and they're all so beastly polite to each other.' With certain exceptions—Daisy developed an interest in local history—they were cheerfully philistine, and any vestige of Celtic fantasy had been lost on the long road from Cornwall. Much more imaginative stimulus might have been provided by Mother's people, but they had a tendency to be distant or dead. There was really only the exotic Sleggs, but to a round-eyed little boy he was worth half-a-dozen run-of-the-mill relatives.

Cousin Fred looked upon 'Auntie Floss' as a substitute mother, and our house was the nearest thing to a home that he recognised. About five years older than my brother George, Fred Sleggs was the eldest of several boys orphaned by the death of Mother's sister in Liverpool. His father had married again. Fred had not seen eye to eye with his stepmother. He had left home whilst still a schoolboy at the Liverpool Institute. It is hard if not impossible to check now upon the details I accepted unquestioningly as a child—that he lived in lodgings on his scholarship money, eating little but bread and pea-nuts—but the picture is completely consistent with the man I later knew, and, what is most important, it was the picture I accepted, and was impressed by, when he used to visit us a few years later. I suppose it was the first whiff of burnt boats that ever caught my nostrils.

When the war came, Fred had just graduated in zoology at Liverpool University. He was only nineteen and it was solely because of the war, we were told, that he was allowed to receive his B.Sc. immediately. He volunteered at once for the King's Liverpools and went into training in Knowsley Park. My earliest memory of him is of a khaki-clad figure arriving on a motorcycle, and teasing Mother with his stories of falling asleep in the saddle as he chugged over the Peakland moors in the small hours.

We boys found him splendid value as entertainment. He would march round the yard balancing the long clothes-prop on his upthrust chin. He could perform impressive tricks such as tearing imaginary sheets of calico and producing just the right sound through his ventriloquial lips. He was a whistler and used to be put to march at the head of the column. He played the mouth-organ and a small concertina. One Christmas he went with us to the Crescent, where to his own concertina accompaniment he sang a harmlessly vulgar ditty of which I recall only the (possibly appropriate) refrain:

> O, O, my tum-tum aches,
>
> O, O, my tum-tum aches …

He became well known as an eccentric in the vicinity of our house. The old cabby, who used to lurk in his little shelter just round the corner, commented on the odd youth who walked up the road with one foot on the kerb and the other in the gutter and his head in the air.

Most of all he entertained us with an endless story. It was called 'The Electric Sledge' and (I would now suppose) was a Jules Verne kind of romance, about some fantastic vehicle ranging the snowy wastes of Siberia. Only a few fragmentary images remain in my mind—the weird blue crackling flashes of the electricity in the icy night, the wolves howling, and the mysterious silent fortress where in every casemate the soldiers lay dead beside their guns.

Fred's letters from camp were so interesting that Mother used to read them to us. He had been promoted lance-corporal for a somewhat odd reason. The orderly officer had come into the canteen at a moment when Fred was standing on a chair and convulsing his comrades with an imitation of a tub-thumping orator. Conscription had not then been introduced and one of the methods of attracting volunteers was to slip a patriotic speech into the programme at the music-halls. Fred seemed just the man for the job and as Lance-Corporal Sleggs he was sent round the Liverpool halls.

However persuasive his eloquence, he was himself often irked by barrack-room life, and on Sundays, he wrote, he preferred to slip away from the crowd and enjoy the solitude of the woods. He had built a den, his dug-out, he called it, even taking the trouble to make a hard floor of concrete. He kept a shotgun hidden under the autumn leaves and would poach some of Lord Derby's game as a welcome variant to Army rations. Mother would purse her lips apprehensively and hope he would not get into trouble but we boys thought it all admirably romantic.

One day our door-bell rang. Mother answered it.

'Good-morning, madam. I am a police officer. You have a nephew, Lance-Corporal F. Sleggs, in the King's Liverpools—'

'*Oh!* Has there been an accident? Is he safe?'

'No, he's quite safe, madam. They have him in the cells actually.' Dazed, Mother led the detective into the dining-room. 'He says he wrote you some letters, and if you have kept them they will substantiate his story.'

Fortunately Mother *had* kept the letters with their weekly bulletins on Fred's private life in his dug-out, and he was quickly released with no worse consequences than the loss of his single stripe. It appeared that his woodland retreat had been accidentally discovered and that the fresh concrete floor had aroused the wildest speculation. It was a period of spy-mania, so it was concluded that the dug-out was the lair of a German agent and that the concrete had been prepared as a gun-emplacement for some improbable hostile weapon. At all events, when Fred made his way through the woods on the following Sunday, there were officers waiting in ambush, who (he told us) chased him through the trees blazing away excitedly with revolvers.

Soon after this he was drafted to Flanders and thereafter, apart from the leaves he spent with us, was in and out of the trenches until the end of the war. He never sustained a scratch and never, according to the best of his knowledge and our own boyish disappointment, killed a German. It was at this time that he began selling newspaper articles, principally to the *Daily Mail*, which in those happy days for the free-lance printed anything up to half-a-dozen short pieces every day. His usual subject was shell-fire. He explained barrages, trajectories, and similar matters fascinating to the patriotic citizen safe at home.

He always took a kindly and flattering interest in his smallest cousin, detecting my embryo literary bent. Bird's Custard had a show-card depicting a bird ingeniously composed of various fruits: it stalked on long legs of rhubarb. I impressed Fred by exclaiming: 'What a strange specimen of averanity!' He reported this to Mother with great delight. Though there was no such word, he explained, *avis* was the Latin for 'bird' and my invention was a logical one. Privately, I thought he was making too much fuss. I had always known the word 'aviary' from the bird-houses in the Arboretum, and had simply coined my own variation of 'humanity'. Still, it was pleasant to be thought clever, even undeservedly.

Words, foreign as well as English, continued to attract me. I was an indefatigable looker-up, occasionally with results that embarrassed even Fred. Once, as a group of us played in the yard, he heard a schoolfellow of Bill's beseech another boy not to be 'a silly twat'. 'You must never use that word,' said Fred in horror, 'Auntie Floss might hear you.' 'Why?' they demanded. 'Why is it so awful? What does it mean?' He refused to say. The others resumed their game of football. I was the one who rushed off to find the dictionary and returned to dance round Fred, importuning him in a shrill voice and with an imperfect Latin pronunciation, 'What's a *pudendum muliebre*?'

When Fred returned after the war he told us that he was going to try his luck in Nova Scotia where he had obtained a post at Dalhousie University. We three boys walked to the station with him. 'Don't say anything to Auntie Floss,' he said, 'it will only upset her—but it may be a very long time before I come back.' I was nine years old and enjoyed the drama implicit in this quiet farewell.

In the succeeding years Fred's letters continued as always to bring a spice of vicarious adventure into our lives. He moved on to the University of Chicago … 'One of my students was shot in a gun-battle last week.' … He described solitary vacation journeys, crossing the Rockies in an old Ford, camping in primeval places … He was 'Professor Sleggs', which sounded very grand to us, for professors were rare in the Britain of the early nineteen twenties and we did not know that across the Atlantic the title was more lightly bestowed. After holding appointments in several universities he finished up in Newfoundland, where he spent his vacations tramping round the virtually unknown stretches of coast and staying at remote fishing settlements. Once he was treed by a bear and had to wait for hours until it disappeared into the forest.

He did not marry. There was a Canadian girl, he told us, but he discovered in time that she was only after his money. Money was important to him because it spelt independence. He was in some sense a miser. His odd childhood, the struggle to support himself even as an adolescent, had set him in habits he could never shake off. In the middle of the nineteen thirties he came back to us. He was forty, and with care, he announced, he would never need to work again. By living simply in bachelor lodgings, and by passing his vacations under even more austere conditions, he had saved the bulk of his salary and it was all salted away in American investments. If Mother was agreeable (and she was) he proposed to spend six months of each year as her paying guest and the other six months in economical expeditions wherever the fancy took him. 'You'll find him terribly uncouth,' I was warned by Bill, who was still living at home. 'He's been by himself so much, or with these backwoodsmen—he tears his food with his hands.' These Johnsonian table-habits must have quickly disappeared in Mother's company, for when I next revisited Portland Road there was nothing objectionable in his behaviour.

For a year or two the arrangement worked very well. My father had died in 1932 and Bill, the last of us to leave home, married soon after Fred's return, so Mother would have had no company in the house except for a somewhat odd little maid. Fred was away for months at a time on his curious expeditions. He spent one freezing Christmas in a tent near the shores of the Wash: he described to us how he had subsisted partly on raw turnips from farm-carts, which he had picked up in the muddy Lincolnshire lanes, and partly on bagfuls of fancy cakes with which he would retire to his sleeping-bag from four o'clock in the afternoon until the winter dawn next day. Once, arriving home on a visit, I met him sailing out of Portland Road on his bicycle, and he dismounted to greet me. He had had an iron framework fitted over his front wheel, such as normally held a butcher-boy's basket. He had filled the space with netting to accommodate a miscellany of camping equipment and temporary purchases. Other kit was stowed fore and aft. He wore a bowler hat, bolt upright on his large curly head. 'I'm just off to Morocco,' he said. In the event, he got no further than Spain. Bill hinted afterwards at some mysterious trouble with the police, likely enough in Spain. Bill thought he had been suspected of tampering with the poor-box in a cathedral. It will hurt nobody now if I say 'not inconceivable'. It must have been just before the Civil War.

The next year he asked me about visits to Russia. I explained the regulations as I knew them. Foreigners could obtain tourist visas only by paying a minimum daily amount, even it they did not use the hotel accommodation and enjoyed free hospitality with friends. This arrangement did not appeal to my economical cousin. What did I think of his chances of slipping across the frontier unnoticed? I looked at him and his bowler hat and his bicycle with the errand-boy attachment and told him as gently as possible that I thought they would be slender in the extreme. As I spoke, a shameful thought crossed my mind, how easy it might have been to disembarrass oneself of this eccentric relative, had one so wished, by giving him the wrong advice. But I had no desire to do so, nor the faintest notion that, as it proved, I was seeing him for the last time.

His departure from Portland Road was dramatic, and, as they say, 'can now be told' without pain to anyone alive. The maid, a most unglamorous creature with a leaning to fantasy which Mother only discovered in later years, made a prim request that she should not in future be left alone in the house with the Professor. Horrified, Mother confronted her beloved nephew and demanded an explanation. With dignity he refused to defend himself. Mother said, with what pain I can imagine, that he must quit the house next day. And next morning he did, without uttering a word of confession or denial, and without leaving an address.

If, as seems probable, he had been misjudged, he never offered any chance to set matters straight. We heard from him, but never received a straightforward message, much less an indication of his whereabouts. He might cut out a review of some book I had written and paste it on a postcard with an enigmatic word or two. Or he might send us a reprint of a learned and to us incomprehensible paper he had published on marine biology. It was just a teasing reminder that somewhere in the world he was still alive and keeping an eye on us.

After 1939 these sparse communications arrived from the Irish Republic. By some indirect means—presumably through other relatives—we heard that he had removed himself there, asserting that he had no intention of being personally involved in a second world war. Also, no doubt, he meant to retain his American investments which he would have had to surrender had he stayed in the United Kingdom.

It was all very sad, and I do not know what distress it must have caused my mother, haunted as she must have been by the fear that she had misjudged him. She never discussed the matter, at least with me, for she had all her generation's distaste for any mention of sex. But Fred had been like another son in her affections, and a kind of trust bequeathed by the sister she had loved so much, and the long estrangement must have hurt her acutely.

The end of the affair came about 1956, when an advertisement in the *Nottingham Guardian* invited Mrs Florence Trease, last heard of at 142 Portland Road, to communicate with a Dublin firm of solicitors. Fred, it appeared, had been living the life of a recluse in a farmhouse he had bought in the Wicklow Hills, and there one day a neighbour's child had found him dying on his doorstep. He had left everything to Mother, though, since he had not provided for her predeceasing him, I suspect it was the simple will he must have made, probably in his Army paybook, when he went to the front some forty years earlier. At all events he had never revoked it. Mother would have been comforted to know that, but she herself had died only about twelve months before, so that Fred had to be regarded as intestate. For my own part I had enjoyed my legacy long ago, the contact with the most imaginative and stimulating character in my childhood.

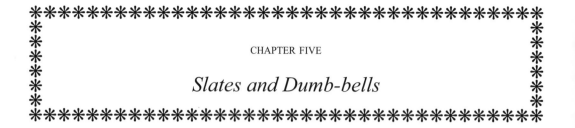

CHAPTER FIVE

Slates and Dumb-bells

MY first school was called Ashbourne House. It was kept by two sisters, the Misses Rogers, in a stucco-faced mid-Victorian villa on the Forest Road, and the educational methods were mid-Victorian to match. But the school was deservedly esteemed for the 'good grounding' it gave. I do not know how old I was when I followed my brothers there, but I could already read.

It was a ten-minute walk through quiet residential streets, past the Arboretum and the massive High School to which I should later proceed. At first I sometimes had Bill for company. The Misses Rogers boldly, if ill-advisedly, kept boys until about eleven and girls as long as their parents were prepared to pay the fees. Bill used to be joined by one of these girls, halfway to school, and I recall bleak January mornings when, with a round woolly cap pulled down to cover the chilblains on the tips of my ears, I had to walk alone on one pavement to provide a moving target for their snowballs from the opposite side of the street. I preferred on the whole to go to school by myself, muttering stories as I trotted along, accelerating to a wild gallop as I passed shadowy gateways that threatened ambushes by Germans, highwaymen or Amazonian Indians.

Having survived these fancied perils, I would clatter down the outside garden steps into a basement lobby, where we hung up caps and coats and pulled off galoshes, and then made our decorous way upstairs into the main part of the house. The first floor provided two spacious classrooms, back and front, but the latter was big enough to hold us all at once, with double rows of desks forming a big L, and enough open space for us to stand in a semicircle round the old coke stove.

There the elder sister, Miss Kate, would open the day with simple prayers, her own bright eyes shielded by a slanting hand as she besought us to remember, among other things, those 'gallant soldiers and sailors at their posts'. She was aquiline, with grey hair and a long skirt which has left me with a curiously persistent impression of a riding-habit. Perhaps this dim early memory is not ill-founded. For Miss Kate ('Crutchy', behind her back) had only one leg—she stood before us, erect as any of our gallant soldiers, crutches tucked into her armpits and with no pretence of an artificial limb, but displaying beneath her hem a wooden leg which (except for its rubber tip) might have supported Long John Silver himself. She used to swing herself about on those crutches with the utmost agility. There is one peculiar thing: not only did I never know how she came to be minus a leg but I cannot remember even trying to find out. It was not something you could ask, and you could scarcely find the answer in the encyclopaedia.

Like all the best teachers in the old tradition, Miss Kate was both lovable and frightening. Miss Julia was not so alarming. She moved quietly on two feet, was rather fleshy of face, and had a cameo brooch just below the high neck of her dress. She taught me when painting a picture of cherries not to show them just as red circles but to leave a bare patch on the white paper, to suggest the gleam of light on the curve of the fruit.

The first days at school were much occupied with slates. The pencils squeaked horribly, but it was fun, when one could no longer clean the slate sufficiently with one's dry duster, to squeeze a wet sponge and wipe out the smudged remnants of earlier work, restoring the oblong slate to its pristine gleaming grey. From slates one graduated to copybooks and then to lined and squared exercise-books. Geography involved a lot of tracing and crayoning of maps, as well as learning the counties of England, their county-towns and the rivers on which they stood. In due course one actually studied a little book called *French without Tears* and from its opening pages gathered the impression that foreign exchange was preoccupied with boys' bargaining over penknives and marbles. Sometimes Miss Julia distributed small cards and coloured wools. Each card was mysteriously peppered with printed numbers, and if one stitched round them in order an outline picture emerged. Each morning one had to be word-perfect in a fresh verse of one's Psalm. I was at the school so long that I was eventually transferred to Isaiah.

Our physical education was confined to 'drill', which Miss Julia supervised, weather permitting, on the lawn. Big girls and little boys, we filed round and round the path, turned about, and wheeled to and fro across the grass. Usually we carried wooden dumb-bells. There were pairs to suit every size of hand, down to the chubbiest baby fingers. We swung them over our heads in unison, we shot them out at right-angles, we clicked them behind our backs. We provided side-splitting entertainment for the errand-boys who paused to watch us over the garden-wall.

It would be consoling to blame my subsequent mediocrity at games on the shortcomings of this early education. Yet George and Bill, who similarly stayed with these two ladies and they were eleven, suffered no disadvantage. George became a dashing three-quarter and Captain of Rugger. Bill won his place in the High School Fifteen at an unusually early age as scrum-half, and in due course also in the Eleven as a slow bowler. They could hardly have done better if they had entered the High School preparatory department as soon as they were old enough. But there was a family prejudice against 'the Prep' because Uncle Syd had suffered from bullying there, so we stayed at Ashbourne House until it was time to enter the main school. Thus, till I was eleven, I never handled a hard cricket ball or kicked a football of either shape, and, lacking the innate flair of my brothers, never afterwards developed much aptitude.

These were not the only gaps in my education. The Misses Rogers were dear good women, they taught us diligently within the limitations of their ideas and equipment, and certainly they gave me the 'good grounding' my parents paid for. I wrote neatly, I spelt almost faultlessly, I got most of my sums right. Otherwise, compared with the pupils of any average infant or junior school today, my generation were deprived children. I was told no stories, handed no attractive books. I heard no music and learned no songs. I did not act or dance, I was shown no famous pictures, my practical experience of arts and crafts went no further than daubing those cherries and stitching those cards with coloured wools.

Not surprisingly I never held a hamster, and the multiplication of mice was a branch of mathematics from which my teachers would have hurriedly averted their gaze.

I remember sadly little of my lessons. I do know that I spent a lot of time, my own task finished, listening to what Miss Kate was teaching the older children. I picked up scraps of history. I can still hear her voice as she turned reluctantly from the excitements of the Stuart period and warned the girls: 'Now we come on to what I always call "the deadly dullness of the Georges".'

Outside school, my general knowledge was supplemented in various ways. I collected foreign stamps: thanks to the printed headings in my album I was well versed in Central American republics and their capitals. There were cigarette cards with interesting pictures and summarised descriptions, *Gems of Belgian Architecture* and a series on vehicles involved in the war ranging from Russian ambulances to a van that transported carrier-pigeons on the Italian front. I took a keen interest in the progress of the war, though my recollections now are oddly eclectic—I remember being unduly distressed by 'the fall of Montenegro' in 1916, yet the Bolshevik Revolution when I was a year older left no impression on my mind, doubtless because its significance filtered through so slowly even to the adult public. My father had a wistful leaning towards geography, and once when he and I were convalescing from some illness we played atlas games in his bedroom. For him, who had grown up in Victoria's time, the really evocative names were the Nile and the Mountains of the Moon, Klondyke and Kumasi and Kicking Horse Pass. He never travelled further than the Isle of Man.

An old lady presented me with an old encyclopaedia in six volumes and several fat albums filled with picture postcards mostly from abroad and a few from as far away as Japan. Therein I first gazed longingly at the blue waters and skies of Garda and Como and Maggiore, and saw the umbrella-pines along the old Roman ways, and grappled with new words like *kursaal* and *plaza*.

George introduced me to Shakespeare. He went through a phase when he liked to marshal us round the fire, 'taking parts'. Unfortunately, the play which appealed to him—or was he perhaps studying it for an exam?—was *Henry V*, especially the prose scenes, and I found myself stumbling over the incomprehensible utterances of Nym and Bardolph, unable to see in what sense they could be regarded as 'comic'. It was not until I got on to *Julius Caesar* that I felt any responsive thrill. About this time, too, I met other verse in a fat, small-type, double anthology called *Gems of British Poetry*. George liked pieces such as 'Horatius' and 'How they brought the good news from Ghent to Aix' and 'The Coming of the Spanish Armada'. I learned to savour such heroic lines as:

> The Mamelukes were tossing
> Their standards to the sky,
> When I heard a child's voice say, 'My men,
> Teach me the way to die.'

The real war was meantime passing over my head, more interesting than alarming. My father was completely exempted from service after his medical examination, Uncle Billy and Uncle Jack were not called up either, and I had no conception of the dangers my younger uncles and Fred Sleggs were facing overseas. Zeppelin raids provided exciting interludes. We would wake in the coldness of the night, the factory-sirens moaning the alarm, Mother in the bedroom doorway with a candle-stick. Out of the warm bed, into slippers and dressing-gowns or draped blankets—we wore night-shirts in those days—downstairs into the cellar, a sleepy file of us groping our way through the darkness, Mother far behind with the one candle calling after us, 'Stick to your father, boys!' We all thought it an immense joke when, having reached the cellar, Dad's voice came from the darkness, 'Whose hand am I holding?' and the maid piped up, 'It's *me*, Mr Trease.'

Mother always blamed the zeppelins for the 'nerves' which began to afflict her at this time and which for the rest of my childhood made her unwilling to walk further than the end of the street alone, to go very far even in company, and to attend church-services or theatres. This nervous trouble had far-reaching consequences for me. I became her companion to a far greater extent than my brothers had ever been. I went with her on shopping expeditions and, as soon as I was old enough to run errands alone—which was very young in those innocent days—I spent much of my time walking long distances to her favourite butcher beyond the hill, or down to the Market Place for the only make of pork pie Dad would fancy, or to the fishmonger's where I was to study the prices chalked on the boards outside and use my own discretion as between plaice and lemon sole. Mother and I got on splendidly. I used to brush her hair when she unpinned it in the evening, and I would count the strokes and lift her hair at the back to reach the reddish-gold lights ('your ginger bit,' we boys called it, unromantically) which were normally unseen. Having her hair brushed was about the nearest thing to selfish, sensuous indulgence that Mother would allow herself. When, a little later, I developed my habit of learning and reciting yards of Shakespeare, she was my uncomplaining audience. Only once did she so far forget herself as to laugh in the wrong place, when as Macbeth I was clutching at invisible daggers. I turned on her in fury, and, as she told people afterwards with something like good-humoured awe, 'he took me by the throat and shook me like a terrier shaking a rat'.

One morning Miss Kate told us that the war was over, and we had won, and we could all go home because there would be no more lessons that day. I reached Portland Road as George arrived, similarly released from the High School. We had a great store of rather splendid flags and streamers, kept since King George's visit to Nottingham before the war. George wanted to borrow them. The Sixth Formers were going 'down town' to celebrate. I thought it all very dashing, but then everything connected with the big school was. I used to stare through the tall gates every time I passed and up at the high tower with its Victorian battlements. In the summer I was taken to Sports Day and was proud of my big brother winning the Hundred Yards or captaining his house in the relay race.

The time was now approaching for me to enter the school myself. More than four centuries old, the High School was reckoned good enough for anyone, and middle-class families who sent their sons off to the minor public schools of the Midlands were regarded as faintly pretentious. Only Uncle Reg, early commissioned into the Royal Horse Artillery in the snobbish atmosphere of 1914, had been made to feel inferior for having attended 'only' a day-school and had determined that any son of his should not be similarly stigmatised. For me, as I have never ceased to be thankful, the High School was the unquestioned next step.

Early in 1920 my father was surprised to receive a revolutionary proposal from Miss Kate. She would like to enter me for the High School scholarship examinations in June. Of course, she insisted soothingly, she knew that I was going there in any case. She had to be diplomatic. In those days the phrase 'scholarship boy' was more often than not used in disparagement, implying that one's parents could not afford the fees and that one might even, like that boy Lawrence, be only a collier's son. Miss Kate must have satisfied my father that his solid bourgeois status was not impugned, and one morning in June, equipped with well-stocked pencil-box, I joined the hundred or more boys waiting on the steps outside the great pointed Gothic doors.

All through the morning and afternoon I scribbled happily. It was exciting, all those separate desks in their lines, separated by yards of bare floor, under the lofty beamed roof of the Prayer Hall. I had never faced even the most informal test-paper in my life. Examinations were a new and stimulating experience, one I should always enjoy.

Once a looming presence brooded over me. It was the headmaster, 'the Doctor', an immense and handsome figure with leonine silver hair, his gown always slipping off his shoulders as though they were too broad for it. In a deep voice, remote as the cloud-layer, he asked: 'Have you really done all you can, boy?' And I answered, in awe yet a little injured: 'I've done it all, sir.'

That summer we had one of our only two seaside holidays, sharing a big furnished house on the Lincolnshire coast with Uncle Jack and his family. The level sands seemed to stretch endlessly to the sea. The dry powdery dunes, with their wiry grass, were dotted with concrete pill-boxes from the recent war, handy for hide-and-seek with my cousins. During that fortnight came a telegram ending 'Congratulations from all at the Crescent', and for a whole day I basked in a glow of self-satisfaction. I felt faintly irritated, though, when they would all go on and on about the 'honour'. What appealed to me was the practical consideration: Dad would never have to pay a school-fee for me again.

Disillusionment came with the letter next day from the headmaster. With this letter my uncertain childhood recollections may be said to assume the dignity of documented history. 'I am glad to congratulate you,' wrote Dr Turpin, 'on the excellent position taken by your son Robert Geoffrey in the recent examination for Entrance Scholarships: he was *second* in the list, the first candidate being quite a year older. The present scheme of the School, however, directs that a preference shall be given to boys from Public Elementary Schools and the Governors, whilst joining in congratulations, were unable to do more than award an *honorary* Foundation Scholarship to your son, as a mark of distinction without financial benefit. I hope that your boy's career in the High School will be successful and full of happiness: he will be eligible in two years' time for the Junior Sir Thomas White Scholarships awarded to boys under 13 already in the school.'

Delightedly my proud parents thrust this missive under my nose. I suspect that my father was secretly relieved that there was to be no taint of charity in this business. But, for myself,

I felt the laurels withering on my brow. All meaning was drained from my little triumph. I went for a solitary walk along the dunes, savagely kicking my feet in the drifts of sand. Among my black thoughts was already an absolute determination to win that Thomas White thing in 1922.

CHAPTER SIX

The Inspiration of the Old Masters

THE High School in those days was exceptionally rich in 'characters'. It possessed not one Mr Chips but several. The first I was fortunate enough to encounter was Wilfred Tyson Ryles, form master of 2A, into whose care passed all the new scholars and the brighter boys promoted from the preparatory department. He was a lean, nervous, wiry bachelor, with a clean-shaven and slightly froglike mouth, alert eyes glinting behind his glasses, and dark hair so invariably sleek that he was rumoured to wear a wig. He had joined the staff in 1883 and was nearing the end of his forty-two years' service. He was known as 'Nipper', partly because of his swift movements and also because he had an elder brother in charge of 3A, whose contrasting weight and somnolence had won him the obvious nickname of 'Jumbo'.

Nipper faced us on that first September morning, the room smelling of well-scrubbed floor-boards, newly filled ink-wells, and freshly opened stationery. There were thirty-three of us, ranged alphabetically, so that I sat in the middle of the back row. He handed out pens, nibs, blotting-paper, timetable forms, and so forth. Then he welcomed us with a long harangue, full of interest and inspiration, of which only one passage remains in my memory.

'It may one day happen,' said Nipper in a tone of deepening solemnity, 'that a boy will raise his hand and ask to leave the room. I may be much occupied—or I may be irritable. I may say "no".' He paused, surveyed the three lines of anxious faces, and wagged his finger. 'That boy must take no notice of my refusal. He must get up quietly *and walk out*.' We listened, appalled by this apparent incitement to mutiny, and no less by its predictable alternative. Nipper's taut expression relaxed into a benign smile. 'Afterwards, he will come to me and apologise for having had to disobey me.' We all breathed again, almost sharing the relief of that hypothetical boy. No one ever knew what bygone catastrophe caused Nipper to issue this annual instruction.

He had no degree and had probably never heard of a diploma in education. Psychology he would have coupled with Physics in that remark, delivered in his high squeaky voice, which once convulsed his colleagues in the staff-room: 'Physics? Don't know a thing about it! Never even taught it!' Today he would scarcely be allowed to teach anything anywhere. He had no qualifications whatever except an adequate knowledge of the subjects, the ability to transmit that knowledge to small boys, infinite patience, and utter devotion to the school.

Nipper was just the man for me, though I realise that my affectionate memories are coloured by the fact that I did well under him. Speed, memory, accuracy were at a premium in Nipper's classes. He would give us a lesson on, say, the *Acts of the Apostles*. Then, economically tearing up sheets of paper into minute squares—sixteenths, I should imagine—he would fire off ten or twenty questions to which we jotted down the one-word answers. Who was the famous goddess at Ephesus? What was the centurion's name? Where did Paul sail to next? This may have done nothing for our development as happy all-round individuals, but it taught me to listen to what I heard, to look hard at proper names and memorise them, and to reproduce what I had learned, all humble skills not without utility in later life. Nipper taught us History, Latin and English as well, all with the same emphasis on correctitude. It was a narrow road along which he led us, but we arrived somewhere, at least, and rapidly.

This new world of competition for marks and places suited me down to the ground. In general, the transition from the sheltered cosiness of Ashbourne House was surprisingly painless. The High School was rough but not brutal. The playground fight was still an institution—the shrill cry would start, and swell to a louder and louder roar, 'Scrap on! SCRAAP ONN!' as hundreds of excited running figures converged from every corner of that hard sandstone desert, to push and jump on tiptoe for a glimpse of the homicidal couple in the midst of the swaying throng. But I was never in a fight myself and saw none of the bullying that my uncle had suffered ten years earlier. Rugger was not bad: at least we were all starting from scratch, because even the boys promoted from the Prep had hitherto played soccer. Though never any good, I quite enjoyed lumbering about in a not very aggressive way. Cricket I did not like. It directed too cruel a spotlight on the poor performer. I did not mind facing the bowler (at least I had often played my back-yard cricket with Bill) but I was sensitive about my inadequacy as a fielder, especially my inability to throw the ball hard and far. I had never learned to, never wanted to. In this respect I suppose I was abnormal. If, throughout my childhood, anyone had placed a ball in my hand, I should have had no desire to do anything with it, and my instinctive reaction would have been to offer it to the nearest boy likely to be interested. This is not how future games-players are made.

Still, I survived the physical challenges of my new life, even the clambering and vaulting and somersaulting of the gymnasium, without any too painful humiliations, and the only hour of the week that I dreaded was 'Singing'. This was taken by a visiting music-master whose heart was clearly, and, understandably, not in the business. The combined Second Forms, about a hundred eleven-year-olds, sat on benches ranged round the great Prayer Hall. The master, aloof at the piano on the dais, would shout the number of the song in our tattered books, and point to some unhappy individual who had to rise and sing the first verse solo. After that, each of us knew whether he was safe for another week, or doomed, since the next boy had to take the second verse and so on, round the hall, and there was never time to complete the circuit. Everyone hated this ordeal. Even those with good trained voices, ornaments of church choirs, were driven by public opinion to sing half-heartedly, while for the shy boy it was pure agony. As we had no fixed places we used to change our seats each week, with much shoving and muttered imprecations, but the master might upset our calculations by resuming at a different point or going round anti-clockwise for a change. As I waited to learn my fate, I used to feel like the Zulus in *King Solomon's Mines* when the witch-doctors were about to perform the smelling-out of their victims.

This was the extent of my musical education. There was no use of a gramophone or any other method to inculcate appreciation. If we all grew up without knowing even Mozart's name, no one would feel responsible. But Nipper would make sure that we got the Latin subjunctive right in 'If Cornelia had not adorned the table with roses …' and that we could point to Pamphylia on the map.

Art was taught in an almost equally narrow manner, though by a kindly and agreeable drawing-master. Art *meant* drawing, with just an occasional dip into the paintbox, and drawing meant dustpans and brushes, wicker baskets, dusters with awkward folds and bottles with baffling reflections. Once in a while we might tackle three daffodils in a jar, and at the end of term be accorded the heady freedom to paint a Christmas card (best effort for the Doctor, second best for our form-master) or even to draw with complete liberty from our imaginations, if these were not by now atrophied. This was my own chance to depict duelling Cavaliers, Brazilian revolutionaries and capering cannibals, to illustrate the unwritten stories fermenting in my mind. The master used to stand over me and make encouraging noises. But as he had never taught us the first thing about the human figure or let us draw from a living model, even my capering cannibals looked as stiff as the hero they had bound to the stake. Needless to say, we heard no more of Michelangelo than of Mozart, and if someone had suggested that there was something to be learned from the Old Masters we should have taken it as a reference to Nipper, Jumbo and other elderly members of the staff.

Most curiously, in a system of education which at least acknowledged the importance of books, there was no effort to arouse our interest in literature. The School Library, as officially designated, consisted of some glass-fronted bookcases in the Prayer Hall, normally locked and reserved for Sixth Form use. 'The Boys' Library' was a miniature room which, when used for lessons, held just four boys and a master. Its walls were lined with a good assortment of adventure-stories, Jules Verne, Conan Doyle, and other authors in well-thumbed, dilapidated editions. This library was run by two prefects and there was usually a queue waiting for them to unlock the door, but I doubt if the authorities ever thought of it as an educational tool.

I made eager use of it, myself, for I was not allowed to visit the children's department of the Public Library, which my father believed to be infested with noxious germs. Instead, he let me have his tickets for the fine library at the Mechanics Institution, one of those early Victorian ventures which, like so many designed for the working class, had long since acquired an aura of middle-class respectability. Its shelves were well loaded with popular novels and books of every kind. I particularly liked, and used to borrow again and again, the heavy bound volumes of the boys' weekly called *Chums*, reading and re-reading the long serials, 'Hurrah for Merry Sherwood!' and 'In the Reign of Terror', both by A.S. Walkey, an absorbing yarn-spinner, perhaps undeservedly forgotten. No one, at school or elsewhere, made the least effort to guide my reading.

In one context the school's indifference was welcome: we were allowed to choose our own prizes. In the autumn, prize-winners collected a voucher from the office, entitling us to go down to a leading bookshop in the town and pick from its stock, or even order, books to a given value. We could use that voucher like a modern book-token, even selecting a handful of cheap editions, provided that for each award there was a presentable volume to receive the crested book-plate and be handed over ceremonially on the platform. I was lucky. All my way up through the school I had to battle with one particular rival for supremacy. He was the steady worker: each spring term, when there were no exams, he was top of the form. When exam marks were joined to term marks, at Christmas and Midsummer, it was I, less diligent but a good examinee, who came first. The prizes, rather unfairly, were awarded on the positions in the final term and not on the whole year. For me it was a happy arrangement. I was introduced to the joys of book-browsing in a well-filled shop and inevitably I developed into a shameless prize-hunter. As I worked my way up through the school more and more special prizes were open for competition and I was sometimes able to reach the cash limit, which was five pounds and in those days purchased a whole armful of books.

They were great occasions, those prize-givings. The staff appeared in evening dress under their academicals, the headmaster was resplendent in his Doctor's scarlet, quite outshining the governors and even the guest of honour. I received my first prize from the hands of the Duke of Portland, who had disappointingly left his coronet and ermine at home. When he began his speech he said how much he appreciated the compliment we had all paid him by turning out in his racing colours. My elders laughed, which I thought unkind of them. Poor Duke! How embarrassed he would be if he realised that our black-and-white ties were our ordinary school colours, not his at all! No, it was the Doctor, not the Duke, who impressed me. For the rest of my school career I cherished two alternative ambitions. I would be an author or a headmaster.

My literary ambitions had by this time met with some encouragement. In my very first term I had discussed with one or two classmates the idea of a magazine to be written jointly and circulated in manuscript. Someone, wiser and more versed than I in school protocol, advised our seeking Nipper's approval. It was a diplomatic step. To my surprise I found my idea made the subject of a form meeting, at which five of us were duly elected as an editorial board. There was to be an issue every term, boys would pay a penny to borrow the magazine overnight, and finally the manuscript would be auctioned, all proceeds going to the 'Lads Club' which the School ran in one of the Nottingham slums.

The magazine which resulted was a lively production modelled not on the decorous printed school-magazine but on what we ourselves thought a magazine should be, jokes and riddles and hobbies but above all fiction in great slabs, as tasty, nourishing and bloody as underdone steak. Nipper seemed delighted with what his boys had achieved—we were always 'his' boys in a fervently proud sense unfelt by other form masters. He bade me carry the magazine to his brother. 'Mr Ryles' compliments, sir, and he thought you might be interested …'

Jumbo, who was my form master in my second year, was portly, comfortable and generously moustached. Coming slowly down the street, he looked rather like a penguin. In school, he was the last of the assistant masters to retain his mortarboard. The two brothers had joined the staff in the same year, but whereas four decades had not blunted Nipper's nervous edge Jumbo was, to put it charitably, a more restful character. Indeed, he was known to fall asleep in class. The nearest to lively excitement he ever displayed was when a boy brought him a matchbox containing an insect for identification. He taught us Latin and mathematics, but entomology was his enthusiasm. He was also reputed to enjoy his pint in the Vernon Arms, adjoining the school. Unlike Nipper, he was married, and in earlier days he had taken boys as boarders in his home.

After a year with his high-powered brother it was pleasant to relax with Jumbo, who was so easy-going that one might have said that discernible movement had ceased. As his top boy I was regularly sent out on private errands in lesson time, to the tobacconist's at the foot of the steep hill or right down into the city centre to his bank—errands performed on foot, since, living so close to the school, I had not acquired a bicycle. On the tobacco expedition I was told to buy toffee for myself. No higher authority ever questioned these long absences from class, and, perhaps more remarkably, no boy ever accused me of being teacher's pet, or whatever it would have been termed in High School vocabulary. Jumbo never showed anything but the most correct and unsentimental detachment towards his boys, and probably had a secret preference for insects. But I do remember a single out-of-school encounter amid the three-day Saturnalia of the Goose Fair, which was then still held in the big central square of Nottingham.

'Ah, Trease!' he greeted me, his paunch quivering with laughter. 'Have you seen these new Climbing Monkeys?'

'Yes, sir.'

'But have you *tried* them?'

'Not yet, sir.'

Privately I had studied the sideshow and decided it was not worth including in my budget. It consisted of a row of toy monkeys climbing poles. You paid your sixpence and turned the handle which operated your monkey, but there was no apparent relationship between the way in which you turned it and the speed with which the monkey went up its pole—or slithered back. It seemed to me a poor sort of race and I preferred to spend my money spiralling down from a high tower on a mat or thundering round and round in a gondola.

'Go back and try them now,' begged Jumbo, pressing sixpence into my hand, and so dismissed me, his eyes wet with tears of uncontrollable merriment.

Like Nipper, he believed in training a boy's memory by drill. Every week, after plodding through our portion of Caesar, he made sure that we had mastered all the fresh Latin words. We had 'standing round', which meant that he planted his armchair against the radiator and we formed up in a curving line, starting behind his right shoulder—the first boy cosily propped against the radiator—and stretching down the long classroom. He tested us, Latin into English, English into Latin, passing the boys who could not answer and moving up the first who did. At the end of the period we 'numbered off' like soldiers, and noted our places for next time. I enjoyed this snakes-and-ladders approach to learning, for unlike the climbing monkeys it did bear some logical relation to ability and effort. Once, over-confidence undid me. I was at that moment head of the line and the questions had just gone by. I was safe for a moment and, lulled by the hot-water pipes, lapsed into some pleasant reverie, unaware that one question was running down the line unanswered. Suddenly Jumbo turned in his chair, peered up at me, and barked: 'Trease, then—"number"?'

'One!' I said.

'Two!' cried the next boy automatically, and the others took it up, so that it reached 'Fifteen!' before Jumbo halted it with a shout, reminding us that he was merely trying to elicit the answer '*numerus*'.

'You were asleep, Trease!' It was a fair comment, but ironical coming from him. 'Go to the bottom.'

No one would have dared to doze in the class taken by 'Beaky', the senior History master, whom we first encountered in 3A. He kept fives balls in his desk and would suddenly hurl one down the room with the velocity of a cannon-shot, if he suspected the least inattention in the back row. I knew this to my cost, for, though I hung on his every word myself, the alphabetical seating arrangement placed me in dangerous proximity to boys less fascinated by the wrangles of Charles and his Parliament. Fortunately Beaky had an unerring aim with any sort of missile, whether fielding in the Masters' cricket-match or shying at coconuts in the Goose Fair, and in class he always threw to miss. The fives balls would whizz terrifyingly over our ducking heads, hit the wall, and give us no more than a thump between the shoulderblades as they bounced back. There was a relief-model of the British Isles above us on that wall. Most of the sharper peaks had been smashed into a semblance of volcanic craters.

R.S. Bridge owed his obvious nickname to his nose, but that aquiline feature was only one of several conspicuous peculiarities—bandy legs, long arms with the swift prehensile action of an ape's, fierce yet humorous eyes, and a voice that could rise to the squawk of an outraged cockatoo. Younger than Nipper and Jumbo, Beaky had recently joined the staff after war service with the Gunners. Legend ran that at one time or another he had broken every bone in his body, and the bandy legs were quoted as evidence. Whatever his age, he certainly had about the craggiest, most weather-beaten face I had ever seen.

Craggy too was his personality. He had no time for fools, no patience with the sentimental or the woolly-minded. 'Bosh, bunkum, balderdash!' he would cry, or dismiss some unworthy book with the contemptuous monosyllable, 'Pap!' If you said something unbelievably silly, he would just stare at you bleakly and deliberately drop his lantern jaw. He had an actor's sense of timing. He knew when to break the silence, when to electrify his audience with a roar, when to surprise them with his quietness and a muttered throwaway line.

Not for Beaky the memory-drill, the fiddling little tests, the snakes-and-ladders games. He talked at us all through the lesson, pausing only to sketch Wolfe's attack on Quebec in coloured chalks on the board—or to whip round with the speed of a Texan gunman and hurl chalk, fives balls or whatever came handy at some incautious whisperer in the class. We listened and took notes. Though the matter of his lessons was suited to our tender years, his method was in essence that of a university lecturer. Our homework was always to write up the material as a continuous narrative in our own words, illustrated with as many pictures, maps and plans as we cared to draw. He collected our notebooks only about twice a term, annotated them scathingly or appreciatively as they deserved, and gave them the marks which determined our positions. If you liked history and could write and draw, it was a most satisfactory system. Beaky made it easy to like history. His racy talk, his humour and his enthusiasm left little need for the fives balls. They were just tricks of his trade.

His walk to school brought him down Portland Road, and, though I never deliberately waylaid him, I was always glad to see him approaching as I came out of our gate. He took us for Geography, too, and taught us to read the local Ordnance Survey maps. One day, as we walked together, he opened my eyes to the newly discovered use of air photography in archaeology. It was the year, too, of the sensational Tutankhamen excavations, and he talked about that.

After the Ryles brothers, Beaky's astringency was a useful corrective. He did not regard us as small boys to be drilled and moulded into young gentlemen. He was irreverent. He shocked me slightly by pouring critical scorn upon *The Swiss Family Robinson*, previously one of my favourite stories. Each boy had to keep by him an approved book for personal reading, and to occupy himself with it if for any reason there was a temporary interruption in the lesson. No 'tripe' was permitted. I myself read *The Cloister and the Hearth* and then struggled some way through Victor Hugo's *Ninety-three*. Beaky's bony and crooked finger was beckoning us forward into the adult world. His mode of address, when exasperated, was 'Good Lord, *maan* ...'

That summer the Junior Sir Thomas White Scholarships were awarded on the results of the ordinary exams. I had always meant to win one and I did. My father, still reluctant to profit by my efforts, told me that he would bank all my fees, then seven guineas a term, to form a useful nest-egg when I left school. The scholarship also carried a cash payment of eight pounds a year, originally intended to ensure that the poorest boy would be decently clad. This too must be mine, Dad insisted, and I could use it as I liked. So at the end of each term I went to the school secretary and collected my cheque for £2 13s 4d. Between them, these twin decisions of my father provided the foundations of life-long independence. The scholarship cheque gave me an immediate personal fund in addition to pocket money and birthday or Christmas presents: I was never again without the price of a book I coveted, or a theatre ticket, or (as I grew older) the cost of a camping trip. As for the main nest-egg, most of it was never touched—it has remained theoretically in being until the present moment, its cash value withered by half-a-century's inflation but its psychological value unimpaired. Whenever I was minded to burn boats, I could draw courage from the fact that I had a hundred pounds in the Post Office Savings Bank which would still be there after the conflagration.

Dad brushed aside thanks for these arrangements. He was giving me nothing, he insisted, these were my own winnings. But he did wish to reward me. Would I like a bicycle or a cricket-bat?

'Please, Dad,' I said, 'could I have a typewriter? Second-hand would do.'

He must have winced inwardly but he controlled his feelings. It was my choice. Without argument he sent me off with his clerk who knew about such things. In a little shop off Bridlesmith Gate we found an old Remington for four pounds, a fine upstanding office model as heavy as a piece of field artillery. For an extra ten shillings it was fitted with new type and I had passed another milestone on my destined road.

CHAPTER SEVEN

Widening Horizons

Now I moved up into the senior school, a promotion I had looked forward to, because my form master would be the admired and amusing Beaky. But when the day came I entered his room with trepidation.

During the holidays my father had been talked into my learning Greek. I did not want to. It meant going on with Latin, which so far I had found dull and wished to drop in favour of Spanish. The school, however, even under a scientist headmaster, tried hard to keep Classics alive, and, as I realised later, studying the records of the years before and after me, was extraordinarily successful in nobbling each top boy as he came up from the juniors. Since I did not succumb to the general propaganda directed at 3A in the final days of the summer term, one of the masters was deputed to call on my father at home. 'Buggy' Woodward (another amateur entomologist) was a formidable bearded Victorian who had taught my father long ago at Loughborough Grammar School, and had thus a most unfair advantage. My own protests were overruled. That August I borrowed Pope's *Iliad* from the Mechanics Library and waded through miles of heroic couplets to demonstrate to myself, since nobody else would listen, that I could if I wished break into the vaunted treasure-house of classical literature without the key of language. My effort was wasted.

What most appalled me was the realisation that I had to face my new form master and confess that I was abandoning my best subject—*his* subject—for ever. Our peculiar syllabus forced the Greek set to drop History, though for four periods a week, presumably in the interests of a balanced education, they were doomed to fiddle about with chemical experiments, learning nothing (I speak for myself) except how to cook their results.

It was with dry lips and a fluttering heart that I went to my allotted seat, that September morning. Beaky took our names and distributed essential stationery, skimming notebooks over our heads with wonted speed and accuracy.

'Now,' he squawked, 'who are the Greek lads? Come on. Let's see you.'

Four hands rose hesitantly like flags of surrender. His eyes raked the room contemptuously, came to rest on me. His jaw dropped. 'You?' he said. I felt like Brutus stabbing Caesar. '*You?*' he said incredulously. 'Good Lord, man …' Words failed him. In the recent scholarship exam my History paper had been marked one hundred per cent. No doubt he had been thinking of me as a potential award-winner at Oxford or Cambridge. I felt about six inches high but I could not explain that this apparent treachery was no fault of mine.

In time he forgave me. He still taught me English, and that term he wrote generously in my report. Twenty or thirty years later, when he was buying my historical fiction for the (by then transformed) school library and grunting his approval of it, I felt that I had expunged my original betrayal. But I was sorry he did not live long enough to read my study of the Grand Tour, dedicated forty-five years after that painful classroom confrontation to the 'memory of R.S. Bridge, a schoolmaster long ago, inspiring, entertaining and terrifying by turns, who taught one boy at least to love History'. He was the least sentimental of men, but I hope the tribute would have pleased him.

Later that morning the four Greekites went along to the little cubby-hole of the Boys' Library. There we met the chief Classics master, who had descended from his Classical Sixth form-room to ensure that our first steps were taken under expert guidance. He was young, new to the school, himself raised in the exacting atmosphere of St Paul's, a Cambridge man from Trinity. He exuded power and soon earned himself the nickname of 'the god'. The god in question would not have been Apollo—rather, I should think, Zeus (for he hurled verbal thunderbolts as Beaky threw fives balls) or Cronus in view of his saturnine expression. He had crisp black hair, a little curly as I remember, and he used to glare at us like a bull.

We took the desks facing him, two and two. He pulled out his pen. 'What's *your* name?'

'Proctor, sir.'

'And yours?'

'Randall, sir.'

He stared at me.

'Trease, sir.'

'And yours?'

'Twelvetrees, sir,' faltered my neighbour.

A terrifying transformation took place. For the first time we saw, what we were often to witness subsequently, the facial warning of a thunderstorm about to break. A dangerously quiet voice demanded: 'Is this some feeble joke?'

'No, sir,' we protested. 'They really *are* our names.'

The sun came out again. 'Ah, I shall call you "Dendrites" and "Dodeka Dendrites".'

We laughed respectfully, though we could only guess at the joke. We were prepared to be called anything.

He then asked us our eventual plans. Proctor and Twelvetrees were starting Greek because they meant to be Church of England clergymen. And they were too, in due course. Even thirteen-year-olds were encouraged to know their own minds in those days. I forget precisely what Randall said, but he was a Roman Catholic, and the wide belief was, true or false, that he was destined for a monastery.

'What about you, Trease?'

All my life I have been plagued by an inability to evade personal questions. I answered, with some diffidence, that I would like to be an author. He received this revelation with kindly interest and asked how I proposed to set about it. It so happened that my father had recently made the one practical suggestion that lay within his sphere of influence and understanding: if I remained serious about this writing business until I left school, he would speak to someone he knew on the *Nottingham Guardian* and see if there was any opening on the staff.

'I thought of getting a job on a newspaper,' I said.

This answer, for some reason, produced uncontrollable amusement, and for the second time that morning I was made to feel very small indeed.

Many years afterwards, enjoying the weekly columns of Katharine Whitehorn, then unborn, I derived a little extra diversion from my memories of her father, A.D. Whitehorn, the man who introduced me to Greek.

For the next three years I progressed in orderly fashion towards what was then called the School Certificate. Superficially my life was that of any well-behaved grammar school boy, who was bookish rather than athletic. For a time my brother Bill remained in the school, a tasselled prefect and my own House Captain. The playing of games was compulsory but not their watching. At home, on Sundays, Bill used to write out the teams for the Wednesday inter-House matches and after realistically providing for half-a-dozen reserves he would hesitate, grin at me, and add my name as a seventh. This ensured that I should make the long journey to the sports ground, carrying all my kit, and provide one supporter at least for the team in which I was most unlikely to play. In actual fact I did not mind watching rugger, though I preferred the more spectacular encounters with other schools on Saturdays, when both touchlines were thickly lined with spectators. I even enjoyed playing for the House when I was bigger and Bill had left, but I did resent what I felt was an injustice he would not have imposed on any other boy. Still, in many eyes no doubt—and perhaps his—I appeared as a priggish swot and some action was needed to cut me down to size.

Bill's own academic interests were minimal. More than once Dad had considered applying the closure to his school career. But Bill's services as scrum-half and slow bowler were so highly valued that the sports masters always pleaded to retain them for 'one more term'. At an early age I had reacted fiercely against comparisons with him and with George, the flashing wing three-quarter. I knew I could not follow in my brothers' footsteps, as well-meaning masters exhorted me to do, so I swung away into an exaggerated disdain for athletic achievement, which if I had been nobody's brother I might never have affected. Bill, as I can now understand more sympathetically, must sometimes have been embarrassed by the reverse side of the comparison.

Quite undeservedly, the family regarded me—with perplexity and conflicting emotions—as some sort of intellectual who had appeared for the first time in their ranks as a genetic anomaly. It was George who, in the event, achieved the professorial chair, the fellowships of learned societies, and the honorary doctorates of more than one foreign university. None of this they foresaw at the time. George's classroom career had been unsensational, his original intentions modestly commercial, and his quiet picking up of the odd chemistry prize had gone almost unremarked. Scoring tries and breasting tapes seemed to the family infinitely more important. So, if at the time I felt the odd man out, the 'clever one', the precocious little horror deviating from a healthy athletic tradition, I was merely sharing a widely held estimate.

On entering the senior school I joined the Officers' Training Corps. I liked this. We wore stiff peaked caps, with an adaptation of the Sherwood Foresters' elegant badge, a stag. We had many brass buttons to polish, carried silver-headed swagger canes, and wore breeches, like officers, ending in carefully spiralled puttees. The stamping and shouting, the slap of hand on rifle-butt, the circular flourish of the bright bayonet whipped from its scabbard and snicked into position, provided a primitive satisfaction and a respectable mode of 'playing at soldiers' open to big boys. It was an outdoor activity at which I could hold my own. I enjoyed the formal evolutions and parade-ground precision, the weekly ceremonial when the company fell in on its markers, and the annual War Office inspection with its march past and General Salute to the visiting brasshat. Equally the field days appealed to me, especially one early in my service when we took part in a scheme involving three other schools, fighting our mimic battle in the dense woodlands of a ducal estate. With another boy I was sent ahead as a scout. We sighted a tall khaki figure, certainly not one of our company, retreating down a narrow path through the shoulder-high bracken. We stalked him, eager to distinguish ourselves by taking a prisoner, and were about to pounce when a gap in the foliage revealed his umpire's armlet. Still, it made a good story against ourselves and inspired my first contribution to the school magazine. This was the usual sort of dignified official organ, its joint editors that year being Eric Abbott, later the Dean of Westminster, and R.J. White, the Cambridge historian, who was to combine academic writing so successfully with thrillers.

From Abbott I received kindness and encouragement in several ways. He was my platoon sergeant, he praised my maiden speech when I attained the debating society, and we acted together. He excelled in 'silly ass' roles, one year convulsing us as Sir Andrew Aguecheek and the next as Humphrey, the ineffective but parentally preferred suitor in *The Knight of the Burning Pestle*. In this play I was making my debut, quite literally carrying a spear in the train-band scene, colourfully arrayed in a mauve doublet with bright blue slashings and hose of emphatic green. A repeat performance was given some weeks later at our youth club in the slums, and on the previous day the boy playing the young lover, Jasper, fell suddenly ill. I was told to go home at once and be word-perfect in the part by the following evening. I managed it, thanks to my earlier habit of learning blank verse for private pleasure. For one night only I contended with Abbott for the hand of the heroine, Luce, played with a suitably reinforced bosom by a boy with the unromantic name of Spanner. Our star performer, the Knight himself, was to become famous in the world of television, though not as an actor. He was Kenneth Adam.

The school magazine was too inhibiting a medium for my fantasies and in any case came out only thrice a year. The first thing I did, after acquiring my typewriter, was to produce a paper for private circulation, not a form magazine or one in any way connected with school, but with every word and every illustration my own work. My model was the popular boys' weekly, my editorial style as pompous as my fiction was sensational. No early issue seems to have survived to embarrass me, but the probable flavour is all too faithfully preserved in the extant copies of *The British Boy's Magazine*, 'Vol. II (New Series)', which began to appear in 1923, after a break, and could be borrowed by school-friends and others for a halfpenny. A typical issue consisted of twelve pages of single-spaced typescript in heavy

The British Boys' Magazine, *written, illustrated and produced by Geoffrey Trease, 1923*

purple ink with action-packed illustrations in water-colour. The first editorial of the revived paper began:

> It is a far cry back to the autumn of 1922, but that was the last time I was privileged to chat to you through the pages of the *B.B.M.* Well, the BRITISH BOYS' MAGAZINE has returned, better than ever, and on somewhat different lines. Comparing it with No. 1, Volume 1, which appeared to delight the Amateur Magazine lovers of Nottingham in 1922, I feel that my alterations are in every way satisfactory. In that first, epoch-making number, there were three serials, which all old readers will fondly remember—'Cedric the Saxon', 'Castaways All!' and 'El Leone the Avenger', and a complete story, 'Lonely Ranch'. This time there are only two serials, but the length of their instalments makes ample recompense. They are: 'The Young Captain!' a tale of South America, somewhat akin to the El Leone stories. 'Fighting the Slavers', a tale of adventure in the Dark Continent. The extra-long complete story 'The Secret of the Yellow City' will, I am sure, be received with delight from all readers …

Having banged the big drum a little more, the editor very properly turned to the vital question of circulation:

> My aim in this new revival is to run an amateur magazine which will really pay its way, and therefore a few facts revealed by the books of the paper, when it ceased publication in 1922, may be of interest. Assets 2*s* 0*d*. Liabilities 1*s* 9*d*. Margin of profit 3*d*. I hope to improve on this however. Also, No. 1. Vol. 1. was *paid for* by 19 people, so that we can estimate that it was read by at least 30. This also can be much improved.

I cannot remember whether it was, but the paper ran for at least six issues and attracted correspondence from its readers, which was either graciously acknowledged (if laudatory) in subsequent editorials, or firmly squashed if it verged on adverse criticism. 'This letter leads me to suspect that my reader is a "Little Englander"; the object of this magazine is to promote the feeling of *Imperialism* among the readers, as its name implies.' One can find fossilized in these schoolboy effusions of 1922 and 1923 all the jingoism, class and colour prejudice, and general historical tushery which pervaded the juvenile adventure stories of the day—and which I was to find myself tilting at, not so many years later. Meanwhile I thoroughly enjoyed the blood-and-thunder. 'Out came his revolvers, spurting flame and death. Every shot told and five men were hit with as many shots.' And in another story a few pages later:

> 'The white dog!' hissed the Arab leader, and his scimitar grated against my cutlass … Backwards and forwards we fought, at times stumbling against the prone bodies of the slain. But his keen weapon, glinting like a great half-moon, grew nearer and nearer to administering the Arab's favourite blow—a keen thrust near the collar-bone, and a cruel wrench, causing the blade to positively *rip* the victim's body from the collar-bone

to the fifth rib. I saw the dark, triumphant face of my antagonist, the curved beam of reflected light raised to strike, and like a flash I ducked, and striking upwards with my left hand, administered a thoroughly British upper-cut. And, because an Oriental can never understand such a blow, he reeled back, a look of almost comical surprise on his face … Ere he could recover from his surprise, I lunged out with my cutlass and stretched him dead upon the ground.

It is fair to say that my values were not derived solely from the books and magazines I read or the spectacular silent films then packing the newly built *de luxe* cinemas. I imbibed them also from my father's *Daily Mail*, and I was an enthusiastic attender of political meetings, the rowdier the better. It was a lively period and Nottingham was a lively place. The Labour Party won one election in December 1923, and lost the next within less than a year. I went to hear Lord Curzon in one hall and one of the early Communist Party candidates in another. I revelled in the smaller outdoor meetings, held in the streets or in the market place. I stayed long after the banners and portable platforms were folded away, until the last half-dozen argumentative listeners broke off the action, and there was nothing for me to do but trudge reluctantly home. Given an essay to write at school on 'The Events of 1924', I began one paragraph: 'In this year died Lenin, and the whole civilised world breathed a sigh of relief.' Not surprisingly, the Debating Society Notes in the school magazine suggested that 'R.G. Trease should try to cultivate a less declamatory manner.'

Soon my private writing took a different turn. I lost interest in lurid serials and the publication of childish magazines. I was only thirteen when I lost my strictly amateur status by selling a brief article to a popular boys' weekly which invited readers' contributions on their hobbies. I earned my first half-guinea with a piece on Amateur Journalism. I followed it up with two more on Stamp-collecting and some other topic. Then my luck ran out. I had not acquired the professional's knack of writing plausibly on a subject of which I knew little, and perhaps the initials R.G.T. were becoming too familiar. It was seven years before I earned another penny from journalism.

The bulk of my writing, though still imitative, was becoming more personal and felt, though the expression of that feeling makes me writhe now with embarrassment at its naïvety. My switch of style and subject-matter coincided, as anyone would expect, with the upsets of adolescence, but only second in importance was my belated discovery of the countryside.

It was ironical, and sad, that my father, the countryman *manqué*, could never communicate his enthusiasm to his sons. Though he did sometimes take us on a Sunday walk, we were bored by the expedition. As a little child I was scared by his impatience when he pointed into the treetops to show me a nest or a bird. 'Can't you see it? There! No, look where I'm pointing—*there*!' He was so quick and knowledgeable, it was the world he had been born to, and he could not believe in the slowness and blankness of a town boy. I would pretend, miserably, that I had seen what I was supposed to see, for I was ashamed to admit that I still had not. I would give a lot today to have a quarter of his country-lore, and to be able to chat freely and naturally with every roadman, keeper, and farm-hand encountered on the road. *He* would stand happily for what seemed like hours, while we sauntered sulkily on to the bend, throwing back impatient but unheeded glances, and groaning to each other, 'Oh, Dad's met one of his old tramps!' Horrible boys (I speak for myself) but if only somehow we could have been drawn in!

I suppose a true countryman does not think or talk much about 'scenery'. My father never wanted much more than the gentle wolds of the Leicestershire border. The little outcrop crags of Charnwood Forest were his ultimate in the spectacular. My imagination nurtured on books and even picture postcards, I demanded more. At last, almost on my fourteenth birthday, I saw my first mountain.

With Bill and one of his friends, and a boy of my own age for company, I went to North Wales. We went absurdly laden by modern standards—we took an army bell-tent with a pole in two sections massive enough for a ship's mast and an immense wicker hamper packed with blankets, primus-stoves, billy-cans and other gear. All this we lugged, with prodigious effort, up a steep and wooded mountainside. A fair-sized stream came plunging down in a succession of cataracts, rocky pools and tall cascades, and there was just one level shelf of grass above the water with enough space to put up the tent. On this terrace we camped for a fortnight, hundreds of feet above the Conway Valley, remote from the world, with a broad panorama at our feet, extending to the distant sea. The fortnight inspired me to a lengthy travel-book, running to a hundred and ten pages plus index and a pompous preface, entitled *By the Waters of Afon Ddu*. Some of it was intolerably facetious, for I was trying with no success at all to imitate *Three Men in a Boat*, which we read aloud in the tent. The rest was turgid. 'The vast panorama of grey, majestic mountains, awful in their splendour … Over the top of Carnedd Llewellyn were rolling the great storm-clouds … We were appalled by the savage, terrifying grandeur of the approaching storm.' We certainly did have appalling weather on that holiday, with thirteen wet days out of fifteen, but it did not deter us from the expeditions we had planned. In that fortnight I discovered for myself a rural world utterly different from my father's lanes and spinneys. Mine was a world of waterfalls and lichened boulders, steep and mysterious woodlands, single rowan-trees spread on the skyline against racing clouds, sinister lakes lashed into white horses—and, for good measure, romantic ruins bearing no likeness to the municipal art gallery that was now Nottingham Castle and the only 'castle' I knew.

This holiday released the first gush of adolescent verse.

> The camp-fire's flame leaps upward to the sky,
> Bathing in ruddy glow the trees near by,
> As with a painter's master-touch. Now red
> As blood, now orange—as if fancy led
> His fleeting brush …

Rather dreadful doggerel, most of it, but as I force myself to look at it again I realise how, to a degree I had forgotten, those simple experiences must have impressed me at the time.

'Just like a maiden blushing,' I re-read—and feel like the maiden as I do so—

> The peaks loom red in the dawn—

and the verse goes on regrettably to 'the glories of the morn'. Another poem, called 'An Old Welsh Garden', reminds me of Gwydyr Castle and its ancient trimmed yews and the cloak-and-sword fantasies I wove out of our visit there.

Our camp by the Dolgarrog Falls was repeated the following summer. A schoolboy's diary, kept irregularly for one of these years, shows that my appetite for the countryside was now whetted. There were 'ripping walks' with one or two other boys to places like Newstead Abbey. My first day-long expedition alone was to Dovedale. Just after my sixteenth birthday I booked my first independent week's holiday, 'bedroom and private sitting-room', on a hill farm in Derbyshire. The farmer's wife looked slightly nonplussed when she saw me, but she had a son Maurice of my age at the Bakewell grammar school and the first evening ended with our all playing *vingt-et-un* in the family living-room, and thereafter I was never alone except from choice. 'A perfect week,' the diary summed up a mixed programme which included solitary walks to Chatsworth, Wingfield Manor and the Black Rocks at Cromford, attempts with Maurice's help to calculate the awesome depths of the old lead shafts in the surrounding fields, and a visit with him to the Matlock Pavilion to see *Tons of Money*.

I had by now become an avid theatre-goer, prepared to enjoy everything from *Alf's Button* to Shakespearean tragedy. The Nottingham Theatre Royal booked all the number-one touring companies, and, except for the depressingly long blank period of the pantomime, almost every week found me on the austere benches of its gallery. Sometimes, indeed, more than once a week, for the Shakespearean companies, the D'Oyly Carte and the Carl Rosa Opera changed their programmes every night. I was just old enough to catch the farewell visit of Sir Frank Benson. After that, we had to take our Shakespeare from the inferior Henry Baynton Company. When I was fifteen I saw *Julius Caesar* on Tuesday night, *Henry VIII* on Wednesday, *The Taming of the Shrew* on Thursday, and *The Merchant of Venice* at the Saturday matinée. What did it matter if the acting was hammy—if one recognised the same two cypresses in Brutus' garden on Tuesday and at Belmont later in the week? I got more from those crude performances than I get from Stratford's ingenious productions today.

For three years I had another theatre to go to. The old Compton Comedy Company, directed by Fay Compton's widowed mother, had re-opened a dilapidated playhouse in the suburbs and was trying gallantly to establish itself in repertory. Night after happy night, I tramped over the hill to see Viola and Ellen Compton as the twins in *Twelfth Night*, as the sisters in *Quality Street*, and in countless other parts. I felt bereaved when the venture folded and those tatty curtains opened no more.

I was lucky in two things that made independent holidays and theatre visits possible: thanks to my father's generosity over the scholarship money, I was never without a few pounds to spend as I chose, and thanks equally to the forbearance of both parents, not indifference but affectionate non-intervention, I was left free to go my own odd way. How much they worried, Dad hardly less than Mother, about my solitary expeditions, I realised only in later years. At the time there was no nagging, only a word of advice about testing strange beds for dampness and watching out for quarries if walking in the mist, and a diffident inquiry, 'Sure you're all right for money?' They could not understand or share my interests, but they masked their misgivings and let me go.

If my theatrical taste was non-existent (or 'catholic' to use a kinder word) my reading was even less critical. I was in a sort of No Man's Land. I had outgrown Henty but the world of adult literature was undiscovered. At school I had started on Euripides, while at home I had not progressed beyond Buchan and Sax Rohmer. Yet my determination to be a writer myself was undiminished. I heard somewhere that '*Roget's Thesaurus* should be on every author's desk' and I still have the copy which I chose as a prize in 1924.

The next summer I sat for my School Certificate, the examination then taken before the academic boys were promoted to the Sixth Form and the others mostly departed to banks and offices. Written tests never worried me. I enjoyed them as a kind of game. The oral French was more alarming, for I had no conversational practice, all our teaching being of a severely literary and grammatical nature. A heat wave was in progress, and the examiner, a professor from the local University College, had established himself in a shady nook among the rhododendrons. At intervals of about five minutes the candidates vanished down the winding path to seek him, and when my own turn came I entered the shrubbery with all the aplomb of a novice hunter in quest of a wounded lion. But the professor, when located, proved the kindest of men. He would ask a question simply and slowly, and as soon as I had uttered a few halting words, enough to suggest that I had caught his general drift, he would interrupt with his next question before I could commit a howler or dry up. After five minutes, in which he had done most of the talking, he dismissed me with a benign smile. I passed. I think we all passed. His name was Ernest Weekley, but if anyone had told me that he was the professor whose wife had run away with D.H. Lawrence thirteen years before, it would have meant little, for I had never heard of Lawrence.

In the holidays I saw an advertisement in which a London publisher invited unknown authors to submit manuscripts, especially poetry. Thus encouraged, I typed out a dozen of my poems and sent them off. Early in September came a flattering response, accepting the book—but on certain conditions. I must help by sharing part of the publisher's risk ... I must understand that this was not at all unusual, and that some very famous authors had paid for the publication of their first books. One or two distinguished Victorian examples were cited. But the sum demanded was out of the question, so I wrote back reluctantly declining the proposition. I could not help asking, in a desperate effort to prevent this open door from closing, whether the risk of publishing the book would be so very great. I had numerous friends and relatives who would be sure to buy copies. I was confident that a hundred could be disposed of in that way.

The publisher replied almost by return post. He discreetly did not comment on my naïve assumption that an author's relatives necessarily fall over themselves to buy his books. But, so impressed was he by the promise of my work, he had reviewed the matter and was able to present an amended offer for a smaller edition in a more modest format. The cost to me would be halved. And, further to meet my difficulties, the payment could be made in small instalments as the book went through its different stages in the press.

The family was by now aware of the agony of temptation I was struggling against. George generously intimated that he would go half-shares. This made all the difference, for I had my scholarship money to cover the rest. A few weeks later I signed an impressive-sounding contract, with much talk of royalties and review-copies and the placing of advertisements.

I went back to school that autumn feeling that the world was at my feet. I was a Sixth Former, I was co-editor with Kenneth Adam of the school magazine, and I was, if not yet quite a published author, at least a poet in the press.

CHAPTER EIGHT

A Dream of Spires

'TRINITY or Balliol—no nonsense, one or the other.'

From Whitehorn, whom I now faced again as my form master, this was an order, almost a divine command, and his precise words are reverently inscribed in my 1925 diary.

He had not taught me for two years, but presumably knew my record. With his forceful personality and Pauline background—St Paul's was reputed to drive its boys to the limit or beyond—he was determined that I should win one of the best Oxford or Cambridge awards.

Somehow I had got on to a conveyor belt with no other destination. The family accepted my fate without enthusiasm. They realised that once a boy had started on useless subjects like Greek he was unfitted for any practical career. Up to that date no Trease had been known to enter a university. Even George, the eventual professor, drifted into the academic life in a slightly unorthodox and casual manner. My father said so little that I still have to guess at his thoughts. I imagine that he considered me a rum lad and regretted my lack of athletic prowess, yet felt some pride in my bookish achievements. If I was really set on college, and could win one of these scholarships, he would back me up. At least I should then have a sure livelihood as a schoolmaster. This was now my official destiny and as I had an incurably didactic side to my nature I faced it cheerfully. Authorship was not an ambition to be publicly proclaimed.

It was usual to spend three years in the Classical Sixth, competing in the last year for the various groups of open scholarships offered between December and March. There were thus about ten of us in the form, the eldest being eighteen. These older boys were prefects and could retire for their private-study periods to the prefects' room in the tower, where they enjoyed a kind of diplomatic immunity. Even the headmaster never trespassed on that winding stair.

Most of my time was now given up to Greek, Latin and ancient history, and the remainder to a little French and English, studied in a desultory way. The serious business of life was Classics, grappling with what seemed to be appallingly intractable unseen translations or with passages of English prose to be rendered into pastiches of Thucydides or Cicero, preparing set books to be construed in class, and gnawing my lonely way through the Platonic dialogue or Sophoclean play assigned to me for private reading. Whitehorn had a scathing tongue and bull-like roar. He was doubtless an excellent schoolmaster, but not for me. One term reduced me to misery. I knew that three years of this Pauline slave-driving would prove more than I could take. There were black moments when I considered a romantic plan to quit school and emigrate to New Zealand, a country I selected because its scenery had so favourably impressed me at the recent Wembley Exhibition.

For one thing I am still grateful to Whitehorn. Whatever work we might be doing for the English master, he insisted that every night we should learn by heart a dozen or more lines from some poem he had chosen. Next morning, before starting other work, we had to stand up in turn and recite, between us recapitulating the poem from the beginning, memorised perhaps a week earlier and repeated daily. Thus I came to know—really know—a vast amount of the best English poetry, Wordsworth, Coleridge, Shelley and Keats, along with *Lycidas* and a number of Miltonic and Shakespearean sonnets. Clearly, it could not have been done in a single term, so I suppose Whitehorn's tradition of daily 'rep' must have been continued by his successor, a very tall, very quiet and gentle Northcountryman named Harold Houghton, whose teaching methods were much more to my taste. For that Christmas Whitehorn left us for Mill Hill, and life thereafter was less strenuous.

Just before Christmas I received the proofs of my own poems, noting proudly in my diary that they looked 'very nice in print'. Another cash instalment was duly remitted to the publisher. Then, in April, came the six author's copies, the slimmest of volumes, dressed in the meanest of bindings, appropriately green. Thankfully I posted the final payment, as I assumed it to be. Two or three days later I came home to find an immense package on the dining-room table. Scrabbling with incredulous and panic-numbed fingers I exposed one hundred copies of my book, sent, explained the accompanying invoice, in accordance with my 'esteemed order' of the previous September. Old as I was, I could not for a few moments stop the tears. They were the first and the last to be shed in a long literary career that has not been without its disappointments,

Somehow this financial crisis was surmounted. My two uncles rallied nobly to my aid, buying several dozen copies each for presentation to their friends. Uncle Jack, the accountant, wrote to me: 'I have just read your book of poems and I am very proud to think that one of our family has found words to express such lofty thoughts so beautifully … I'm rather flabbergasted … your book certainly came as a shock and surprise.' His heart was sounder than his poetical judgement. The poems were bad, I think, even for a fifteen-year-old. Many were about 'friendship' and were lushly sentimental in a way that would not have stood the sophisticated scrutiny of today. Crudely, I needed a girl, but was so naïve that I did not recognise my need. I knew no girls. Had I been at a boarding school I might have sought compensations that were not offered in a day-school environment. But it is a wonder that our new headmaster did not go through the roof, for he had come to us from Rugby and Dartmouth, and was much concerned with combating precocious sexuality. In Nottingham, however, he felt that the main moral danger lay in what he described, with a curl of his lip, as 'calf-love' and 'pavement-lovemaking'. Had I only realised it, a little of that would have done me a world of good.

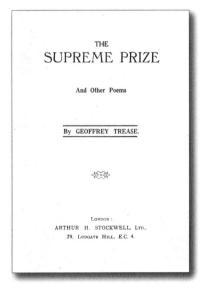

THE

SUPREME PRIZE

And Other Poems

By GEOFFREY TREASE.

LONDON :
ARTHUR H. STOCKWELL, LTD.,
29, LUDGATE HILL, E.C. 4.

Title page of The Supreme Prize

Fortunately, my slim volume contained one eminently respectable poem on Crich Stand, the Sherwood Foresters' War Memorial beacon-tower in the Derbyshire hills—though even that, come to think of it, was startlingly phallic in appearance. Still, anything to do with a War Memorial was, in 1926, above criticism, and this poem could quite safely be reproduced in the school magazine and serve as an unfair sample of the whole collection.

Needless to say, the book sold virtually no copies and was stocked by no sane bookseller. It was no doubt advertised in a few obscure journals (the publisher was scrupulous to fulfil the letter of our agreement) and a handful of insignificant 'mentions' were secured in local newspapers. Then the embarrassing little volume sank quietly into oblivion.

Of more consequence to my future as a writer was the arrival of a new English master, Garry Hogg, only seven years older than myself, whose own literary career was to begin long after mine, but whose influence upon me at this stage was immeasurable. Good-looking, articulate, humorous, with a twinkling quizzical eye, he possessed a southern sophistication and charm to which some of the pawkier Nottingham folk did not respond. I did. One night he took some of us to a lecture at the University College and gave us coffee afterwards at a local cinema. 'Any of you chaps ever write anything yourselves?' he asked lightly. 'I'd always be interested ...' My ears went up like a gun-dog's.

Shortly afterwards I was away from school with a poisoned foot, caused by a rusty nail in my football-boot. I would not now believe it, were the fact not recorded in the school magazine, but I was apparently a member of the House Fifteen, small indication of brilliance but proof that I was not utterly inept. During those ten days of immobility I remembered Hogg's invitation and dashed off a three-act play.

The title, *The Nine Ladies*, did not relate to any conspicuous feminine interest, which my inexperience would have made me singularly ill-qualified to handle. The 'nine ladies' were a circle of prehistoric stones, eerily located in a dark little wood on a Derbyshire hilltop, near another farm on which I had just spent one of my solitary holidays. The form and style of the play were determined by what I had most recently seen at the Theatre Royal. As I had been equally impressed by Esmé Percy touring in Shavian repertory, *Pygmalion* one night, *The Doctor's Dilemma* the next, and so on through the week, and by Hamilton Deane's petrifying dramatisation of *Dracula*, a somewhat incongruous mixture was the result, with pseudo-Shavian discussions and macabre melodrama in equal proportions. The prologue, set in prehistoric times, showed a human sacrifice in the stone circle, with the high priest's knife and the curtain descending simultaneously. The period of the play itself was modern. The high priest was reincarnated as a Welsh doctor who roved the moors at the full moon, content at first to slaughter the odd sheep but impelled at last to seek a human victim, in which enterprise he was abetted by his sinister and crazy Oriental servant. It was, though I say it, good rousing stuff, when the Shavian influence did not slow down the action. There were minor traces, too, of *Outward Bound*, *The Ghost Train* and *The Green Goddess*, popular successes of the nineteen twenties that I had recently enjoyed.

Perhaps the play was not as bad as it now sounds. Garry Hogg was encouraging when he read it: I suppose any enthusiastic English master, presented with a full-length play in his first term at a new school, could hardly have failed to respond. Some time afterwards, when its worst crudities had been tactfully smoothed out, he persuaded me to send it to a publisher—'persuaded', because my unhappy experience with the poems had made me cautious. I still have the two-page letter which came back with it from Geoffrey Faber, chairman of Faber & Gwyer, as they then were. He quoted his reader's report, ending with the query, 'Does he write novels?' (How my heart leapt that a publisher's reader should ask such a question without apparent irony!) Faber went on to say he had read the manuscript himself and endorsed the reader's criticisms. 'I should like to suggest to you,' he continued, 'that you should try your hand upon a novel ... Novels of this genre offer much more scope; and good ones are few and far between ... If you do act on these suggestions, we shall always be pleased to read anything you send us.' It was three or four years before I took his advice and attempted a novel, and, sad to say, Faber's were among the numerous firms that rejected it, but that long personal letter from a great publisher (who, if he guessed my youthfulness, said nothing about it and took me seriously) helped to keep the wavering flame alight within me.

Before that, however, a stimulating friendship had developed with Hogg. He was to be married in the Easter holidays, but for his first two terms he was in lodgings near the school, and so within a few minutes' walk of Portland Road. I doubt if he realised what he was letting himself in for when he issued his casual invitation to 'drop in some evening and borrow a book'. For the rest of that winter, sometimes twice in one week, I might have been seen hurrying eagerly along that foggy street, a handful of books under my arm, a fresh poem or two in my pocket, straining my eyes for the chinks of light between the venetian blinds of his sitting-room on the ground-floor front. Seldom was the window dark, but how black my night when it was! Fortunately for me, the intended bride was living at the other end of England and my new friend had not too many calls upon his time. Even so, I shall always look back with amazed gratitude upon the infinite patience and good-humour with which he received my continual—and protracted—visits.

In that shabby little villa, where the narrow hall was half-blocked with his bicycle, the Aladdin's cave of adult literature was suddenly opened before me. Belloc, Chesterton, Meredith, Hardy, Yeats, Synge, Galsworthy, Gissing, and countless other authors were discovered in those few months. During Hogg's absence in the Christmas holidays his landlady was instructed to let me borrow as many books as I wanted, though he made the realistic proviso that every loan should be recorded in the notebook provided. He knew his books and their precise whereabouts as a shepherd knows his flock. Writing at New Year from his home at Harpenden, with J.C. Squire reading *The Ancient Mariner* over the wireless in the background, he commented: 'It *is* a magnificent poem, you know. There is a copy of it, rather nicely illustrated, two from the right end of the bottom shelf, if you like to have a look at it.'

He was an indefatigable correspondent. He mentioned once that he had written four hundred letters in the preceding twelve months. And they *were* letters, long, articulate, and full of matter, the sheets covered in a fluent minuscule hand that almost demands a magnifying glass. I have kept only a handful of the many he was to send me during the years that followed, but this early one survives and helps me to think myself back into that almost antediluvian period of my life.

'Dear Trease ...' I was 'Trease' for a long time and he was 'Mr Hogg' until my schooldays were over. 'Many thanks for your delightful letter ...' The adjective seems not to have been intended ironically, though it might deservedly have been so. For I had written to him from Fallinge, the moorland farm near the Nine Ladies, where I had stayed in the summer and was now spending the first few days of the New Year. It was a remote spot, reached by a winding track through woods. Beyond it, the grouse-moors climbed higher still to a skyline of weather-beaten gritstone, one of the many 'Edges' that tower above the Derwent valley. In January it was a weird *Wuthering Heights* kind of landscape, not the ideal holiday setting for a lonely and moody adolescent, and parts of my letter had clearly betrayed this. The more cheerful passages had evidently described the charms of life in the farmhouse itself—my private sitting-room with its fragrant log-fire and gentle lamplight, and the splendid meals that awaited me when I came in from a ten-mile tramp, turkey and chicken, mincemeat and apple-pie and cream, and the long evenings of reading and writing until I carried my candle up to my feather-bed.

I was revising *The Nine Ladies*. Though the school dramatic society was presenting *The Rivals* in February, and I was myself struggling with Sir Lucius O'Trigger's brogue, Hogg had secured the headmaster's hesitant permission to put on my play for two nights as an extra production in the summer term, provided that no one's examination work was jeopardised. On Hogg's advice I had undertaken a careful study of William Archer's *Play-making*, and acquired thereby such an obstinate prejudice in favour of 'the well-made play' that forty years later it hindered me from writing for, and even deeply appreciating, the contemporary theatre.

'You have perhaps done some more to your play, by now,' wrote Hogg. 'We will have a good talk about it, with a couple of pencils, next term, and collect our cast before the Easter holidays. Do you want to take a part in it yourself, or produce it? You'll have to decide that point, of course.'

I decided to produce. Before that, with some tactful suggestions from him, I cut and rewrote until a quite actable text emerged. That spring, he was preparing the new house he had bought for his impending marriage. My memories of discussing and revising the play are interwoven with incongruous recollections of helping him to lay crazy pavement and slip cork lino under the feet of the bath. He named the house 'Coverdale' and had screwed on the gate the separate metal letters, bought from Woolworth's. When he returned from his honeymoon a school-friend and I devoted some little time to deciding how best these letters could be rearranged, and then went round in the dusk with a screw-driver, so that the next morning he emerged to find that his address had been changed overnight to 'A Clever Do'. It was not hard to guess where the guilt lay. The same afternoon I received a laconic postcard in that familiar minuscule script: 'Stout work. G.L.H.'

My play was duly produced in June, and was, for its author at least, a heady occasion. A curtain speech was demanded on the first night and again on the last, which was unfortunately also the next. My parents came. Dad's comment was, 'The *cheek* of the kid!' It epitomised the family's attitude to publicity and self-display of any kind.

My friendship with Hogg was quite undiminished by his marriage. I was invited up to meals and his wife always gave me a warm welcome. Privately, perhaps, they were not sorry that they had bought a house three miles away and on the highest hill above the city, protected by gradients that made even the staunchest cyclist dismount. But if my visits were ever thoughtlessly over-frequent, they were both too kind to let me suspect it.

There was nothing at all unusual in such social contacts between staff and pupils, though I think they meant more to me than most. As the university scholarships loomed nearer I used to be invited down to Houghton's on regular evenings with my particular friend and fellow-candidate, W.D. Haden, who later, as headmaster successively of the Mercers School in Holborn and the Newcastle Royal Grammar School, achieved just the kind of career I used to dream of for myself. With Houghton we read Martial's epigrams and anything else which might come in handy for the examination. After an hour or two Mrs Houghton would enter firmly with a tray of coffee and sandwiches, and the session would dissolve agreeably into general chat. There were occasional visits also to the homes of masters supervising the editorial work of the magazine, and of another who wrote incidental music for my play. Altogether, I must have been on visiting terms with about half-a-dozen, which might understandably arouse the suspicion, quite unfounded, that I was developing into an overgrown kind of teacher's pet.

In fact, I had several close friends among my contemporaries, not all in the Classical Sixth and very diverse in character and interests, ranging from another future headmaster (of Canterbury Choir School) and his brother, later provost of a northern cathedral, to a boy who became a dedicated Communist Party member. It sounds as though they had one thing in common, a basic seriousness, not to say solemnity, matching my own. If they had, it was less obtrusive. My memory of them is of acting the fool and of playing elaborate tricks upon the masters and other boys. With such friends I shared walking tours, camping trips or one-day expeditions. We met for the theatre and went to each other's homes. But my trouble was that I had always too much time on my hands. I lived too near the school and lost none in travelling to and fro. Once home, I worked fast and sometimes, my masters hinted, skimpily. I knocked off my prep like a journalist meeting a deadline. Then the evening or the week-end stretched emptily before me. I used to walk miles through the city streets, sometimes three miles each way to visit Haden on the far side of Trent Bridge, sometimes with no objective save to kill the time until sleep. Poems used to form themselves in my head. I can remember often pausing under the foggy halo of a gas-lamp, pulling out an old envelope, and scribbling down the new-minted lines before I forgot them.

I was writing very different stuff now—rondels, sonnets in the colloquial style of Rupert Brooke, taut little verses in the manner of Housman, whose melancholy sentiments chimed all too often with my own moods. Hogg had introduced a new textbook, *The Golden Book of Modern English Poetry, 1870–1920*. It stopped just short of Eliot, but I was devouring the Georgians, Masefield and Flecker and the young poets of the recent war, not least among them Siegfried Sassoon. My own views on war spun round like a weathercock, and the juvenile jingoist of a year or two earlier had become practically a pacifist.

This transformation had its funny side. In the September of 1927 I entered my final year at school not merely as head prefect but as company sergeant-major in the Officers' Training

Corps, the highest rank open to a boy. A fortnight later the debating society passed, by a two-to-one majority, the motion 'that military training in schools be superseded by some less war-like instruction'. I spoke in favour of the motion. The fat was in the fire immediately. The master commanding the Corps summoned a lunch-time meeting of all N.C.O.s and harangued us with tight-lipped fury. A disgraceful debate had taken place which should never have been permitted. Since it had been, cadets had a clear duty, either to oppose the motion or to remain silent. I asked how in that case a fair discussion was possible, since the non-members of the Corps (about half) could easily be accused of not knowing what they were talking about. When we were dismissed, I stayed behind and offered my resignation. It was refused, and I was more or less bound over to keep the peace until I left school. I must perform my ceremonial duties on parade—I should have been sorry anyhow to give up all that delicious play-acting, the stamping and strutting and screaming and saluting—but no more would be expected of me, and I could retire to the prefects' room and check the roll-books. No one really wished to prolong a row which had already gone further than we intended, and we let it go at that.

It is fair to remember that in 1927 Britain and France were the dominant military powers. No one thought Mussolini a menace, Hitler was unknown, Bolshevik Russia though hated was also despised, and Japan had not disclosed her aggressive plans in Manchuria. It seemed reasonable enough for the British to query the armaments of their own apparently invulnerable Empire.

A few months after the O.T.C. affair I relieved my feelings in a poem called 'Satan on the Fives-court'. I visualised the Devil looking down upon the school playground, and went on:

> The O.T.C. came filing out in field-day panoply,
> And Satan winked his ancient eye and scratched his hooves in glee.
> 'Is memory dimmed so swiftly of the passion and the pain?
> Are good pre-war conditions so soon restored again?
> Is that dreamed hour forgotten, when they heard the barrage cease,
> And spring came in November with the trumpets of the Peace? ...
> The war is barely finished, the war to finish war,
> But see the fine old Public Schools preparing hard for more!'
> Just then the Sergeant-Major, all majestic and aloof,
> Came out, and Satan's laughter nearly rolled him off the roof ...

I had the sense at least not to embarrass my co-editor by trying to publish these subversive lines in the school magazine.

At the beginning of December I went up to Oxford, alone, to compete for the first batch of scholarships. Most of my contemporaries were trying for Cambridge, where the links with the High School were much stronger—we had had only four Oxford headmasters since 1513—but Houghton, though himself a Cambridge man, believed that the more literary

O.T.C. camp, Strensall, 1926 (Geoffrey Trease, as a Sergeant, at the near end of the front rank)

emphasis of Classics at Oxford would suit me better than the philological bias of his own university. There was no question, at this stage, of trying for Balliol, for that college had its examination in January. My own group comprised New College, which I put down as my first choice, Queen's, and four more. The examination was held in term-time, so that the usual vacant rooms in the colleges were not available. Hogg, who had been at Wadham, recommended me to his old landlady in St John's Street, and she agreed to lodge me for the three or four days I was to be there.

For the past year I had been gradually building up for myself a vision of Oxford as some kind of celestial city, Lionel Johnson's

> City of weather'd cloister and worn court;
> Grey city of strong towers and clustering spires …

and Flecker's,

> With her fair and floral air and the love that lingers there,
> And the streets where the great men go,

and Andrew Lang's

> … land of waters green and clear,
> Of willows and of poplars tall,
> And in the spring-time of the year,
> The white may breaking over all …
> And Autumn with her crimson pall
> About the towers of Magdalen roll'd:

> And strange enchantments from the past,
>   And memories of the friends of old,
> And strong Tradition, binding fast
>   The flying terms with bands of gold—
> All these hath Oxford: all are dear …

My mind had become a feverish anthology. I knew my 'Scholar Gipsy' and *Jude the Obscure*. But nothing, poetry or prose, worked so yeastlike in my fancy as Compton Mackenzie's *Sinister Street*. I must attain this celestial city. Failure was unthinkable.

I suppose I had worked hard. The headmaster had footnoted my last report, 'Must not overwork and should take physical as well as mental exercise.' He knew nothing of those long late-night walks through the city. Some of the other comments on that report make amusing reading. My tutor, bless him, described me as 'a thorough sportsman', which I treasured as the most inaccurate remark ever made about me until, during the Second World War, I overheard my superior officer assuring Western Command over the telephone that 'of course, Mr Trease is a soldier first and foremost'. More realistic was Hogg's comment on my English work for him: '… must beware of indulging in intellectual superiority …' My Classics had improved, though my prose style was 'just a little too simple' and in the ancient history I was criticised for answering too briefly at times. Perhaps the struggle had already started within me between the scholar and the author.

Anyhow, I caught the train to Oxford in fighting mood and reasonably confident. On arrival I went to tea in New College with a former schoolfellow. The dream had become reality. I was actually walking through twilit quadrangles, finding the right staircase, eating the honeyed toast brought up by the scout from the J.C.R. 'You'll be very happy here,' my host told me, bolstering my confidence. I did not need telling.

For the next three days I sat at a long table in New College hall, with a hundred or more rivals, desperately covering the long foolscap sheets and carrying up the completed efforts to the aloof invigilator on the dais. It was all much as expected: an essay, a general paper, passages from Latin and Greek from which one had, with much head-scratching, to unravel or guess a meaning and reproduce it in good English, and pieces of English prose which contrariwise must be transmuted, with all the low cunning of the faker or the parodist, into something that might have been written two thousand years earlier. 'Low cunning,' I say. Yet there was a better side to it. I have never really regretted that disciplined practice in the turning of abstract and often ambiguous English into the concrete and precise Latin or Greek which had no place for woolly thought.

I enjoyed that three-day tournament. I have little memory of the evenings. I imagine I walked a little in those magical streets of which I had read so much. I was played out and probably went to bed early. I did not believe in last-minute cramming. I just read for a little while, Demosthenes or Tacitus or whatever would set my mind on the right wave-length for tomorrow's paper. On one evening the thirty or so candidates making New College their first choice were summoned for interview. The butler showed us into a long panelled room, adorned with the arms of bygone wardens going back to the fifteenth century. The interviews were short, but we were called in alphabetical order and, as the room gradually emptied, I realised that I was going to be the very last. It was nearly half-past ten when I faced the warden, the historian H.A.L. Fisher, and the flanking dons. The interview was conducted in the urbanest terms. My headmaster's letter had mentioned my play and this was the main topic discussed. There were probing questions and somewhat embarrassed replies. *The Nine Ladies*, when subjected to the scrutiny of several Oxford dons, did not emerge as a highly intellectual creation. But they bade me a very civil good-night and I left without undue dismay.

My most vivid memory of that period is of the morning, a week later, when the results were expected in *The Times*. I rushed out into the winter darkness before breakfast and went down the hill to the newsagent's. I unfolded the paper in the shop and read the small print. New College and two others of the group announced their awards. My name was not there. I went to school in a daze of misery, sure that I had failed, for the other two colleges had been my second and third choices. The headmaster was incredulous—which was flattering but not comforting—and wrote off to Oxford to inquire what had happened. I had not the heart to go down to the newsagent's the next morning, but before I left for school the postman delivered an impressive communication headed 'The Queen's College, Oxford', and beginning, 'I have the pleasure to inform you that you have been elected to a Foundation Scholarship at this College, and offer you my congratulations …'. An hour later, after morning assembly, the school was cheering the announcement of a half-holiday, and the keen golfers on the staff were eyeing me with a new geniality.

One's life can turn on the most trivial of incidents. When my headmaster received the answer to his inquiry he was told that it had been touch-and-go whether New College would give the scholarship. While deliberating, they heard that Queen's would rather like me, so they passed me, figuratively, across the walled lane that separates the colleges. I am still wondering whether, in so doing, they really affected the whole course of my life thereafter.

CHAPTER NINE

Higher Education?

In 1928 it was the accepted thing, at least in my circle, to complete the school year and go straight on to the university after the summer. Doubtless there were boys elsewhere whose parents preferred to remove them from boarding school and dispatch them on a few months' foreign travel. But the economic conditions of the time provided none of the opportunities that students now take for granted. There were no jobs to be picked up easily: with high unemployment the real workers needed all that were going. In any case, middle-class dignity would not have allowed an educated boy to consider the dirty but highly paid manual labour which many will cheerfully tackle today. Hitch-hiking was scarcely heard of: one's range was limited by one's feet, one's bicycle, or the fares one could pay, and the holidays provided time for all the travel one could afford.

So I remained at school for two more terms and enjoyed it, or some of it. Not all.

Nottingham High School prefects, 1928
(The author, then Head Boy, seated second from left, between the Headmaster,
C.L. Reynolds, and W.D. Haden)

Sometimes I sat on the battlemented balcony outside the prefects' room, staring moodily at Nottingham's undulant skyline, saying to myself, 'Never—however long I live—will I forget what this was *really* like, and pretend that this was "the happiest time of my life".' But it was not school, so much as life in general, that produced my adolescent gloom. My generation was, by modern standards, laughably immature. We accepted the hierarchical system of offices and prizes, we relished the petty dignities that we had earned by long years of respectful subordination. To be Captain of the School or Captain of Boats was an honour which, in our enclosed little world, took on an importance incredible to our grandchildren.

Oxford, too, assumed that one was still studying, not lorry-driving or stravaiging about in Nepal. Queen's sent me a reading-list. Naturally, having secured my scholarship, I did not over-exert myself. It had been a long haul and I was glad to relax. I was free, among other things, to take on the lengthy role of Doctor Faustus in the February play. But I did not try to follow up *The Nine Ladies* with another piece of my own. My writing in those last months was confined to seventeen poems. One sonnet, 'The Middle-aged', captures my prevailing mood of revolt, and I find it salutary to make myself re-read it now.

> You old ones say we young are always tragic.
> > We are. But you have made the tragedy,
> You, gross and dull, who have forgot the magic
> > The world once held for you, the poetry,
> The lost cause to be fought for; you, forgetting
> > That mist-hung road on which you turned your backs,
> Turned to your Sunday paper and your betting,
> > Your smoke-room tales, cigars, and income tax.
> If we are discontented, is it strange?
> > We know you had our dreams. Shall we too say:
> 'Too young to start yet', then, 'too old to change'?
> > Shall we too pass unsatisfied away?
> Rather we strive to keep, O worldly wise,
> > The vision which once shone in your young eyes.

These lines appeared in the school magazine and rather saddened Uncle Jack, who had been so unduly impressed by my earlier verses and now felt that I was being less than fair to his own age-group. He was a county councillor with a social conscience, and as a chartered accountant he knew that income tax was an unpleasant reality no one could ignore. Indeed, I was later glad of his professional services myself as I began to degenerate into a materialistic middle age. My more taciturn Uncle Billy, the stockbroker, made no comment on the poem, but he liked a good cigar and I can only hope now that he did not imagine I was attacking him personally.

The family in general must have viewed my development with some misgivings. The scholarship was all very fine, but as Auntie Minnie told me in her blunt, Girl Guide Captain way, I should not find it enough. I should need what she called 'parlour tricks'. She advised me, for a start, to take up tennis. I was never very good, however, at taking advice.

Still, when October came, I caught the Oxford train with the good wishes of them all, and the trunk which had preceded me contained many a generous family gift—a picture, a table-cloth, a coffee-pot, and other items to bring a semblance of home into the shabby impersonality of my college room.

I had never set foot inside Queen's, but photographs, eagerly studied after the award of the scholarship, had familiarised me with the cupola-crowned gateway on the High, the splendid library, and the barrel-vaulted hall with its portraits of royal patronesses and eighteenth-century worthies. Though one of the oldest colleges, founded in 1340, Queen's had been completely rebuilt in the time of Anne and the first Georges. If its cool elegance did not appeal to my unformed taste as strongly as the Gothic picturesqueness of some other colleges, it was mine now and I was prepared to be fiercely proud of its distinctive traditions—the Boar's Head ceremony with its Latin carol, the ancient Founder's Horn still used as a loving cup, and the silver trumpet by which Queen's men, alone in the university, were called to dinner instead of the more ordinary bell.

My rooms were in the back quad, and when I walked into my sitting-room I realised that there was something to be said for Georgian spaciousness. Ample shelves and cupboards flanked the fireplace and two lofty sash windows looked across the quad to a blazing tapestry of Virginia creeper on the other side. The cushioned window-seats concealed coal-bunkers. Every week the coal-man humped the heavy sacks up the innumerable stairs to my second-floor rooms. There was no plumbing anywhere near. All the bath-cubicles and lavatories were concentrated in a subterranean headquarters and I was comparatively lucky in that I had only to go down into the quad and walk a few paces to the very next doorway, which also led to the junior common room. Even so, I was glad to find that my scout, a cherubic Welshman named Thomas, brought a can of hot water when he called me in the morning.

My first day was a little lonely. I knew not a soul in Queen's, and, of the few schoolfellows coming up as freshmen to other colleges, my one particular friend, Haden, was not due at Wadham until the morrow. Queen's was historically a northern college, founded by Queen Philippa's Cumbrian chaplain and subsequently endowed with numerous close scholarships, tied to North Country schools. It was thus a place without exaggerated social pretensions—there were no fox-hunting types standing in doorways, cracking whips, as they were said to do at the House. Queen's had a high proportion of rather sober characters with limited means, who would have to make their own way in the world. As such, it might have been tailored for me.

In those days it was reckoned that an undergraduate could live decently, if not luxuriously, on less than £250 a year. A Rhodes Scholar from, say, Australia found his £400 allowance adequate, though he had no home to go to in vacations and would expect to include some European travel. In my own case the High School had added a £60 leaving exhibition to the £100 of my foundation scholarship, and if my needs had justified it I could have got more by applying to my city. This was not necessary, for I had all those accumulated school-fees now to be drawn on, and Dad assured me that I had only to ask for anything extra within reason. His one anxiety was that I should not 'get into debt', the legendary fate of young Oxford gentlemen. So, having introduced me to his own bank manager, he instructed Bill (who was then plodding painfully through his accountancy exams) to buy a cash-book and show me how to keep proper records of my expenditure. I have it still, reminding me that I paid 14*s* 6*d* for my long scholar's gown and 12*s* 6*d* for the surplice I should need when it was my turn to read the lesson in chapel, 5*s* for two second-hand volumes of Demosthenes, 1*s* 3*d* for 'a cake and two oranges' and £11 for life membership of the Union. Punctilious though I was in entering my expenses to the last halfpenny ('scones 3½*d*') I was never worried about money and was never conscious that I was denying myself anything that would have made life richer.

But that is rushing ahead. My first twenty-four hours, as I say, were a little solitary. One of the second-year men on my staircase spoke to me kindly in a voice that was later to become familiar to millions on radio. The black-and-white name-board told me he was 'W.E. Davis'. Twenty years later I met him at a reunion and learned that he was at the B.B.C. 'Oh,' I said, 'I've been doing quite a lot for North Region—features for Norman Swallow and Children's Hour stuff for Nan Macdonald.' 'I know,' he said, and explained that he was working with 'Uncle Mac' in London. 'You mean you're *David* Davis?' I cried. I had been pleased to renew acquaintance with one I still remembered, after all those years, as the first Queen's man to offer me a helpful, welcoming word, but I was doubly pleased to feel that I had already established my B.B.C. connection. Later, when David succeeded to the headship of Children's Hour, he produced those of my scripts which were not written for Manchester or Birmingham. Our working relationship was most agreeable but we kept it correctly professional and it owed nothing to the old college tie.

In fact, apart from the exchange of a smile and a word on the staircase, I had no further contact with him at Queen's after that first day. I found my own level with the men of my own year, first at the scholars' table in Hall, then in a wider circle inside the college and beyond. Probably the most interesting freshman at Queen's that year was John Newsom, who already exhibited signs of that cheerful flamboyance which marked his subsequent career. I was impressed by the adventures he had already had, sleeping in casual wards to study the life of vagrants and working as a deck-hand on a tramp steamer. I was equally impressed, and envious, because Basil Blackwell was publishing his first book, *On the Other Side*. I was never a close friend of Newsom's, but we often talked and he had a powerful influence upon me.

My first formal duty, that week-end, was to wait upon my tutor. T.W. Allen lived out of college but held his tutorials in a bleak room on the next staircase. When he had scathingly demolished your Greek prose composition, he would hand you his own version of how it should have been done, and, while he called in the next victim, dismiss you to make a fair copy of it in the adjacent bedroom, an unused icy apartment permanently shrouded in dust-sheets.

Allen was as bleak as his rooms. He sat—and I do not blame him—with a travelling rug spread over his knees. His face had a certain distinction. It exuded contempt. His fierce moustache had a faintly Prussian air, and he had a curious trick of jerking his head upwards and sideways, as though his stiff collar irked him. His walk was odd, too, for he brought down one foot with much more weight and deliberation than the other. In the summer you might meet him portentously proceeding along the street, not so much limping as momentarily pawing the ground, a panama hat crowning that distinguished head and a pair of white tennis-shoes encasing those presumably painful feet. Never would he betray the least sign of recognition that you were one of his pupils. The icicle eyes pierced you. Outside the tutorial, you did not exist.

No time was wasted at that initial interview. He made no inquiry about my interests or what I would like to choose from the numerous options offered by the syllabus. He dictated which lectures I should attend as though he were ordering a meal from a waiter. 'You will attend Mr Higham's lectures on Aristophanes … Dr Poynton's on the *Poetics* … my own, of course, on the Homeric Question.'

The comparison with the ordering of a meal is appropriate. Allen's most human characteristic was his love of good food, and his reputation as a gourmet was considerable, though I had no chance to test it, since he never offered me as much as a cup of coffee, let alone a meal. It is said that once a guest at high table, who knew his fame as a Homeric scholar, remarked deferentially: 'I suppose, Mr Allen, you go to Greece quite frequently?'

'Never,' said Allen, with a snort and a twist of the head.

'But—but with your interests—and surely you were given an honorary degree at Athens—'

'The Greeks cannot cook,' said Allen, closing the subject and returning his attention to his plate. Thanks to his insistence, the kitchen staff at Queen's *could* cook. We were reputed to have about the best chef in Oxford. Even we undergraduates used to get a superb four-course dinner for our two-and-threepence, with game in season and sometimes elaborate sweets.

Unhappily, the excellence of our cuisine was not matched in all fields of collegiate life. The Provost, J.R. Magrath, had been an admirable character in his day, but he had been elected a Fellow in 1862 and was now nearing the end of his sixty-eight years as a don of the college, half-a-century at its head. He survived like some ancient tortoise, but I never saw him. With his deputy, a clergyman named Walker, I recall just two personal conversations, at the beginning and end of my university career. At the first he informed me that no one had written any good novels since Jane Austen, though William de Morgan's were not without merit. I did not find him sympathetic.

There were, of course, some brilliant dons at Queen's, such as the future Lord Franks. But in my first year I encountered no one but Allen, and a superannuated Christ Church don who tottered in to read the *Georgics* with us. When the General Election of 1929 was looming, he informed us that if the Socialists won a majority he would retire to Metz. The particular attractions of that city he did not define.

Allen's lectures on the Homeric Question were intolerably boring. I sympathised instinctively with his concern to prove that Homer had been a poet, not a committee or an evolutionary process, but the detailed evidence was tedious. I noted that, though it was a university course and open to all, no men came from other colleges. There were some girls, frowning and earnestly scribbling, but otherwise only ourselves. We could hardly cut our own tutor's lectures, though it might have been a way to test his awareness of our existence as individuals. That was the trouble. I had a most uncongenial tutor and, since he was also the Senior Tutor, I did not know whom to appeal to for a remedy.

I envied my friends who had approachable tutors with whom they could discuss their work, their preferences and difficulties Haden used to tell me about Maurice Bowra at Wadham. It sounded like another world. Yet I realise now that my own experience was by no means unique. James Lees-Milne must have been up at Magdalen, a very different type of college, at this time. In his autobiography, *Another Self*, his bitter recollections of the 'authorities' match my own.

Unless an undergraduate was outstanding, he writes,

they did not care a damn whether he sank or swam. He would have no encouragement, no help. Tuition was minimal. His tutors were either too busy or too lazy to be bothered. So long as he attended the prescribed number of lectures he would not be penalized in any way. And who the hell can learn from lectures? ... A student does far better to read the stuff quietly in his room ... But he does need personal guidance as well ... My three years at the University were a complete waste of time, a blank in my life over which I do not now care to linger.

As a Classics man, reading Honour Mods and then Greats, I was committed not to three years but to four, and should be nearing my twenty-third birthday before I could tag 'B.A.' to my name.

Life, fortunately, was not all work. It was reckoned that a steady average of three hours a day—real work, that is—was enough to cover the ground. This modest limit was surprisingly hard to attain. The morning was usually consumed by a couple of hour-long lectures, perhaps at ten o'clock and twelve, and in widely separated colleges, so that there was not much chance to settle down to any private study before lunch. The lectures themselves could not honestly be counted as 'work' in any productive sense. It was not done to work in the afternoon. One was expected to play games or at least take healthy exercise. I walked with like-minded friends, either along the riverside paths or further out into the real country, to Otmoor or some Roman villa in the Cotswolds, or in the summer term took a canoe up the Cherwell from Magdalen Bridge. Tea-time might arrive and conscience would refuse to admit that one's mastery of the Classics had been so far advanced not one iota that day. If one was not too drowsy after the healthy exercise and the anchovy toast and walnut cake beside the roaring fire, one *might* manage an hour or two's solid reading, or wrestle with the weekly prose-composition for Allen, before the sweet blast of the trumpet in the cloisters called one to snatch up one's gown and rush down the rumbling stairs to see what that chef had devised for dinner. Too often, though, one had friends to tea or was accepting a return invitation in another college, and the talk went on and on. In my first year the sheer novelty of possessing a room of my own in which I could entertain my friends was an intoxication I could not resist. I remember once realising that for the next ten days ahead I had either invited men to tea or committed myself elsewhere. When *was* the work to be done? After dinner, perhaps, by a powerful exercise of self-discipline? But what a waste when every night there was so much going on outside! In that first year I saw and heard two of the authors I most venerated, Belloc and Chesterton—indeed, I nearly enjoyed the fatal distinction of being trodden on by Chesterton, for I was sitting on the floor in the central gangway at his packed lecture when I turned my head at the welcoming applause and saw that gargantuan white waistcoat looming over me like a summer cloud. Bertrand Russell, William Temple, Masefield, Osbert Sitwell … the celebrities passed through Oxford in a ceaseless stream. To a youth from a provincial city, who practically speaking had never seen any famous person in the flesh, every notice-board offered some fresh enticement.

I had at least enough sense to realise that I could not do everything. I had been tempted to join the O.U.D.S. but knew that my acting was not good enough. I had come up with some vague hopes of opportunities in university journalism, and on the first Saturday of term I called at the offices of the *Cherwell* near Folly Bridge, had a brief conversation with two rather grand young men, and handed them two poems in an envelope, which they accepted without apparent excitement or curiosity. As the weeks (and eventually the terms) went by without any news—the editor lacking the energy even to reject unwanted contributions—I dismissed the matter from my mind. I should not have been so quickly discouraged had not my interest concentrated itself by then upon the Union.

Here, in the Thursday night debates, was a field open to all, even though the beginner had little hope of being called until the last half-hour or so, when his audience had dwindled to the white-tied officers and a handful of his impatient competitors. I made my maiden speech quite early in my first term and felt my future assured when I read the *Isis* report: 'Mr R.G. Trease (Queen's) was a delightful surprise, and performed a feat I have never seen done before—he roused the Union to interest after 11 o'clock.'

Ours was not a strong Union college, but by a happy coincidence it was a Queen's man, Roger Wilson, a Quaker from Manchester Grammar School, who that term defeated Quintin Hogg and became, after Christmas, the first Labour man ever to be elected President. Wilson noticed and encouraged me. The next term, he gave me a chance to speak 'on the paper', to be, that is, one of the first four speakers, named on the printed notice of the debate. He even thoughtfully arranged the loan of tails for the occasion, for few of us possessed more than a dinner jacket. My account-book records the purchase of a white waistcoat for half a guinea and a tie for two shillings, and towards the end of my second term I was able to read, on every notice-board:

QUESTION FOR DEBATE
'That Oxford today is not worthy of its traditions.'
Moved by Mr J.P.W. Mallalieu, Trinity.
Opposed by Mr R.G. Trease, The Queen's.

I can remember nothing of the debate or the voting, only the elation with which I sailed down the High just before midnight, and the thought that a scholar's gown, worn over full evening dress, was the most splendid attire a young man could aspire to in the drab twentieth century.

Quintin Hogg won the presidency for the summer term. The other leading lights of that period included Michael Stewart, sitting like an alert little fox at the Secretary's table, Boyd-Carpenter and Edgar Lustgarten. Derek Walker-Smith was a freshman like myself. The standard of oratory, judged by the traditional Union standards which exalted the epigram, the paradox and every sort of verbal pyrotechnics, seemed to me amazingly high.

I began to cherish ambitions. I did not fully realise, what time would have taught me, that to win votes and climb the ladder of office called for more than polished rhetoric. It was advisable to belong to a strong Union college and come from a big school with numerous Old Boys who knew your name and would give you their votes if only from a sense of loyalty. Still more desirable was it to join one or other of the political associations.

I never did this. My ideas were still in a state of flux. At one presidential debate the visiting speakers included Oswald Mosley, a minister in the newly formed Labour Government. He was supporting a motion in favour of Socialism. I went along certain of at least one thing: I should have to vote against him. Mosley made an excessively long speech, far too long for such an occasion, but of such compelling brilliance that I felt no impatience. I knew I was being carried away, just as one knows, after a certain number of drinks, that one would be ill advised to give an immediate answer to some catchy proposition. I would not let myself vote with Mosley, but I could not vote against him, and when the house divided I could only abstain. It was odd to recall years later, when I regarded myself as a convinced Socialist, that I owed my conversion to a man by that time stigmatised as a turncoat and a Fascist beast.

What else stands out in memory from that year?

There was a great frost in February. The Cherwell was solid jade, the Meadow and Mesopotamia put on a new Scandinavian beauty. Even the Isis froze and the Torpids could not be rowed. The cold water in my bedroom jug was a block of ice for a fortnight. As my scout was off duty between lunch and dinner, he always left a can of water on each landing so that we could fill our own kettles at tea-time. During those weeks I had to stand the can on the hearth and thaw its contents first.

As so often, the severe winter was followed by an idyllic summer. I missed the full benefit, for, within a day or two of enjoying the May Morning ritual, I woke up with the strong conviction that I was starting mumps. 'Better report to the Dean, sir,' Thomas advised me. 'He's a medical doctor. *He'll* know.' The Dean confirmed my fears. 'Go to your room and I'll come up and see you.' I obeyed. Luckily it was a fairly mild attack, as adult attacks go, for he never came near me and no other doctor was sent. Thomas moved my bed into my sitting-room and for the next three weeks he was the only person allowed across the threshold. From my tutor, needless to say, there was no word. Only for one reason had I cause, indirectly, to be grateful to Allen: invalids, Thomas explained, enjoyed the same menu as High Table, and, as my swelling subsided and I was able to eat normally, I did benefit from the critical attention my tutor had always lavished upon the college catering.

Friends came, stood on the landing, and chatted through the doorway. In the third week Thomas informed me, presumably on higher authority, that I might take the air in Christ Church Meadow, so long as I kept my distance from all members of the college. With Finals looming for the senior men, I must not contaminate anyone. The enforced solitude at least enhanced my appreciation of the heart-catching beauty that surrounded me on every side in that early summer of halcyon sunshine. I saw the Oxford the poets had led me to expect.

When I returned to normal life the term was half over, yet somehow I packed a remarkable amount into those last four weeks. It was a light-hearted time, with much desultory paddling of canoes up the leafy tunnels of the Cherwell, much enthusiastic reading and discussion of what we regarded as modern poetry—no mention still of Eliot—and much hilarity. My closest friends drank little. Perhaps words and ideas were sufficient intoxication. Certainly there were times when our high spirits might have convinced a casual passer-by that we were rolling drunk, though a pint of beer or cider, if that, would be all we had taken.

Of my three particular friends that term one, a fellow scholar of Queen's, was to take a double First and go to Nigeria in the Colonial Service, while the others, at different colleges, were to become professors respectively of theology and, of all languages, Romanian. This gives a misleading impression that the company I kept was excessively serious. The reality was quite different. But all those three, I came to recognise, possessed—behind the mask of fun and absurd fantasy—something I did not, a good academic brain and the pertinacity to use it.

None of my circle was actively concerned in politics—many did not even join the Union, much less share my interest in its debates. No one had journalistic or literary aspirations, no one afterwards went into publishing. In short, in my time at Oxford I met no 'useful people', and it never occurred to me then that such contacts could be the most valuable by-product of a university career. If I had thought of it, and set out in the most calculating spirit to cultivate that kind of friendship, I wonder if it would have made any difference in the long run?

At the end of each term there was the 'don rag'. One by one we climbed the stairs to the Senior Common Room to face the Pro-Provost and Fellows seated at a long table and hear a caustic report on our progress from the tutor concerned.

'Mr Trease', said Allen, jerking his distinguished head and twisting distastefully inside his collar, 'had the misfortune to contract—er—mumps, at the beginning of the term. This misfortune appears, however, rather to have—er—fortified his reading than to have interfered with it.'

Fair enough. Once the first days of the illness had passed, I had worked quite steadily throughout my quarantine. I forget what else Allen said, but it was nothing drastic. At an earlier don rag he had informed his colleagues that I could not write English, and this had hurt more than anything he could say about my Greek.

The Pro-Provost murmured something in dismissal. I bowed to the learned assembly and withdrew in good order. I was looking forward to a long summer in which I planned to alternate several short trips with spells of work in the undistracted calm of Portland Road. I went down from Oxford with no inkling of any crisis ahead.

CHAPTER TEN

Drop-out 1929

THE first break in my reading schedule was slightly out of character. I went to the conference camp of the Student Christian Movement at Swanwick in Derbyshire.

I was not a member, nor was I particularly pious. We had never been a church-going household. My father roundly declared that he had attended enough services in childhood to excuse him for the rest of his life, and Mother's 'nerves' prevented her, during my formative years, from taking me herself. However, a school friendship at thirteen had led to my attending a Sunday afternoon children's service in another parish, and then, as adolescence worked within me, I went on to individual appearances at matins in my own church, where I sat at the back and politely declined invitations to join Granny and the aunts in the family pew. In due course, entirely on my own initiative, I got myself confirmed and used to take Holy Communion at the fairly long intervals then considered reasonable in what I still regarded as the Protestant faith. True, my addiction to Belloc, Chesterton and the early novels of Compton Mackenzie stirred a few wistful hankerings for the brighter colours of Catholicism, but fundamentally my interest in Christianity sprang from social conscience rather than mystical fervour. My temperament was ill-suited to prayer, contemplation, and ineffable ecstasy. I was concerned with problems of peace and poverty. Even those juvenile verses written at school serve now to date the dawning of my social conscience, when I could not write about the gaiety of the Goose Fair without pointedly contrasting it with the permanent situation of the working class as I observed it in the back streets and alleys not ten minutes' walk from my own home—the fate, I ranted angrily:

> Which makes them dwell in unloved homes, 'mid fish-saloons and bars,
> With line on line of washing hanging 'twixt them and the stars.

This preoccupation had been strengthened at Oxford in a variety of ways, from conversation with contemporaries like Newsom to powerful sermons delivered at St Mary's by preachers like Temple, F.R. Barry, and Studdert-Kennedy. And so far, despite Mosley and all the other eloquent political speakers at the Union, I hoped for more from the churches than from the parties.

Even so, I doubt if I should have thought of attending the camp but for my future-theologian friend, Bob Leaney of Hertford, who was also to join me later on a walking tour.

Once at Swanwick, I did not regret going. Students had come from all the British universities. Colonial bishops, missionaries, social reformers, Christian intellectuals and fraternal foreigners swarmed, denominational differences laid aside. We slept and ate in tents and vast marquees, and participated in seminars, lectures, services and lighter forms of entertainment. It was all interesting and often amusing too. The mansion itself was crammed with female Student Christian Movers, but I must confess with shame that they did not move me, though presumably they shared all our day-time activities. Clearly I was a late developer even by the standards of my own generation. Bob's heart was already given to the girl he married as soon as he had taken his degree.

The camping we planned for a few weeks later was to be rather different from the canvas-town existence of Swanwick. In preceding years I had covered a good deal of fresh ground—the Lakes, Shropshire, the Wye Valley, the Malverns and the Forest of Dean—but now I wanted to return to my beloved Peak district, show it off to Bob, and penetrate to the wilder corners I had never seen. We were to travel light and sleep rough, though the lightness must have been relative.

'My spirits soar,' Bob wrote from his home in Birmingham. 'My room is littered with packs, tents, stoves, water-bottles, sleeping-bags, Oxford texts, S.C.M. publications and pyjamas ... I have found our tent without any difficulty, very light and small when packed ... I have bought a Meta solid fuel stove, so we shall not want meths. I think, though, we'll definitely try to make fires ... I'm trying the sleeping-bag this week-end. Laurence has already surreptitiously tried it on the floor in his bedroom and says if anything it is too hot. It is rather a lovely thing ... I am getting on pretty well with work so that I shall be able to enjoy our hol: with a beautifully free conscience. Aeschines' *In Ctesiphontem* is a sight more gentlemanly, interesting and persuasive rationally than the bombastic *De Corona*.'

The hot summer continued. At Swanwick I had nearly given myself sun-stroke, and when our tour brought us to the great Derwentwater reservoir on the Yorkshire border it looked like a half-emptied bath. The high grouse-moors and bogs were utterly devoid of shade. At night we sometimes did not need the tent. By day the glare was dazzling and our packs pressed leaden on our shoulders, soaking our shirts with sweat. Once, after a particularly gruelling midday tramp across the desolate peat bogs, we were cheered by the sight of the first stone wall in the distance. We made for it, promising ourselves a rest in its shade, only to find that the three o'clock July sun was falling almost exactly along it. There was a stripe of shadow about six inches wide. We flung ourselves down and thrust our peeling noses gratefully into it.

It was a grotesque landscape, beautiful and also alarming. The map was peppered with place-names worthy of the scene. The Salt Cellar, Cakes of Bread, Raddlepit Rushes, Featherbed Moss, Snake Pass, Slippery Stones, Cranberry Clough, Madwoman's Stones, Ringing Roger, and—all too ominous—Lost Lad, were well up to the standard of the Nine Ladies that had caught my fancy long ago. That brown-green wilderness was as stark as any country in England, and the grouse-shooters meant to keep it so. One could walk for hours without a glimpse of human occupation. All the more attractive were the little hamlets, sunk deep in tree-bowered dales, with sometimes a packhorse bridge, a mill, or a seventeenth-century manor-house built of the same grey-white stone.

Home, then, for another stint of the Homeric Question, Aristotle, Juvenal, the *Georgics*, with notebooks and texts and the huge open dictionaries covering the table in our cool north-facing dining-room ... In August another week's walking, in the West Country I had never seen, and this time alone.

The railway companies used to issue reduced holiday return tickets, but only to specified resorts and for precise periods, either eight or fifteen days. This explains the otherwise puzzling fact that I set off for Weston-super-Mare, a town in which I did not propose to linger a minute longer than necessary. It was as far west as I could afford to take the train, and, since I could not spare time or money for a fortnight, I had to cram as much as I could into a week.

The idea of hitch-hiking had barely begun to impinge on the British consciousness. Someone, Newsom most likely, had introduced me to this revolutionary notion that there was nothing inherently shameful in asking for a lift, and as I strode through the unexciting outskirts of Weston early that evening it came back into my mind. The unpremeditated decision was almost instantaneous: smooth Somerset was not enough, I would go to Cornwall, the land of my forefathers, and I would hitch-hike. To lend precision to my resolve I would go to Boscastle, where I knew that Laurence Giles, my closest friend at Queen's, was staying with his family. It would be fun to surprise him. I vowed that I would be at Boscastle tomorrow and without spending a farthing on public transport. Elated, I quickened my stride, and those haunting lines of Hardy rang in my head, apt for my mood:

> When I set out for Lyonnesse,
> A hundred miles away …

Nowadays, when any truant school-child seems able to ride the overnight lorries from Scotland to London without difficulty, it is hard to invest my little Cornish jaunt with the romance and adventure which it held for me at the time. But the north coast road I meant to follow was not a route used by long-distance lorries, and the traffic, as I soon found, consisted mainly of holiday-makers' cars, crammed with children and luggage, and of locals always about to turn down the next side-road. Drivers were not expecting hitch-hikers. There was no recognised signal with which to identify oneself, which meant that once one entered a built-up area there was nothing for it but to march forward until the last houses fell behind. This did not worry me unduly, for I intended to walk a fair mileage. Free lifts were a supplement, not a substitute.

That evening I got through Bridgwater and saw the noble curved backs of the Quantock Hills stretched like a sea-serpent against the tangerine sky. It would soon be dark and I ought to be thinking about a bed. But in my exhilaration I pressed on, prepared (I told myself) to sleep out if necessary on the beach of the Bristol Channel. It would be no new experience. Under Belloc's inspiration I had spent more than one night alone under the stars, in woodlands or in a haystack or on the moors. It was fortunate that the necessity did not arise on this occasion, for it would not have been easy to grope my way down to those desolate shores in the darkness, and I should have found their stratified rock ledges, mud and puddles less comfortable than the soft sands of Lincolnshire which I mistakenly supposed to be typical of English beaches. But soon after leaving Bridgwater I was given the third and last short ride of the day. My benefactors dropped me at a lane-end near (I now suppose) the village of Kilve, where the Quantocks sweep down to the coast at their northern end, and the road wriggles past them to Minehead, Porlock and the west. I saw a light in the gloom and heard a man chopping sticks. I walked forward and spoke to him, and in a few minutes—so easy were such matters in those days, or perhaps so great the need of farmers' wives and cottagers to pick up another five shillings—I was fixed up with a bedroom and was sitting down to a lavish cold supper.

If a gipsy had then appeared (and the Quantocks were a great place for such folk) and told me in what circumstances, in another five years, I should myself be a cottager only a few miles from that spot, I should have scoffed at so palpably absurd a prediction.

I was on my way next morning as soon as I could swallow my bacon and eggs. I was only sorry that I had to gulp down the equally delectable scenery at the same brisk pace, but I had my vow to keep. A tradesman's van gave me a few miles' lift towards Minehead. The Quantocks and the Brendons were tossed over my shoulder, Selworthy Beacon pushed up its isolated hump against the sea to my right, Exmoor rose sombre and immense in front. I need not have worried about rushing past all the scenery. Once I had started to clamber up Porlock Hill the gradients banished any hope that a motorist would stop to offer me a lift. I was committed to several miles of stiff climbing, with plenty of enforced opportunities to stand and contemplate the view. And a good view it was when I had cleared the lower woodlands—the expanse of the Channel with the misty hills of South Wales far beyond, the purple of the heather and the gold of the gorse rolling across Exmoor to the summit of Dunkery, and ahead, along the indented coast, a glimpse of the sliced red cliffs of Devon.

I was off my one-inch map, had been long ago. I knew only the names of the chief places I had to pass through: Lynton, Barnstaple, Bideford, Bude. The distance that day was about a hundred miles, trivial by today's reckoning, but I walked about twenty-five of those miles and used a dozen different vehicles to cover the remainder. It is thus not completely inexplicable that sunset found me somewhere on the border of North Cornwall, still short of the objective I had set myself, and increasingly uncertain where I should spend the night.

It was then that I was offered the final lift of that long day. I had begun with a baker's van, now it was a limousine that slid to a discreet halt beside me. Though I had made no kind of signal, I expect I had turned my head wistfully at the sound of a car. My weary gait, my knapsack and the late hour spoke for themselves, and my college blazer may have helped. We wore blazers a lot in those days, and people—wisely or not—accepted them as evidence of respectability.

A patrician lady bade me get in. The chauffeur got out. A spare rug was deferentially spread over my sun-burnt knees. We glided forward again into the gloaming. I suppose I was questioned and gave a satisfactory account of myself. At all events, my benefactress assured me that they would be passing within about three miles of Boscastle and would drop me at the turning. Meanwhile, late though it was, I really *must* see Crackington Haven. The chauffeur was instructed to make the necessary detour. We drove past Poundstock, where my great-grandfather was born, and plunged down a steep by-road towards the sea. Somewhere above us, under the black sky, was the little hill-top church of St Gennys, where my ancestor, Peter Trease, married Joan Sharp in 1740. I am sure this information would have delighted my kindly companion, but I did not possess it myself until about thirty years later. Then I knew only vaguely of my family's Cornish origins. I had no notion that the dark countryside around me was the particular corner in which every other churchyard held the bones of my forebears—men like John Treese of St Minver's, who was fined sixpence in 1606 for an assault 'that drew blood', or the Rev. William Treise, Rector of St Mabyn, 'reckon'd a profound scholar, and his compositions extraordinary', but ejected in 1662 for nonconformity.

We reached the Haven, crept through the water-splash at the bottom, and paused for a few moments so that I could admire the wildness of the place, most of which I had to imagine, though a certain luminosity from the breaking waves did a little to define the shape of the cliffs. Then we drove on, climbing out of the Haven, and a few minutes later I was deposited at a desolate turning on Tresparrett Down. A signpost, illegible by now, pointed in what I was assured was the direction of Boscastle. A gibbet would have been more in keeping with the spirit of the place at that hour. As the red rear-light of the car went winking round the next bend, I felt a slump in my morale for the first time in that endless day. I had no idea of my surroundings. In the daylight, I suppose, I should have seen rather prosaic fields enclosed by steep Cornish banks with a riot of fuchsia and hart's-tongue fern. But I felt as though I had been dumped on a blasted heath and might encounter a spectral huntsman at any moment. The fact is, I was dead-beat and famished.

I heaved my pack on to my shoulders and plunged down the lane. 'Down' was the right word, for the gradient steepened until the tarmac seemed to be falling away from under my feet. The night was abysmally black. I could not even say with Hardy that 'starlight lit my lonesomeness when I set out for Lyonnesse ...'. Not a twinkle pricked the gloom. There was a constant, rather sinister murmur, a blend (I fancy) of the wind on the heath and the sea somewhere below. Though my feet rang on a purposeful road, which presumably led to a safe and civilised termination, I could not quite suppress an absurd fear that at any moment now this sharply slanting surface would finally curl over into the vertical and propel me into some maelstrom. In three-quarters of an hour I saw no light from house or vehicle.

Then, suddenly, I was in the village that climbs the hillsides around the little land-locked harbour, and the street was full of chattering people. I had arrived just as the weekly film-show ended in the hall, and most of the population were drifting home in sociable clusters. I fell into step with some lads and inquired what hope there was of finding accommodation so late. One youth immediately assured me that there would be a bed at his auntie's, and in no time, just as on the previous evening in Somerset—was it only twenty-four hours ago?—I found myself welcomed in, and sitting down in the mellow lamp-light to cold ham and stewed raspberries and Cornish cream.

The next morning I enjoyed the surprise on my friend's face when I appeared at his lodgings at breakfast-time. I knew where he was, of course. We were all copious letter-writers, in that respect closer to the eighteenth century than to today. It would have been unthinkable not to exchange holiday addresses.

I had no intention of intruding, however, upon what seemed a close-knit family group, including two sisters and a huge, hirsute and ebullient sheep-dog. I wanted to see local places, notably Tintagel, that were already over-familiar to them, and I dared not stay long in Cornwall at all. It was a long road back to the railway-station at Weston-super-Mare, and I did not wish to cover it at the same breakneck speed on the return journey. I took a walk with Giles and I lazed on the beach with them all, but I made my usual solitary explorations. I had just begun to keep a random notebook, a habit encouraged by Garry Hogg and continued in a desultory manner ever afterwards. It helps me now to recapture moments from those days—my first Cornish tea in a cottage-garden at Trevalga, looking over shaggy fields that curved to the lip of the cliffs and the satin-smooth Atlantic beyond, and a rest in the shade by the Camel, 'a little brown stream, overshadowed by great trees and fringed with ferns … A Cornish girl, with a long auburn plait, rides by on a pony whose tail sweeps the ground.' It will be seen that I was beginning to observe the life around me, but detachedly.

My return journey was without special significance, though as a mere holiday experience it was happy and rich in impressions. Hitch-hiking broke down my natural shyness, gave me an excuse—indeed the necessity—for contact with strangers, and prevented the megrims. Nor was the contact limited to friendly motorists.

At Bridgwater, in the bookseller's doorway, I was addressed by an elderly lady with a direct though agreeable manner. The encounter is worth mentioning, because quite unexpectedly we were to meet again.

'Excuse me,' she said, 'but are you in the Bedford First Fifteen?'

I saw she was staring at the Queen's eagle on my blazer pocket and the misunderstanding was cleared up. 'Have you been up St Mary's tower?' was her next question. 'Oh, but you must. That was where Monmouth climbed and saw the King's troops in the distance across Sedgemoor.' She took me across to the parish church and waited while I went up the tower. Then she conducted me to an old house, opposite Judge Jeffrey's lodgings, where the local prisoners had received their summary sentences after the battle. 'Sold to an American!' she commented explosively. Finally she insisted on giving me lunch in a splendidly panelled restaurant close by, where she was received with obvious deference. As we ate, she quoted Lewis Carroll, and Virgil in the original, and mentioned the good time she had once had in Alaska. She was an Admiral's widow and, being a fair mathematician, had herself worked at the Admiralty during the late war. More recently she had been helping out in some capacity at a boys' public school, and, having finally retired to a flat in Bridgwater, was missing young company.

'And where are you making for now? Glastonbury tonight? Then you must stay at Chalice Well. It's a guest-house. *Was* a monastery—modern, of course—but the R.C.s moved off when someone bought the Glastonbury ruins and gave them to the C. of E. The R.C.s knew then they'd *never* get back into Glastonbury and make it a big centre for themselves. The original Chalice Well is in the garden, they'll show it you—*you* know, where Joseph of Arimathaea hid the Holy Grail—'

Mrs Shipster gave one little time, and no encouragement, to plead ignorance.

At last I continued on my way, crossing the heat-hazy levels of Sedgemoor through that early September afternoon. My notebook reminds me of my pleasure in little things like the creamy-rich syllables of the names on a signpost, 'Chedzoy' and 'Weston Zoyland', and a talk with a man operating an old cider press, the layers of apples on straw, squashed together by wooden beams as he tightened the hefty iron screws. And on Mrs Shipster's instructions, not to be ignored, I called upon a friend of hers, a woman painter living in a caravan which proved to be an immense pantechnicon with empty shafts slanting down to the grass. I slept that night at the guest-house, which proved to be rather feminine, jumperish and vegetarian, and as pure as the ever-flowing Chalice spring. I was sufficiently affected by the atmosphere to slip out next morning before breakfast and walk barefoot up the pilgrim's path to the top of Glastonbury Tor. But later in the day I was sitting in a pub at Priddy, on the top of the Mendips, with a young man I had met on the road. He was returning to Cheddar, and was sure that there was a vacant room in the same house, so I went with him and thereby saw Cheddar Gorge to great advantage, for we descended it in the late evening, when the last picnickers and parked cars had vanished, the show caves were shut for the night, and the limestone ravine had regained its pristine dignity, with jagged cliffs against a rose-pink sky.

Next day was the eighth of my tour, and I made for Weston-super-Mare. It had been a varied and eventful week, but quite how eventful I did not immediately realise.

It was time to attack my books again. Breakfast over, I carried my armful into the dining-room, Liddell and Scott's enormous dictionary, Oxford texts, annotated editions, notebooks … I opened them and laid them out, I pulled up a chair, and then I received my instantaneous, blinding, damascene revelation. For instantaneous I now recognise it to be, though for some weeks I deluded myself that I was keeping an open mind and that nothing irrevocable had been decided.

I could not go on. I was bored to death with this musty scholarship, this wearisome gibberish concocted by the pedants. 'An excellent example of where the Riccardianus, backed by the Arabic, restores omissions in the Paris MS …' And, 'Lobel has conjectured', 'Van Leeuwen emends', '*commendat Eust.*' and—most absorbing of all—'*24 post 25 posuit G, postponi voluit P5.*' What had this to do with poetry? As Yeats put it, in 'The Scholars':

> Bald heads forgetful of their sins,
> Old, learned, respectable bald heads
> Edit and annotate the lines
> That young men, tossing on their beds,
> Rhymed out in love's despair …
> … Lord, what would they say
> Did their Catullus walk that way?

One year of Oxford at its driest, unrelieved by one flash of inspiration, humour or understanding from any don concerned with me, had suffocated the enthusiasm with which I had gone up from school. I told myself that if I went on like this for another three years I should hate the Classics for the rest of my life.

It is easy to say now that I had never had the stuff in me to make a true academic, that I really never amounted to more than the 'clever boy' who shoots his bolt at scholarship level and fades out when confronted with the exacting discipline of an Honours course. But no one had suggested it then. And I had never for one moment toyed with the fantasy of a fellowship, let alone a chair. I had dreamed of being a headmaster, perhaps, but never a don.

Now, I gloomily persuaded myself, that dream was out. Even if I choked back my nausea and stomached three more years of the Oxford course, I could not see myself taking a good degree. And how far would a poor one take me, lacking as I did what Auntie Min termed 'parlour tricks' to make up the deficiency? I ought to have been scared. This was September 1929—perhaps I *should* have been scared if I had foreseen the economic conditions that lay just ahead. But, ridiculous as it may seem, that so-modest hitch-hiking adventure had given me a little nerve, as well as clearing my mind.

For the last month of the vacation I lived with my secret. I could not discuss it with my family. I justified my silence by reasoning that I did not want to upset them until the issue was decided, and that so far it was not. I made myself set out my books again on the second day, but my revulsion was as strong as ever. Still, I remained open to argument—argument, that is, by the college dons, the only people who could help me. For that reason I did not write to Queen's, announcing my intention to abandon my course. I would go up to Oxford in the usual way, tell them how I felt, and hear what they said.

I did confide in Garry Hogg, who was appalled but offered prudent advice. 'What do your people say?' I explained why I had not told them yet, and no one must. 'If I do leave Oxford,' I told him, 'I don't want to come home until I've found some sort of job and can keep myself.' I knew how fatally easy it would be, otherwise, to go back to Portland Road and hang about while a forgiving father looked round for a suitable 'opening', probably in some friend's business in the town. 'What *will* you do then?' Hogg asked. I cannot remember what I answered. But the last entry pencilled in my notebook before I went up to Oxford runs: 'Emigration to U.S.A. Cheapest passage—about £21. Passport with visa. Two birth certifs., six photos. Medical examination at Liverpool. Waiting list: probably 3 or 4 months to wait. The support of someone in U.S.A. required.'

I knew nobody in the States. But before I had time to worry about surmounting that difficulty, Hogg came out with a sensible counter-suggestion. 'Look,' he said, 'if you do leave Oxford—*if* you do—I have an aunt who runs a settlement in the East End. I could write to her if you like and see if she'd take you on for a while. You'd live in, and earn your keep—it'd be quite hard work, mind you. Still, you'd be independent and it would give you time to think about the next step.' I snatched at the suggestion eagerly. It chimed well with my growing interest in social problems. And the obvious contrast between slumland reality and dreaming spires gratified my urge for self-dramatisation.

Meanwhile, I went up to Oxford as if nothing had happened. I moved into the better rooms on the same staircase that I had applied for in June. I took the test papers on my vacation work. As college representative for the Union I went diligently round the freshmen, touting for members. In the common room someone came up and said: 'Congratulations!'

I stared at him. 'On what?'

'Your poems in the *Cherwell*.'

I found the first issue of the new academic year. The incoming editor had printed those two poems I had handed in, just twelve months earlier, and long since forgotten. It was mildly ironical, especially as one of them was called 'End of a Phase', but there was no deep significance. I was not quitting Oxford because of any disappointments in university journalism, which I had never made any further attempt to enter.

I went to see Allen and told him I was thinking of resigning my scholarship and leaving Oxford immediately. I cannot remember a word he said. But if there had been the slightest attempt on his part to probe the reasons for my discontent or to suggest remedies, I should not have forgotten. It was much the same at subsequent interviews with the Pro-Provost and the chaplain. Nobody said, 'Quite right, your work has gone to pieces, you'd better go.' Nobody, on the other hand, offered a word of encouragement. I remember only one remark. The Pro-Provost said stiffly: 'Well, Mr Trease, if you go down like this, you will have wasted a hundred pounds of the College money.' And I know I answered: 'Yes, sir, and I am extremely sorry. But I feel that if I stay I shall waste another three hundred.' That debt, at least, has since been repaid.

I received a more generous response from my old headmaster when I wrote to explain what I was doing and why I must, with apologies to the governors, resign my leaving exhibition. A shy man, gauche in manner and misleadingly stern, he was at his best in a personal letter. He wrote me three pages in his own hand.

> Once upon a time, when I had just made a decision which was to affect the whole of my life, and when my boats were burned, a matter-of-fact, 'sensible' but tactless friend said to me, 'We think you are making a great mistake.' … I expect you will have many friends who will say the same sort of thing, but I will try not to be one of them … I am sorry and disappointed that your Oxford career has been cut short, partly for your own sake and partly because my job is the School, and I am anxious to add to its laurels. Still, I am not without hope that you will have some contribution to make to the latter, not by degrees and such like things, but in your own way. Don't get it into your head that you have let down the School or anybody else … Your year at Oxford has not been wasted, I believe, and if it hasn't, neither has the Bishop Exhibition.

Hogg's aunt, Muriel Lester, had by now agreed to accept me as a resident worker at her settlement in Bow. I was thus able to say truthfully, when people plied me with questions, that I was going down to do social work. At the same time I was anxious that no one should be under any misunderstanding—I knew I had no vocation, no capacity to surrender myself to a cause, and I should have been embarrassed if anyone had supposed that I was sacrificing the joys of Oxford in a spirit of lofty idealism. On the other hand, I could hardly proclaim to the whole world, and least of all to the college authorities, my persistent dreams of literary glory. I must have confided in my friends to some extent, for the 'Oxford Letter' published in the school magazine that December contained a surprisingly accurate reference. 'There is one big bombshell of news this term—the permanent forsaking of Oxford at the beginning of term by Mr Trease (Queen's). This was, to most of us, quite unexpected. It appears that Mr Trease is temporarily taking up social service in London, but that his ultimate ambition is to write …'

My affairs were wound up, my books and most of my possessions ready for dispatch to Nottingham—where, of course, my family had been told what was happening. Just thirteen days after the beginning of term, I took my suitcase and made my prosaic departure without benefit of torchlight or muffled drums. The Cardiff-to-London coaches used to stop in front of Queen's. I stepped on board, and away we went down the High.

For the rest of my life, at recurrent intervals, I was to dream myself back in Oxford—always aware that it *was* a return and that many years had elapsed, yet facing the dons again, anxious to complete my unfinished business.

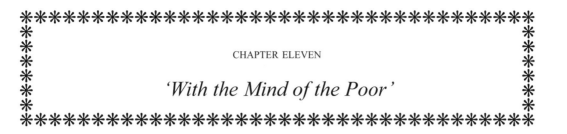

CHAPTER ELEVEN

'With the Mind of the Poor'

I HAD never been to London alone. Indeed, my knowledge of the capital was limited to two or three single days of schoolboy sightseeing. So, rattling along underground by the shabby District Line, past twenty-odd stations from Hammersmith (where the coach terminated) to Bromley at the very east of the East End, I gained a slightly daunting impression of the vast unknown city spread invisibly above my head. I had almost given up hope of seeing that surface world again when I emerged at last into the murky twilight of a featureless and deserted street. Bow Road would have welcomed me with lights, traffic and Cockney animation, but Bromley station was fractionally nearer to the settlement. The fog wrapped round me, flavoured with soot and the fumes from the local soap-factory.

Kingsley Hall proved to be a bright oasis. It stood on the corner of two mean streets, tall between the terraced slums, its newish brick not yet completely grimed. The tiled entrance was freshly scrubbed and through glass doors beyond I saw an expanse of polished floor. Upstairs I found the living quarters and met my future colleagues.

Muriel Lester was out. I was lucky to catch her in England, even, for she was a tireless traveller, much in demand as a speaker, one of those magnetic, dynamic women who can hush conferences and bring tears to every eye. For the moment I could take stock of the place and its people, unblinded by her radiance.

I was handed over to a burly youth, rather like a red-headed, freckled, benevolent bear. He too was named Geoffrey, so I thereafter was known as 'Jay-Two'. His father was a stained-glass artist and he was fairly fresh from his public school. He led me up another flight of stairs and we emerged upon a concrete-floored landing which gave access to the flat roof. This roof was divided into two areas by a row of cell-like bedrooms, with three opening our way, the men's side, and about seven with their doors facing in the opposite direction. For a week or two, Geoffrey explained apologetically, I should have to doss down on the landing. He produced my mattress and bedding, and took me downstairs to high tea.

The welcoming faces round the table were predominantly young and feminine. I can see them now. Else, a plump *fräulein* from the Ruhr, and keen-eyed humorous Knappett (always known by her surname) who wore her hair in the then-fashionable headphone coils, and used to join Else in singing sweet German folk-songs in the firelight … Miss Buck, genteel and elderly, angular, astringent and Anglican, who ruled the kitchen while everyone else shared domestic chores on a rota … Muriel's secretary, whose name has escaped me into undeserved oblivion, for she was a pleasant young woman, hampered by deafness … Elsie, with whom I *did* make real contact as time went by—she had had to mother her orphaned brothers and sisters when she was fifteen and now at the ripe old age of twenty-one was revelling in the freedom she had just attained … and Nell, lovely Nell, who improbably came from a home only ten minutes' walk down the Mile End Road, but had an exotic, possibly Huguenot surname, a refinement of voice and feature, and a response to poetry.

The men, besides Geoffrey, were a pallid tubercular young collier named Ray and a vaguely middle-aged character whom I always thought of privately as 'the Scoutmaster', since he appeared to possess no trousers and was invariably attired in khaki shorts.

For an aspirant writer, anxious to study human nature, Kingsley Hall was a living laboratory.

At breakfast next morning I met Muriel Lester. It was as if the lights had gone up. In the first minute people always knew they were in the presence of an extraordinary woman.

During those months I gained some notion of what it must have felt like in the Dark Ages when ordinary mortals had to associate with saints. Inspiration alternated with irritation, the latter always in her absence, as her radiance faded. When she was there, her charm was irresistible. She had exercised it in the White House and in the viceregal lodge at Simla, in Gandhi's *ashram* and in the mountain-top lair of a truculent Chinese war lord. No wonder she was never allowed to get inside the Kremlin or Berchtesgaden. Her saintliness was of the Franciscan kind, warm, down-to-earth, gay as a bird. She got the best out of everybody by believing and expecting the best, and her strength of will made it hard to prove her wrong. It is easy to romanticise such characters forty years later, but I wrote in my notebook at the time, using the past tense for objectivity: 'She never spoke ill of anyone. Indeed, she tended to praise them too much. Everybody was, to her, "*almost* perfect". Her praise was ready and frequent, her blame rare but terrible … She was amazingly human, rejoicing in food like a schoolboy, loving songs and good company.'

Gradually I learned how she and her sister, Doris, had come to Bow before the 1914 war. Comfortable middle-class young ladies, travelling into London by train from Essex, they had been appalled by the landscape of slums and the throat-catching stenches that seeped through the carriage-window from the soap-works. They looked down into those back-yards and alleys and saw a life they felt they must do something to alter. 'But', Muriel used to say, quoting Gandhi, 'one must approach the poor with the mind of the poor.' Nothing could be accomplished by genteel philanthropy. So the girls established themselves in a typical terrace house with a tin bath hung outside the kitchen door. By 1915 they had taken over an old chapel and named it Kingsley Hall in memory of their brother. They had made it a harmonious rendezvous for all who chose to come—conscientious objectors, soldiers on leave from the trenches, Belgian refugees and blameless Londoners who were cursed with German-sounding names. In peace-time the sisters had learned, as the first Salvation Army lasses learned, to face drunks and toughs. Now they had their premises mobbed by hooligan patriots and raided by police in quest of deserters and foreign spies. They survived everything, and after the war, without compromising their Socialism and Christian pacifism, achieved an unlooked-for respectability. Their work drew support from all sides. The new Kingsley Hall was subscribed for by men like Galsworthy, A. A. Milne, and countless others. In the next street stood Children's House, benignly ruled by Doris, a sweet but less strongly fibred character. Young people's activities were concentrated there, ranging from an officially approved nursery school to the youth club which became one of my own special responsibilities. In the short time I was there we had private visits from the Prime Minister's daughter, Ishbel MacDonald, and from Mrs Baldwin, the wife of his antagonist. If those visits had clashed, it would not have mattered in the least. Muriel would have convinced us all that it was a delightful coincidence and tremendous fun.

What was Kingsley Hall *for*? What did we *do*? The answers to those two questions I began to learn from the first morning. With its twin foundation, Children's House, the Hall was 'for' the people in the back-streets that lay around it—it offered them religion, social gaiety, education, professional counsel (such as a 'Poor Man's Lawyer') and the most personal consolation in their troubles. As for what we did, we did whatever needed to be done.

No menial labour was employed. Our first job was to keep the building clean and tidy. 'One must approach the poor with the mind of the poor.' When the Bow people came into the Hall to join a discussion group, watch a play or read in the library, they had a hard day's work behind them. Anyone who preached at them or tried to improve their minds was more willingly listened to (Muriel reasoned) if he had put in a fair stint of what they would consider 'real' work beforehand.

That first morning I was roused from my fitful slumber on the concrete landing by the devilish clangour of a bell on the roof. Geoffrey was standing there, tousled and dressing-gowned, tugging at the rope with fervour. Fresh from Oxford, I found nothing unreasonable in this infliction of a tocsin on the whole neighbourhood merely to awaken our own small community. Later, when I wondered, I realised that it was not resented. Most of our working-class neighbours were stirring anyhow and the Hall bell offered them a handy time-check in an age when people had not begun to rely on the radio.

It was still dark. We had to dash along the open roof to the men's bathroom at the far end. There was not a minute to waste and I soon fell into the proletarian habit of the evening shave. Huddling into our clothes we ran downstairs for the twenty minutes of silent prayer with which the day began.

Tall candles were lit in the main assembly hall, known as the Place of Worship, though it was used for all kinds of meetings and other activities. Low, rush-seated, tall-backed chairs like *prie-dieux* were ranged in two files of five or six each, every chair as far as possible from its neighbours, islanded in an acreage of parquet on which the candle-flames gleamed. That floor was Muriel's pride and joy. It had to be kept immaculately polished—not with any mechanical aid but with a long-handled, heavy-headed, rag-wrapped implement we called the 'slosher'—and it must be austerely bare. For services, concerts and meetings, it was filled with seats, screwed together in lengths of about half-a-dozen to comply with safety regulations. After each function it was the men's job to open a big trap in the floor and manhandle these sections into the basement. Next morning, the hall had resumed its dim religious atmosphere, supposedly conducive to meditation. I have no doubt it was—to some. I myself had no talent for such exercises, and the daily sessions, squatting on those rush seats, did nothing to uplift my spirit. I was always ready to depart when the signal was given, grab my broom, and start on my pre-breakfast assignment.

A typed list hung in the kitchen, sharing out the routine duties for the week. There were some specifically male jobs such as stoking the boiler, hosing down the flat roof, and heaving those accursed rows of seats in and out of that hell's-mouth trap-door which led to the basement. There was the cleaning out of the Gents after last night's dance and social. And there were all the other domestic chores shared equally with the women—sweeping, dusting, polishing, and scrubbing. At some of these I was pitifully inept. I could not get the hang of washing a tiled floor and used to leave the entrance lobby awash with unmopped water. But it was the boiler that reduced me to the deepest humiliation. It either would not light for me at all, or stealthily went out, or developed such an infernal heat that steam began to issue from the radiators and catastrophe seemed imminent. My failures would have been more frequently noticed had not Bill Coote come to my rescue.

Bill was a cadaverous stoker from the gasworks, a regular habitué of the settlement. He claimed to have stoked boilers in ships all round the world and to have acquired his two knife-scars in Rio de Janeiro. He was a reader and a well-informed Socialist, with two incongruous *bêtes noires*, Lord Northcliffe and General Booth. Working different shifts as he did, he would pop in and out of the place at all hours, and would linger in the kitchen till nearly midnight, leaning on the sink and entrancing us with his stories. It was he who first introduced me to rhyming slang and the racy idiom of the East End. 'Narsty corf, Jay-Two,' he would admonish me. 'Wanna watch that—or yer'll be puttin' on yer wooden overcoat!'

Life was not all stoking and cleaning. As the day wore on there was library supervision and similar light duty, while at night, when the building filled up with people from the neighbourhood, one might be acting in a play, participating in a discussion-group, handing out coffee, volunteering as dance-partner, or running the youth club in the old Hall round the corner. The point was, one was on duty from morning till night except for two hours, usually taken in the slack period during the afternoon. Meal-times were regulated. We were not supposed to linger at table longer than twenty-five minutes. The rules were observed by common consent. Meals were our social time and letters must not be read over breakfast. It was permissible to take jam with margarine, but not with butter.

For all our typed duty-roster and the Hall's programme of public events, nothing was ever too rigid and there were continual variations. The Lesters retained a cottage in Epping Forest which was used for people who needed a break. At Hallowe'en Muriel insisted that all of us who could be spared should make a flying visit to the cottage, get a good breath of forest air, roast chestnuts round the fire, sing and tell ghost stories. I gained another, rather different, view of the forest a month or two later when I conducted an all-night walk through its spectral glades with the youth club. One afternoon Doris took us all up to the Italian Art Exhibition then at Burlington House: she had kept control of a little fund of her own money, with which to provide such treats, whereas Muriel's private income had been made over to trustees, who (I was told) accounted for their expenditure at a public meeting every year in the Town Hall. Probably it was Doris's fund that paid for the fifty or so children I helped to escort to *Peter Pan*. I forget. I find it easier to remember the charming child who bit me when I strove to restrain his anti-social behaviour on the Underground. Once Muriel sent me at short notice to deputise for her and address the crowded congregation of a North London chapel, and another time I represented Children's House at a conference of youth leaders. Life was full of incident. I was only sorry that, because of a smallpox outbreak, Muriel forbade all but urgent visits to people in their homes, and I thus did not get the close insight into East End conditions that I would normally have gained.

One special task she found for me—probably in tactful compensation for the dreadful hash I made of scrubbing and stoking. She had not long before made a lengthy visit to India, staying much of the time with Gandhi, who returned the compliment when he came to London for the Round Table Conference in 1931 and made his headquarters at Kingsley Hall instead of a West End hotel. Muriel wanted to write a book about her Indian experiences, but was over-modest about her literary abilities. She asked me to help her with the rough draft she had made, and I spent many a congenial hour, nominally on library supervision but effectively on editing and polishing what was later published under the title of *My Host the Hindu*.

There was not much time to think of writing anything of my own. Muriel wisely insisted that each of us should have one day off in seven, but she no less wisely encouraged us to get right away from the Hall after breakfast and stay out till bed-time. My usual day was Wednesday, which was good for theatre matinées, and enabled me at a pinch to fit in two different plays. In addition to our board and lodging we all received seven shillings a week in cash, and this could be made to stretch a long way when West End theatre galleries cost one-and-sixpence and the Old Vic fivepence, and a meal of fish-cakes, date-pudding and custard, and a cup of coffee, could be bought for a shilling at a Lyons teashop. The rest of the long day could be pleasantly eked out with free entertainment provided by the British Museum or the Strangers' Gallery in the House of Commons. I began to know my London.

It was Doris who asked me to write something. Each month she edited a page in a Sunday School paper called the *New Chronicle* and needed three or four short articles on any topic that could be made to seem vaguely relevant. I wrote her a piece on Poetry and Religion, thereby earning my first guinea since my schoolboy efforts seven years earlier, and starting a connection with the *New Chronicle* which continued long after I had left Bow and she had ceased to run her own page. It was a tiny and obscure beginning but it marked my real début as a journalist.

That winter in Bow taught me far more than my Oxford year. The hard physical work was salutary. It brought me down to earth. Living with dedicated idealists cleared my mind of some of its woolly sentimentality: I saw at once the impressive power of such idealism when incarnated in a dynamic character like Muriel Lester, and its dangerous power of self-deception. I had never really seen myself as a neo-Franciscan, but had I done so I should have known after a few months at Kingsley Hall that it was not the road for me to tread.

My eyes had been opened in other ways. I had seen something, if not enough, of the workers and the way they lived. I had mixed more closely with people who, though mainly middle class and educated (my family would have held this inconceivable), accepted Keir Hardie Socialism, the old-style Labour Party, and the original propagandist *Daily Herald* as providing the obvious guide-lines for a decent life. And finally, for the first time in my life, I had lived under the same roof as several young women.

The result of that was predictable. In January—I can still date it from a sonnet called 'Breakfast Thoughts'—I fell painfully in love. 'And not before time,' I can almost hear the impatient reader exclaim. The object of my passion was Nell, Nell of the exotic musical surname, the fine eyes, and the short-cropped hair that left little gleams, like gold dust, in the nape of her neck. My feelings ripened the faster when we had to act together in that ancient one-act farce, *Ici On Parle Français*, I as the comic young Frenchman and she as the heroine I pursued. The depth of those feelings may be gauged from my begging her, one day, to let me scrub the kitchen floor in her place. 'Go to the devil,' she told me sharply. At other times she was much gentler in her discouragement, but she did convince me that I had no hope. 'I'm Bow,' she would reiterate doggedly, 'you can't alter that.'

This sad affair precipitated my departure from the settlement towards the end of February. I had been thinking for some time about the next move, for it had been understood all along that Muriel had taken me only on a temporary basis. Now I wanted to get away as soon as possible. The question was, where?

A possible answer was suggested by an advertisement in the *Daily Telegraph*. A 'well-known author' was in need of a 'young literary assistant'. I applied and was summoned for interview at an office in Great Russell Street.

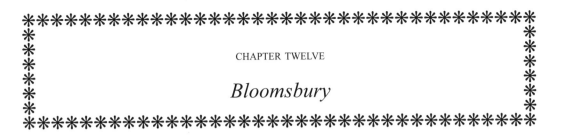

CHAPTER TWELVE

Bloomsbury

THE author proved to be a middle-aged little man with all the nervous fluency that often compensates for an unimpressive physique. *Who's Who in Literature* listed his published fiction. He also wrote short stories for magazines on both sides of the Atlantic. It was not with his own creative work that he required assistance, but with a grand project he outlined to me with persuasive eloquence.

The idea of book clubs had just reached Britain from America, but had not yet developed into its modern form, so that publishers were viewing any new proposal with a cautious open-mindedness, half afraid of missing the bus and half afraid of being taken for a ride. This particular scheme was not to offer the public certain volumes, selected for them, at cut price, but to supply any new book at the normal price but post free to any part of the country. Therein lay the crux. Trade agreements, designed to protect the bookseller, decreed that postage must be paid by the customer up to a certain minimum order. This difficulty could be overcome if would-be customers joined a club and promised to take books at least up to that value in any one year—I believe it was three pounds, that is, five shillings a month in an age when the novel cost seven-and-sixpence. Everything obviously depended on whether the trade would turn a benevolent eye and allow that annual commitment to be regarded as a single book-buying transaction, even though in fact it involved posting half-a-dozen separate packages during the year. If the deviser of the scheme could get away with it, he would have cracked wide open a vast potential market, for who would not order books by post if it cost him nothing extra?

'Obviously,' I have just said. At the time, to be honest, the issues involved were *not* obvious to me. I had not heard of the Net Book Agreement and I had no conception of the powerful forces that would be deployed against the revolution my interviewer planned.

He came now to the point. He wanted not one 'literary assistant' but a dozen. There would be a variety of jobs to be done when his scheme was launched. In particular, the club would issue its own journal, containing thumbnail reviews of the best hundred books published each month. His assistants would require training to write these, training that he would give us in a series of evening meetings spread over the next month or two. By the end of that period he would be ready to start the book club. There would be impressive central offices and a national publicity campaign. For us, a guaranteed job at three pounds a week minimum, and who knew what possibilities thereafter?

The little man struck me as a shrewd judge of character and a person of decision. He did not embarrass me with searching questions as to my knowledge, abilities or experience. Indeed, the sole question I recall was, had I the nominal premium of fifteen pounds which he was compelled to ask, to protect himself from time-wasting amateurs? When I said yes, he seemed no longer in doubt that I was exactly the type of young man he was looking for.

Farewells said in Bow, I had time for a brief visit home before taking up my abode in Bloomsbury—the old Bloomsbury, that is, before its destruction by London University.

A search of newsagents' notice-boards led me hotfoot to Francis Street, off the Tottenham Court Road, where a furnished flatlet at twenty-five shillings a week seemed just within my means. Downstairs was the receiving office for a laundry. The two top floors were occupied by a young couple, though on the lower one they used only the back room as their drawing-room. The front had long ago been divided to make a miniature two-room flat, with an entrance lobby holding a gas-ring and a tiny sink. It had just been vacated by one of their friends and they were anxious to find a tenant who would be tolerable at such close quarters. The bath, for instance, was in their kitchen upstairs, and as there was no lock on the door baths were best taken 'by arrangement'.

We took to each other at sight. 'We had a stream of the oddest people after the flat,' Patience told me later. 'You were the first possible. We thought you were a student. *I* said, a theological student.' She had been a nurse at the Middlesex. She was warm-hearted and laughed delightfully and I revere her memory. Petey was a lean, saturnine young man, with a Charterhouse and Cambridge background, side-burns, and a taste for Wilde and Beardsley. His kindness, too, I have not forgotten.

Thanks to the abbreviation of my Oxford career, I still had some of my original nest-egg, so that, although I guarded it jealously, I should have no serious financial worries until the book club started. I reckoned that the promised three pounds would be enough to live on and that was the amount I meanwhile withdrew from my post office savings. As a check for the first week or two I resumed my Oxford habit of keeping precise accounts. My first week in Bloomsbury cost me £2 14s 4d, which included a theatre visit and a volume of D.H. Lawrence. I seem to have lived on brown bread, cheese, honey, oranges, bananas, corn flakes, milk, jam, marmalade and cake. Only in the second week did I treat myself to a couple of eggs.

Besides the rent, six precious extra shillings had to be earmarked for my share in the daily services of the charwoman, an entertaining character with one eye and a Dutch name, Vandermeer, acquired by marriage, for she was pure Cockney, if 'pure' is the word. 'If this is "service",' she once groaned as she knelt to brush the stairs, 'I'd rather be a kept woman. *And* I may say,' she added, tilting her homely face to roll her one eye at me, 'I've 'ad me chances.'

That ancient cash-book brings everything back to mind. I see the pleasant olive-green earthenware plates, the yellow coffeepot, the gas-fire paling as another penny becomes due, the tiny bureau by the window, just big enough for the typewriter carriage to travel from side to side … That typewriter, a small portable bought on the instalment system, was a slightly alarming but quite unavoidable expense. The ancient machine in Nottingham would not meet my future needs.

I see too the view from my high window. Heal's staff entrance opposite with the salesmen and cabinet-makers streaming in and out … the railway vans with their massive feathery horses clopping by to Euston and the other termini … a glimpse of Whitefield's Tabernacle at the end of the street and the red buses sliding to and fro … I hear a gentle tap on my outer door, and there is Patience on the landing with a covered plateful of meat and vegetables and some charmingly unconvincing excuse that it would be wasted otherwise. Sometimes she asked me to dinner upstairs, sometimes she and Petey took me out, either across the road to Antoine's in Charlotte Street or down the Charing Cross Road to Tokiwaya's, where they taught me to eat exquisitely delicate Japanese specialities with chopsticks and to sip *saké* alternately with the pale tea. They were so tolerant of my brashness, not least of my half-baked political dogmas. Petey, I suppose, was temperamentally apolitical, though with the basic right-wing instincts which stir when an assumed security is threatened. His father had known Tsarist Russia, and they had White Russian friends who had lost everything in the revolution only a decade ago, yet Petey never showed the irritation I must have caused him. With a quiet smile he would merely refill my glass.

Meanwhile I met my future colleagues when we assembled for our first training session at the author's flat in Great Ormond Street.

We were a well-diversified group. There was a sallow, signet-ringed Harrovian, and a pale-haired bespectacled New Zealander, rather older than most of us, correct in the black coat and striped trousers of a City clerk, and very quickly designated as our eventual office manager. The women, rather in the majority, had certain common qualities of youth and good looks. There was Miss Smith, who was tired of working in an Oxford Street bookshop. There was a particularly glamorous creature whose promise seemed scarcely literary, even to my inexperienced eye. One girl truly stood out from the dozen or so of us—Barbara Nickalls was so tall that she stooped and hunched her shoulders, making dangerous gawky gestures with a cigarette in a conspicuous holder to emphasise her staccato remarks.

Barbara and I drew together at once. She too had been to Oxford, where she had taken an English degree, and by this time she had tried teaching and one or two other short-lived jobs. We found we shared many interests, enthusiasms, and occasionally, as the weeks went by, forebodings. We fell easily into a comfortable elder-sister–young-brother relationship. She lived in a girls' hostel close by, and when she wearied of feminine society she would stalk round and ring my bell, catch the key I threw down to her and come up to make toast with me at the gas-fire.

Once she took me down to Newbury for the week-end. 'You'd better bring your dinner jacket,' she said, 'Mummy is rather old-fashioned.' Mummy proved a gracious hostess, the first person I had ever met who could end a sentence quite naturally with the words, 'don't you know', clearly enunciating every syllable. Barbara's father, Vivian, had been a notable rowing coach, though never so much in the public eye as other members of the family. His other interests were soldiering and foxhunting—we went to a point-to-point that Saturday afternoon—and I fear he must have found me a dull companion when we were left alone over our port that evening. A year or two later Barbara helped him to write his memoirs, which were published under the appropriate but somewhat awkward title of *Oars, Wars and Horses*, and had to be hurriedly withdrawn when one of his Etonian contemporaries threatened a libel action over the ambiguous narration of some schoolboy incident.

Knowing Barbara, straight after my East End experiences, brought home to me the world's infinite diversity. We argued incessantly, but never quarrelled. With her true-blue background she considered me 'an utter Bolshy'. Ironically, she ended her days as an active, even militant, member of the National Union of Journalists. She was working for the *Bristol Evening Post* when she died as the result of cold and exposure, covering the air raids on that city.

Those training sessions in Great Ormond Street were of enormous value to me afterwards, both as a writer and as a reviewer. Whatever he was not, our future employer was a craftsman in fiction and had the rare gift of being able to break down the creative process into its components. His immediate aim was to make us competent judges of new novels. We were to find out what, basically, the author was trying to do; to assess how far he had succeeded; and to consider the relative value of his objective. In showing us how to do this, our tutor could not avoid at the same time showing us how to write. In any case, as he admitted, he was covering roughly the same ground as he had marked out five years earlier in a course of lectures delivered to embryo writers and then published. He gave us each a copy of this book. I still treasure mine as the most practical manual I have ever found. It may have nothing to teach the writer of the amorphous 'serious' novel, for it is concerned with technique and structure, with opening and climax, with the infinite variations on Polti's classic 'thirty-six dramatic situations', with the creation of character and atmosphere, and the working out of a plot-outline from 'the indispensable incident' with which every story must begin. All these things were to be relevant, however, when I began to write children's adventure stories, in which plot and climax have never lost their traditional importance. The Great Ormond Street evenings were my apprenticeship as a storyteller.

There were other incidental benefits. I was introduced to some notable prose that was fresh to me, Liam O'Flaherty's *The Black Soul* in particular, and T.F. Powys' *Mr Weston's Good Wine*. And I was stimulated to begin writing steadily myself.

For the moment we had only the two or three evening sessions every week, and those who had jobs carried on with them until the book club started. I for my part sat in my little room tapping out my first novel, which was called *The Anvil* and was inevitably autobiographical. It had been growing in my mind for some time. Odd scraps had been scribbled down in Bow. Now it poured out and its eighty thousand words were completed in two months. Barbara said she liked it—she could hardly say anything else, for I had just read and praised a typescript of her own. She added darkly that my novel would 'finish' me with my old school, a prediction which surprised but did not deter me. It was a time when it was almost fashionable for first novelists to be expelled from their Old Boys' societies.

Once my manuscript was dispatched to the fortunate publisher of my choice, I looked round for fresh employment. My nest-egg was dwindling. I had sold another article to Doris Lester for her page and my future employer had given me odd jobs for which he had paid me three or four pounds in all, but I was compelled to badger him for a firm date on which my guaranteed salary would begin. There were, he explained, unforeseen delays.

Vital negotiations were still in progress with the Publishers' Association and he had not yet signed the lease for the offices, but all was going well. Meanwhile, worn down by my importunity, he gave me work in the small temporary office where our original interview had taken place.

He and his secretary, Eileen Bigland, herself afterwards well known as a writer, were between them trying to see most of the publishers individually and explain the scheme. My task was to telephone about half the firms in the Year Book, make appointments for one or other of my superiors, and type letters of confirmation. With the optimism of youth I assumed that all people, including directors of publishing firms, maintained my own Greenwich standard of punctuality. I made out schedules committing my unfortunate superiors to appointments at widely separated addresses and half-hourly intervals. I would have them in Bedford Square at eleven and on Ludgate Hill at half-past, and then expect them to appear in Albemarle Street, without a bead of perspiration, as the clock struck twelve. If two successive interviews were both in Covent Garden, I felt that a fifteen-minute gap was ample. They had complained that they could never fit in all their appointments. I was doing my best to help, only to be ungratefully accused of making them run round like scalded cats.

I was happier, and no doubt they were, when the club started at last and I could begin the work for which I had been trained. We had been lucky enough to secure the ground floor of 100 Great Russell Street—lucky because the number linked up with the name of the book club and its monthly journal and the whole conception of offering a choice from the best hundred new books. Review copies streamed in. Each of us was given an armful. Though primarily trained to assess novels, we had to tackle anything. On the afternoon before press-day it was discovered that we had only ninety-nine reviews. I was handed Sir Oliver Lodge's latest book and told to bring back a hundred-word evaluation in the morning. Two words would have sufficed. The title was *Beyond Physics* and the most honest review would have been, 'Beyond me'. Having my bread to earn, I cloaked my ignorance in a hundred.

Our great enterprise was beginning to move. It was not in every respect quite what we had dreamed of, but these were early days. At least we were drawing our promised salaries, lining up each Friday to sign for our tiny buff envelopes. Barbara and I had sometimes exchanged unworthy suspicions that this stage would never be reached. We saw now how ill-founded these had been, and how little we deserved, faint-hearted sceptics that we were, to share in the glory to come.

On the third Friday Barbara and I adjourned to a café along the street to celebrate our solvency. Her expression was inexplicably strained. I tore open my envelope. With the money I pulled out a typed slip and read that my services would not be required after the following week. I went white with a variety of emotions in which fury became quickly predominant. I held out the slip across the table. Barbara said:

'I know. I was expecting you'd get that. I think everyone knew.'

'*I* didn't,' I said. 'I've not been given the slightest idea. What does it mean?'

She said I was being got rid of because I had made a nuisance of myself with awkward questions. It was true. My need being acutest, I had always taken the lead in demanding the fulfilment of promises. As a result, I was probably about the only member of the group to have recovered the fifteen-pound premium.

What stung me was the humiliation. I was so green a youth, I had never realised that educated people could receive anything so vulgar as 'the sack'. Even when drunken or incompetent, they were given face-saving hints and confidentially counselled to seek other employment. To receive without warning that curt slip in my pay-packet, as if I were one of a thousand redundant labourers, was as though someone had spat in my face. It provoked the same reaction. I swallowed my coffee, went straight back, stormed into my employer's room, and said things which it was long afterwards a comfort to remember. I gather that I said them loudly enough, also, to provide considerable pleasure for my colleagues in the outer office.

My bruised pride was soothed by what followed. Within a fortnight Barbara and all the others, bar two, were also out of work. Of those two exceptions one, the conspicuously glamorous girl, had suddenly vanished: it was said that she had gone abroad as secretary to a well-known author. The other, the efficient Miss Smith, had been retained by the creditors to sort out the confusion in the abandoned offices. The book club that had been founded to end book clubs had succeeded at least, with amazing rapidity, in ending one.

CHAPTER THIRTEEN

Grub Street

PETEY and Patience were all sympathy. 'This mayn't be of any interest to you,' Petey began diffidently, a few days later. 'You might not even be able to do the work. All the same …'

I rushed off to a large building near High Holborn, where, on the sixth floor, the Blank Publishing Company produced three glossy magazines I had never seen or heard of.

Their format was opulent, large and lavishly illustrated. They opened with one or two general articles by well-known popular journalists like Ursula Bloom and Godfrey Winn. Then came features on specific subjects—a particular private school, a corner of the New Forest with an exceptionally comfortable hotel, the work of a new interior decorator. The contributors of these pieces were unknown to me, but after running through a few copies I realised that they must be men and women of tireless enthusiasm and acute discernment, and utterly devoid of snobbery. They recognised merit wherever found. A back-street shop in Burnley would be commended as *An Epic of Enterprise*, while a suburban kindergarten was as likely to appear under the caption *Facing Tomorrow* as the most illustrious public school. Indeed, I soon found, more likely.

Could I write this sort of material if supplied with all the data? I agreed to try and was taken to the journalists' room. Crammed into a tiny smoke-hung space were the editor, his assistant, and two personable young women, all typing like machine-gunners making a last stand. I was introduced and welcomed to the only vacant desk. The managing director withdrew and my new colleagues surveyed me with amiable interest, showing no impatience to resume their feverish labours. 'Better keep one machine going, Belinda,' the editor murmured, and one of the girls reluctantly went back to her typing. It was soon explained to me that the journalists' room was a sanctum seldom entered by anyone but the office-boy bringing and removing work. The managing director never came near it in the ordinary way. He knew nothing about writing and was happy so long as he could hear the typewriters rattling when he passed our door. It was quickly impressed upon me that I must not overwork. About three thousand words a day would do splendidly. If we averaged more than that, one of us would be out of a job—and I could guess which one.

With the help of one other man who worked at home in the country, plus the 'celebrity' articles (inexpensive syndicated material which had been published already elsewhere, but which served admirably as window-dressing), all the editorial copy for the three magazines was produced in that small room. Belinda, who faced me across our touching desks, was a good shorthand typist. The other three were fluent and versatile writers. The two men, I learned, did a good deal of free-lance journalism in private collaboration, largely for second-class Sunday newspapers. They ghosted the work of a famous aviator, the then Master of

Sempill. They wrote his book, *Air and the Plain Man*, and supplied his regular articles for the *Field*, of which he was nominally aviation correspondent. Our assistant editor, known affectionately as 'Uncle Ern', could not himself fly but had a genuine interest in the subject and a command of technicalities. The editor supplied the more popular journalistic ideas and touches. The Master of Sempill supplied his signature and pocketed half the money, though, to do him justice, he conscientiously read every word that appeared under his name. Once he sent back an article with the marginal query, 'This is very interesting if it is true, but it is new to me', and Uncle Ern was able to reply gleefully, 'It comes from a paper read to the Royal Aeronautical Society—you were in the chair.' The last member of our department impressed me greatly. Maboth Moseley had had two novels published and was acquainted with William Gerhardi and other 'real' authors. One Sunday she took me to a party Stephen Graham was giving at his house in Frith Street to celebrate his latest book, *St Vitus' Day*. I knew Graham's work—his adventures, tramping in Tsarist Russia, had enthralled me at the height of my Belloc period—and that hilarious party in Soho gave me a glimpse of the bohemian literary society for which I hankered. I was sorry when Maboth left the firm and I lost touch with her.

Our work, though humble and ill-paid, demanded a certain knack which not everyone possessed. A pile of large manilla envelopes lay on a table and was frequently replenished by the office-boy. Each contained the correspondence relating to one particular firm or institution on which an article had to be written, together with a variable amount of raw material as a basis. There might be brochures, newspaper clippings, even a handsome company history. There might be little more than the illiterate jottings of our representative in the field. Whatever the quantity and quality of this material, it had somehow to be shaped into a plausibly reading article which suggested that the concern in question—its name introduced quite casually in the second paragraph or so—was of such outstanding interest that it merited notice in a national magazine. Each envelope was marked with the length of the article to be written, anything from about fifteen hundred words down to four hundred, determined in what seemed to me at first a strangely arbitrary manner, bearing little reference to the importance of the subject.

At first the editor picked out the envelopes for me, with some regard to my competence and interests. When he found that I could tackle anything, I could make my own choice. We all played fair with each other. We knew the material must be kept flowing in roughly the sequence in which it arrived. The editor explained the general idea—the puff should not be obvious, but clients varied, and some liked it laid on with a trowel. I should need about half-a-dozen different pseudonyms, each kept for one range of subjects. It looked bad if the magazine contained several articles under the same name, and clients liked to feel that they were being written up by specialists. So I had one personality when I discussed educational matters and spotlit individual schools, another when I wrote of country inns and West End restaurants, a third for kennels and riding stables. When Maboth left us and we could find no replacement, I took over the feminine topics and became 'Elizabeth Severn'.

'But who reads our papers?' I asked in my early callow period.

With cynical smiles the two men put me in the picture. The basis of the company was the well-known superiority of editorial publicity over straightforward advertisement. Many a famous newspaper and magazine quite obviously provided such publicity in return for space bought in some adjacent advertisement column. Puff papers like ours had merely extended the idea.

Typists in the next room were sending out thousands of standard letters to addresses culled from directories and specialist journals, chosen according to the geographical areas at that moment being 'worked' by our twenty eloquent representatives. These letters, and any that followed them up, were worded far more thoughtfully than any of our articles: they had to stand up, if necessary, in a county court—and in that arena I believe our far-sighted managing director never knew defeat, even before the most hostile judge.

The first letter indicated that the institution had come to the notice of our editor, who wished to feature it in an article which he was sure would be of wide interest to his readers 'and, with your co-operation, increase our modest circulation'. No charge would be made for publishing the article and there would be no obligation to advertise.

Needless to say, this approach brought a good number of delighted replies, and the nearest eloquent representative then moved in. On his assessment of the possibilities a second letter was dispatched. The editor (who had to sign all these letters but had otherwise nothing to do with the business) was sure that a most interesting article was going to emerge, but its appeal—and the space devoted to it—would naturally be increased if it were suitably illustrated. Who could have disagreed? He would like to send down a photographer … 'You will appreciate', the letter continued, almost as an afterthought, 'that the blocks made for these pictures will be of no further use to me, but may on many future occasions be of service to your company …' Who at this stage in the proceedings could be so churlish as to reject the suggestion that he take the blocks 'off our hands' when finished with? And who, already hooked by the bait of free publicity, was going to risk the project's falling through? Such rhetorical questions could be multiplied. How many knew that the rate quoted for the blocks was several times the normal trade charge? How many paused, before signing their consent, to consider how quickly square inches mount up and that it might be prudent, if a little ungentlemanly, to set a limit on their commitment?

In fairness to my ingenious employers it must be said that a number of firms knew precisely what they were paying for and were well satisfied with what they got. One large company was so pleased with its write-up that it ordered ten thousand copies of the magazine and a quarter of a million reprints in leaflet form. The tourist bureau of a remote Mediterranean resort swore that the number of British visitors had doubled since the publication of our article. In the journalists' room we could only imagine that some lone Englishman must have returned for his honeymoon. But apart from these exceptional cases there were many concerns—hotels and private schools being obvious examples—which could obtain in this manner a professionally written account of themselves, apparently carrying an impartial editorial recommendation and for that reason more persuasive than a conventional brochure.

Others, by contrast, had no notion of what they were letting themselves in for until it was too late—if then. I once had the macabre pleasure of writing up an ancient Oxford college—I doubt if our managing director could have distinguished such an institution from a third-rate private school touting for pupils and I often wonder how the eventual payment was shuffled through the bursar's accounts. Some people, shocked by the bill for the blocks, had to be taken to the county court. Here the full malign beauty of the procedure became apparent. They had signed the authority ... They had previously expressed a wish to have the article illustrated ... Whatever their expectations of wider publicity, the magazine had made no inflated promises ... 'I see in this first letter', the judge would remark, 'that the editor specifically refers to "our *modest* circulation".' And once at least a judge turned to our managing director, the picture of affronted benevolence, and said, 'As a matter of interest, Mr So-and-so, would you mind giving us some idea of what your circulation is?' Whereupon the managing director would answer with manly frankness that of course it fluctuated but on occasions it had topped the eleven thousand mark. Whatever the judge thought—and the recurrence of these cases in certain areas caused some judges to become very pensive indeed—there was never anything he could do but order payment of the bill.

None of this concerned us in the journalists' room. It was a job and at a time when jobs were desperately hard to come by. I worked in that office all through the worst of the 1931 economic crisis. From our high window we looked down on the unemployed demonstrating in Kingsway—sometimes on flying bricks and flailing batons. If you had a pay packet, however slim, you clung to it.

I started at forty-five shillings a week, which ended at one o'clock on a Saturday. I wrote four, five, even six short articles a day, the equivalent of a novel every five weeks. Even so, there was nothing feverish in the tempo, unless we heard the managing director's voice in the corridor or saw his tall silhouette through the opaque glass door. We had a dozy or gossipy period between lunch and our four o'clock tea and bun. So long as at least one typewriter went clacking on ...

I learned to work fast and accurately, to master an unfamiliar brief, and to find an angle from which it could be made interesting. All that was useful experience. Less useful was the continual danger of falling into clichés. It was not the haste that created the danger, it was the frequent necessity to write a long article based on vague and scanty data, for the length was determined by the total area of blocks likely to be paid for. Also, some of the businessmen who would have to approve our drafts positively liked clichés. Even eulogy made them uneasy if expressed in anything but conventional words. So sometimes we had to use clichés, just as we had to pad our insufficient material. The main thing was to know that we were doing so, and not let the infection creep insensibly into our normal style.

I picked up a lot of useful, if superficial, knowledge on commercial, industrial and other matters. I also learned some more about human nature. Some of that knowledge came out of the big buff envelopes, but not all.

CHAPTER FOURTEEN

Revolting Youth

Soon after starting my new job I received a letter which transformed my Bloomsbury existence.

The writer explained that he had just enjoyed my novel in his capacity as publisher's reader, but I must steel myself against its rejection. His own favourable report had been overruled by his employer. 'V.G.' was a highly temperamental man, and the fate of a manuscript might hang on the mood in which he sat down at his desk. My correspondent had broken professional etiquette by writing to me, but he had deduced from my novel that I came from Nottingham, as he did, and for this and other reasons he would like to meet me. His flat was in Guilford Place, not ten minutes' walk away. Would I come to supper?

Jon Evans proved to be a quizzical, faintly faunlike Welshman of my own age. Had he gone to the High School, we should have been Sixth Formers together. He too had walked out of his university, London, but in his case to get married.

Kathleen was a brilliant fellow student, determined to follow her vocation as a psychologist. London University cared nothing if students lived together illicitly, but if her marriage became known officially she would automatically lose her grant. She and Jon were thus compelled to reverse the conventional situation: only their close friends must know that their cohabitation was in lawful wedlock.

In his urgent need of a job, Jon had presented himself to Victor Gollancz, a new publisher whose flair and flamboyance had made his imprint immediately outstanding in the trade. 'I don't know that there's anything you can do,' Gollancz had said. 'Still, you can stick around for a little while, and we'll see.' Jon had stuck, making himself useful and sometimes, I suspect, indispensable, though for a long time, he told me, he figured on no payroll and drew his salary from the petty cash. He was still to be with the firm as literary adviser more than forty years later.

Through him I was drawn into a whole new group of friends.

There was then an excellent literary weekly, *Everyman*, edited by C.B. Purdom. It had recently published, under the heading 'The Revolt of Youth', a young woman's letter which seemed to Purdom to voice the frustration of the young in 1930, their blend of cynicism and idealism, their desire to change the world and their disenchantment with existing movements. Letters of support poured in, filling the columns week after week. There were too many to publish, and some were too good for the wastepaper basket. They were S.O.S. messages from the isolated. Purdom handed the whole lot over to his original correspondent, E.M. Barraud, and suggested that she was morally bound to do something with them. Jon was one of the first with whom she made personal contact and I came in on the second wave.

We soon found ourselves creating yet another of those organisations at which we scoffed. We called ourselves the Promethean Society. Prometheus, in his defiance of the Olympian establishment, seemed to us a suitable hero.

Broadly our outlook was what is now termed, with some historical inaccuracy, 'humanist'. In each bonnet was a favourite bee. Pacifism was mine. But, although our priorities differed, we were in general sympathy on many 'progressive' policies. We felt that if in turn, as chance offered, we all supported whatever campaign was in the public eye, we should be far more likely to get something done than if we dissipated our strength in more specialised organisations.

Our major prophets were Freud, Marx, Wells, Shaw, Lenin, Trotsky, Gandhi and D.H. Lawrence. We did not worry unduly about reconciling the contradictions. We thought a great deal of, but rather less about, the work of Havelock Ellis. We admired macabre German films and dynamic Russian ones with rows of tractors churning up the collectivised black earth. We assumed that religion had been forever disproved by Darwin, Huxley and Frazer, whom we took as read. I myself was going through an inevitable reaction against my recent experiences of religious enthusiasm at Kingsley Hall. We believed, Social Credit being the latest gospel, that the world's poverty could be cured by a simple change in the financial system. War could be abolished by disarmament, if necessary unilateral, and by non-violent demonstrations such as lying down in front of troop-trains.

Half-a-dozen groups were set up, corresponding to the dominant enthusiasm of the individual member—economics, art, and so on—and people were put in touch with each other all over the country. In London we held crowded meetings in Gower Street and elsewhere. No subject, needless to say, aroused more lively discussion than 'sex reform', on which E.M. Barraud herself conducted a zealous group. Babies were out of fashion. It was self-evident that no intelligent progressive woman would voluntarily produce them—what about her career, and what about Armageddon looming ahead? This group agitated for birth-control, but since, in spite of all their efforts, children were still conceived, they demanded the legal right to abortion. If children none the less were born, the best thing to do was to dispatch them as soon as possible to a school run on A.S. Neill's principles and give their parents facilities for easier divorce so that it would not happen again. In contrast to all this, the unmarried mother and her child were popular figures. So, of course, were homosexuals of both sexes.

It is easy to smile at the extravagances of that short-lived movement, struggling forward all those years ago to the permissive Paradise so largely, and with such wry faces, now attained. Yet I owe much to the Protheans, both in terms of personal friendships and in the further gaps they filled in my unbalanced education, showing me—even if in distorting mirrors—many facets of life that were entirely new.

Jon played a restrained and sensible part in these activities. He edited the monthly magazine we founded and called (since there was then no other review of that title) the *Twentieth Century*. It was not merely an organ for our own manifestos and effusions. Jon was uncannily skilful at obtaining free articles from people like Havelock Ellis, Sir Norman Angell, Fenner Brockway, Gerald Barry and R.L. Megroz. He kept the paper going for years. We used to go round the theatre queues selling it, much to the fury of the buskers on whose carefully demarcated pitches and time-schedules we were in our ignorance trespassing.

I myself ran the Active Peace Group. I harangued apathetic audiences on Hampstead Heath and demonstrated at the Hendon Air Pageant and joined in the march to Hyde Park on May Day. Some of us tried to break through to the Japanese embassy. The literary part of my brain registered the novel impressions—the ring of hoofs on a Mayfair pavement, the rhythmic rise and fall of mounted policemen's long staves on heads and shoulders in front. The May Day theme that year, 1931, was protest against Japanese aggression in Manchuria and the inertia of the Western powers. We were made to feel very disreputable and cranky at the time, but within eleven years the Japanese had taken Singapore.

The Prometheans included some odd young people but they attracted also a number who afterwards demonstrated their effectiveness in various fields. One became editor of a great newspaper, another controlled a B.B.C. region, and several became recognised authorities in the columns of the quality press. My own Active Peace Group was typically varied. It included a Norfolk pig-farmer who was last seen on the beach at Dunkirk, an Aberystwyth lecturer, Pat Sloan, who became head of English broadcasts for Moscow Radio, and W.N. Warbey, who entered Parliament in 1945 and was for long the stormy petrel of the Labour Party.

It was Bill Warbey who conceived the idea of persuading a world-famous figure like Wells to refuse payment of his income tax as a protest against armaments. Wells had recently published *The Open Conspiracy* and saw some reflection of his ideas in our Promethean movement. He wrote back:

47, Chiltern Court, Clarence Gate, N.W.1.

Dear Trease and Warbey   22. vi. 31.

I'm busy. I don't want to be interrupted by distraint and have to go to prison. But the logic of Warbey's letter is sound. When would you like to come and talk about it? Is Sunday next any good?

Yours,

H.G. Wells.

We had a memorable evening alone with our revered prophet.

He welcomed us in a drawing-room that seemed leather-walled with the bindings of old books. We had a cold Sunday evening supper, grapefruit, meat pie and salad. He talked, but saw that we talked too. Russia's Five-year Plan was failing, he warned us. 'The trouble' (I wrote in my notes straight afterwards) 'was Stalin—"a Georgian romantic", who had no appreciation of Europe and was shutting the door against the West.' The conversation ranged from sexual freedom to disarmament and his own dream of the World State. He questioned us about the Prometheans. 'You must find a basis!' he insisted in his high-pitched voice. 'Someone must find a basis!'

But, as he had warned us, he was not going to risk imprisonment for refusing to pay income tax. I was scarcely in a position to lecture him on that score. I had never paid income tax and I sometimes wondered glumly if I ever should.

Though these intoxicating new interests filled so much of my life outside office-hours it was not to the exclusion of everything else.

I still enjoyed the friendship of Petey and Patience, who tactfully repressed their misgivings about my wilder activities, and I still saw Barbara Nickalls, who declined to be drawn into them. She had found herself a job with a big publishing group on Ludgate Hill, editing a literary monthly, *The Bookfinder*, which was primarily a shop-window for the innumerable volumes issued under their dozen different imprints. I used to review and write articles for her. She made me grow a moustache so that she could print my photograph. 'I can't let my readers think they are having their books chosen by someone who looks so young,' she said. The portrait I now find as embarrassing as the caption she gave it: 'the young journalist who voices the ideals of revolutionary youth'. At the time I expect I was flattered.

My novel was meanwhile going the rounds. It went to Barbara's firm. Again (as she told me in confidence) the first reader recommended acceptance. But the second, in this case a country clergyman, expressed the fervent hope that the firm's good name would never be sullied by such a filthy book. In the course of a year or so I collected a dozen rejections. Then—if it was not the thirteenth firm it should have been—I received the dreamed-of acceptance. It was a new company, but Jon's highly successful firm was also new, and my unhappy schoolday experience of publishing had shown that long establishment guaranteed nothing. I behaved with caution, showed the agreement to my office colleagues, and was assured that this time everything was aboveboard. It was a straightforward royalty contract, with no question of the author's contributing a penny. True, there was no advance payment, but for a first novel in the depressed conditions of 1931 that did not seem unreasonable. Exhilarated, I signed the agreement, and with no less exhilaration, a few months later, received the catalogue, announcing *The Anvil* among the 'forthcoming publications'. Alas, the next communication came from the Official Receiver, notifying me of the firm's bankruptcy. When, after due formalities, he returned my manuscript, dog-eared but still unpublished, I was too dispirited ever to send it out again.

To judge from its effect on some people who read it, perhaps it was as well.

In that first year in Bloomsbury I had been given an introduction, through a friend of Mother's at Nottingham, to a Fleet Street newspaperman. He was a popular habitué of the Press Club, where he first entertained me, and though now dead he is probably remembered with well-deserved affection. For that reason I will not identify him. Reticence may be out of fashion in autobiography, but I should hate to hurt surviving members of a family that began by showing me such kindness.

After that preliminary inspection at the Press Club, I became a regular visitor to their sixth-floor flat in Gray's Inn Road. They were an all-journalistic family, mother included. The elder daughter, B., the same age as myself, had served her apprenticeship as a cub reporter and now had an editorial job on one of the better women's magazines. J. was still at her convent school, but soon to begin her career as an illustrator. Life had been tough for them. Father had been the victim of a recent newspaper amalgamation, and had had to start afresh in middle age, building up a free-lance income with the help of his many Fleet Street connections. But there was no cynicism in that home. It was a place of geniality and immense warm-heartedness. Something of the Dickensian spirit seemed to have drifted across from Doughty Street close by. The father adored Dickens, and it was the first matter on which we differed, but at this stage amicably enough. The family were united by all the old-fashioned values and the adversity they had so lately experienced.

It was natural that the elder girl and I should draw together. It began, I seem to remember, with two press tickets to *The Barretts of Wimpole Street*, when I was invited to supply the black-tied escort. Other evenings developed from there. After a late Saturday night affair I would be given a shake-down at Gray's Inn Road and become a week-end guest. One Sunday, riding on the top of a bus to Hampstead Heath, we decided to become unofficially engaged. Her parents agreed, on condition that we did nothing impulsive until I had found a better job. Father insisted that I join the N.U.J. and kept his eyes open on my behalf. On another Sunday I took B. to Nottingham on a day-excursion to meet my parents.

The idyll did not last long. She read the carbon copy of my novel, then still going the rounds. I doubt if it shocked her—she had great toleration and humour, and, while not supporting me in all the extravagant pronouncements I used to deliver at their fireside, would always defend my sincerity against the opposition. Alone, she would tease me gently, which was just what I needed.

It was a different matter when her father picked up the typescript. I was summoned by telephone at the office, not to Gray's Inn Road, but to a man-to-man parley at the Press Club. Did I realise that if this novel was published it might do me lasting harm by giving people a completely erroneous idea about me? I stuck to my guns, with all the obstinacy of twenty-one. If anyone accepted my book, I could not bear the thought of turning the offer down. We parted politely, but the seeds of parental disapproval were sown.

They sprouted quickly. A few evenings later the talk turned to Epstein's new sculpture, Genesis, just then the subject of scandalised outcry. Though I knew little of art I began from pure cussedness to defend the work. The argument changed its ground to Radclyffe Hall's recently banned novel, *The Well of Loneliness*. My host was vehement. Such unnatural women were not fit to show their faces in decent society. I could not let that pass. I explained that I knew such a couple among my Promethean friends. Far from being monsters, they were very likeable young women with far more highly developed social consciences than most. Surely their private life was their own affair? They were good citizens.

The argument tailed off. I expect my hostess, always the peace-maker, interrupted with a pot of tea. Her husband slept on the matter. Or perhaps he did not sleep. Next morning—it was Sunday—he posed the blunt and fatal question: had I ever permitted his daughter to meet these women? Only one answer was possible. Yes, they had met at a little party in my flat. Next question, would I promise to sever all contact with such undesirables? Again, only one possible answer. No. Though in deference to his opinion I would not bring his daughter into contact with them again, so long as she was a member of his household. This answer was judged unsatisfactory. I was banned from his home forthwith.

There began then a painful struggle, not to be recounted at length, but too important to me at the time to be suppressed. It had its wry humours, too, easier to relish after forty years, and possibly it enshrines a mite of social history, though I fancy the situation was already untypical even in 1931. Many girls, especially young London journalists, would have snapped their fingers at paternal dictation. But this was a very special family, bound by the strongest ties, and I can understand now, much better than then, the agonising tug-of-war to which poor B. was subjected.

Early in the affair her father did agree to my calling on him one evening, but before I could leave Francis Street I was called to the telephone on the landing upstairs. It was his wife. She explained that her husband was so agitated that she did not feel it safe for us to meet. She herself would slip downstairs and talk things over with me. For the next half-hour we paced the dark Bloomsbury squares in mournful conference. It was then that—though normally a woman with a strong sense of humour—she let fall the remark that I preserve gratefully from the wreck of my romance: 'The trouble with you, Geoffrey, is sex. Thank God, there was nothing like that in *our* married life.'

After this unhelpful exchange of views things went from bad to worse. At lunch-time I used to race through Covent Garden and waylay B. as she emerged from the offices of her magazine. 'I know you are not supposed to see me,' I would say, 'but if you won't lunch with me I shall make a scene in the street, so you can tell them you had no alternative.' We had some thoroughly miserable lunches together. Her father countered these moves by ringing me at the office with an ultimatum: if I did not cease to molest his daughter he would communicate with my parents and demand (again the precise phrasing is indelibly inscribed on my memory) that I 'be put under restraint'.

Captive princesses can be rescued. Nothing much can be done with princesses who are free to walk out across the draw-bridge but shrink from the open gate. Easter was approaching and I was planning to spend the precious four days in the Black Mountains, which I had worked out to be the nearest true 'mountains' within reach of London. I challenged B. to go with me. Needless to say, I caught the midnight train to South Wales alone. Walking those desolate grassy ridges I knew that I was beaten, though for many a month afterwards I refused to acknowledge my defeat to anyone else.

CHAPTER FIFTEEN

Bargain Basement

HILL-WALKING, when I could get it, represented one of the few links with my old pre-London existence.

Visits home were rare. I did not enter my week-end freedom until Saturday lunch-time. My two weeks' annual holiday was conscientiously divided between Nottingham and the Peak or the Lakes. My parents, no great travellers, visited me once in Bloomsbury, but Mother and I exchanged long letters every week and she sent me occasional food-parcels, including the new white Stilton which seemed unobtainable south of the Trent. I relied mainly on letters also to keep up with my old friends, though occasionally someone from Oxford would turn up at my flat, and Garry Hogg appeared once and drove me to his people's house at Harpenden.

The hill-walking was important to me. In those silent prayer sessions at Kingsley Hall—sessions to me so regrettably unhelpful—I used to close my eyes, shut out the flickering candles and the hunched figures, and fight my personal unhappiness with the pictures I conjured up of Great Gable cairn swimming out of the mist or the jagged dragon's teeth of the gritstone edges running mile after mile above the Derbyshire dales. That world existed too, I reminded myself desperately, and I should get back to it some day.

In the two and a half years I spent in Bloomsbury I made good use of my time. From Bank Holiday week-ends I squeezed every possible moment and travelled long distances to reach what I regarded as 'real' hills. My Black Mountain Easter began with arrival in Newport about five o'clock on Good Friday morning, a journey up the dark valley in a workmen's bus, and an hour or two's steady slog through the drizzle before the joy of an enormous breakfast beside a bright fresh fire at the Angel in Abergavenny. The next Easter I spent on Dartmoor, again travelling overnight from Paddington and marching out of Exeter before anyone was awake. On the Monday night I returned similarly, dozing fitfully in the train, and had just time for breakfast, bath and shave, before reporting at the office at nine. Thus, by sacrificing two nights' normal sleep, I could get four full days and walk about eighty miles.

One summer I managed to revisit Cumberland. Another, when I was about to leave London and could spare two weeks, I joined a little party of four others, and walked over the Pyrenees from France, down through the long and in those days solitary valleys of Andorra, into Spain. For the rest, I had to content myself with brief sorties to the tamer hills of Surrey and Sussex. On these day trips I found a welcome companion in a North Country girl who had recently joined our happy little band in the journalists' room. She was another 'Muriel', but my *avant-garde* friends outside, a little intimidated by her moral integrity, referred to her guardedly as my 'beautiful Wesleyan'.

By June 1932 I had been two years with the puff-paper company. For the second half of this period I shared an unfurnished flat in Lamb's Conduit Street with Neil Renton, a young advertising man I had met at the Promethean Society, who remained a close friend until his death some thirty years later. We equipped the large rooms in a most rudimentary manner. I had a sleeping-bag on a divan, and refused to let Neil spoil the look of the other room with the conventional iron bedstead he had brought up from his Dulwich home; he was so good-natured that he let me bully him into discarding the head and foot and supporting the bed itself, unsteadily, on boxes. It was hardly surprising that his parents, when they came up to visit him, declared that he was living in a slum. But at least they had no cause for fear that, with such spartan furnishings, we had much chance to lead a life of unbridled immorality.

When our twelve-months tenancy expired, Neil decided to return to home comforts in Dulwich, and I knew that I should have to seek cheaper quarters alone. The estate agents received our notice with little show of regret. There had been complaints from neighbours after we had used our uncarpeted rooms for a meeting of some thirty vociferous rent-strikers, and our occasional practice of starting poster parades from the flat had done nothing to endear us to the other tenants.

A larger question presented itself to me: should I stay in London at all? My wilder political enthusiasms had burnt themselves out, my love-life made no progress, and I was getting nowhere as a writer. My hack's salary had been advanced, by several infinitesimal rises, to three guineas a week, supplemented by the rare extra guinea or two earned by an article in some minor paper. My hapless novel lay forgotten in a drawer. I was unlikely to write another, or anything of consequence, so long as I had to turn out three thousand words a day in the office. Yet I could not even feel sure of the office-job. There were nearly three million unemployed that year. The air was full of menacing rumours. Sackings, pay-cuts and bankruptcies were the order of the day.

Though in quitting Oxford I had turned my back for ever on any thought of a serious teaching career, I still had the didactic itch, and indeed have never lost it. In those days there were countless private schools, only slightly caricatured by Evelyn Waugh and other young novelists of the period, where an unqualified person could earn a pittance so long as he was a 'gentleman'. I made a swift calculation. If I went to the agencies at once I might find such a post for September. By the autumn my present job might have foundered under me and it would be too late to get into a school.

After three interviews I was accepted by a moribund academy at an Essex seaside resort. It combined the functions of a prep school with the education of a few older boys: I was to teach History and English to School Certificate level, plus junior French and Latin, for a salary of a hundred pounds a year, resident. Later, the headmaster confided to me that he had rejected half-a-dozen London University graduates in my favour. 'I wanted someone I could take into my wife's drawing-room,' he explained. So Mr Trease, 'sometime Scholar of the Queen's College, Oxford', embarked with what dignity he could assume upon another stretch of his zigzag career.

The headmaster was a kindlier and more enlightened character than his remark might suggest. He was struggling to keep a school alive whose whole *raison d'être* rested on snobbery. Our day boys came largely from the local shopkeeping families who sought the cachet of fee-paying education at something grandly called a 'College'. Our boarders were often the children of separated couples who wanted to dispose of them respectably at cut-price fees. Some of these fees were terms in arrears. The headmaster kept the boys as long as he could, not wishing them to suffer more than they had already suffered from their feckless parents. To keep this leaky ship afloat the poor man religiously ate a Rotary lunch once a week, in the hope of picking up fresh pupils from the local bourgeoisie.

In his humanity and conception of education he was far in advance of his junior partner, a saturnine bachelor whose main idea was to build character on the cricket-field. It was an incompatible partnership. The assistant staff soon learned that almost any uncongenial extra duty could be avoided by hesitantly mentioning the instruction to the other partner. 'Mr A. has asked me to …' produced the reflex response from Mr. B., 'No need at all!'

There were four of us in the little staff-room. Roger, with whom I also had to share a bedroom next to the senior dormitory, was a tall, bespectacled nineteen-year-old, best described in a phrase he often applied to his various friends in London, 'a chappie from the Poly'. Ruby, the matron, was a doctor's daughter, refreshingly ribald in contrast to Roger, who was an earnest Anglo-Catholic and used to don, in the evening, what he referred to as his 'sanctuary slippers'. Marian, my senior by a term's service, taught the smallest boys. She had previously been teaching at her own old High School in the Fens, but had been a victim

Marian Boyer with some of her pupils, Clacton 1932–3

of the staff-cuts in that crisis year. We established a certain rapport from the very first day, when a particularly stupid remark of Roger's stung me to the impulsive question, 'Excuse me, Mr Blank, but *what* excuse did your parents offer?' It was no doubt indefensibly rude of me, but I cannot wish it unsaid. It was the first time I made Marian laugh. It was what my first Bloomsbury employer would have called 'the indispensable incident' and it was the opening of a long and happy story.

The work, both the teaching and the leisure-time activities, I found enjoyable, if sometimes testing. My half-dozen School Certificate candidates had the advantage over me in that they had at least failed the exam on the same History period, the term before, whereas I had never even studied it. I had to learn fast. With the juniors quick wits and firm discipline mattered more than knowledge. When an angelic nine-year-old in the Latin class lisped the innocent query, 'Please, sir, did the Romans have *hens*?' one quickly learned, from a perceptible heightening of expectancy throughout the room, to be prepared for the ambiguous supplementary that was about to follow.

Marian Boyer, late 1920s

Winter in a seaside town can be grim, especially on the bleak East Coast. There were few diversions beyond an occasional charity 'ball', polite black-tie affairs, tickets three-and-sixpence. I agreed, reluctantly at first, to make up a foursome with my colleagues. Then, when the matron fell ill and was eventually replaced, Marian and I used to go by ourselves. Roger, a thorough handyman, had already rigged up his own electric bell device for waking the senior dormitory on his own duty days without having to leave his bed. Now he concealed wires under the staff-room doormat so that another bell would ring at his bedside when we came back from the dance, and ring again when we re-emerged, our good-nights said. Unfortunately for this ingenious plan we must both have stepped over the trap the first time, and, though the bell rang as we parted, he was no wiser about the duration of our farewell. I heard the bell myself, and guessed its meaning. It did nothing to sweeten a Perrin-and-Traill relationship.

Secretly, that spring, Marian and I decided to get married. There could be no question of our remaining at the school. There was no married accommodation—and probably there would be no older boys left to make a job for me, anyhow. But, rested from the two-year drudgery of my puff papers, I was renewing my faith in myself as a writer, a faith which Marian, defying reason, and with a courageous loyalty that still humbles and amazes me, seemed prepared to share.

It was not quite the complete economic madness it may sound. Marian had friends in Bath. Their tall Regency house had an unused basement which could be ours rent-free if we had it redecorated. I still possessed about a hundred pounds of my boyhood nest-egg, and we reckoned that, with no rent to pay, this would keep us going for a year, while every guinea I earned would prolong that year by another few days. Even in my limited leisure at the school I had earned a few such guineas. With nothing to do but write, I could surely expand that income many times?

Orphaned early, Marian had been brought up by an uncle, an Evangelical and rigidly teetotal clergyman. When she broke our news to him he wrote and asked me if I could 'support her in the comfort to which she had been accustomed', a ticklish question I found easier to parry in a carefully phrased letter than face to face. There was, in the conditions of that period, no suggestion that Marian should go on working, and little chance that she would have been able to. Married women were not supposed to take jobs that other people needed, least of all in teaching. Her uncle generously continued her small dress-allowance and so, with a few pounds a year of her own, she was independent of me in that respect.

My own family reacted to my latest imprudence with their wonted stolidity, masking their apprehension with acts of goodwill. Only many years later did I hear by accident that

Marian and Geoffrey before their marriage, Clacton

Geoffrey and Marian Trease on their
wedding day, 11 August 1933

Bill had commented gloomily, 'I can see I shall end by keeping Geoff.' My father had died in the previous September. He thus missed the anxiety, but he also missed knowing a daughter-in-law he would have dearly loved.

On the first evening of the summer term I handed in my notice. Within the hour Marian went to the headmaster's study to do the same, and was asked the reason. Soon his delighted wife was at the staff-room door. 'Quite a romance under our roof!' she cried. As the term passed she became a little sterner. Late one evening she was tapping on the staff-room door again. 'My husband and I are waiting to go to bed, Miss Boyer—you must realise we can't possibly do so while you are in here with Mr Trease!' Life was like that in 1933.

We were married at a village church in Cambridgeshire in August, on my twenty-fourth birthday, and after a week's honeymoon at Capel Curig we took up residence in Bath at Lansdown Place.

Our 'bargain basement' looked bright and welcoming. There were no houses opposite, only railings and a grassy slope falling steeply to the city, so that our elegant tall windows showed more sky than most people see from the ground floor. At night we could cross the road and gaze down into what looked like a vast bowl, jewelled with lights. Marian had given the decorator a colour scheme which, though he muddled her directions, broadly achieved the sunny effect she wanted. We occupied only the big front room and the long butler's pantry adapted as a kitchen, ignoring the dank flagged premises at the rear and the wine-cellars that descended mysteriously to still lower depths.

In my incurable naïvety I had assumed that, if I gave appropriate instructions to railway companies, road carriers, friends and furniture shops, we should find on arrival in Bath that Saturday afternoon that all our possessions had been delivered. Not so. For the next week we had to manage with a single piece of proper furniture, mercifully our bed-settee. The only other arrival was a massive oblong packing-case, crammed with fish-knives, cut-glass bowls, and all the other wedding presents of least immediate utility. The packing-case itself was invaluable. Standing parallel with the settee, it gave us a table for our meals and a desk for my writing. Luckily my typewriter went everywhere with me, even on honeymoon.

It was vital that I should get to work at once, and I did. That autumn I poured out little articles and short stories to every market I could think of. Perhaps one in six was accepted, always in some minor publication which paid about a guinea. After a few weeks an inquiry came from the puff-paper company. Would I help them out by taking a regular batch of work for so many shillings per thousand words? I was reluctant to mount that treadmill again but I dared not refuse. By the end of the year, and my first four months as a free-lance, I had received less than twenty-three pounds, ten of which came from the hack work. So I was glad to have it.

Yet there was a gleam of light ahead. As my feverish mind quested hither and thither, turning over a dozen journalistic possibilities, a new idea suddenly presented itself. Children's stories, but children's stories such as there had never been before …

While in London I had come across a book translated from the Russian, *Moscow Has a Plan*, in which a Soviet author brilliantly dramatised for young readers that first Five-year Plan which had already captured the imagination of the adult world. I did not want to write books like that, I could not, but Ilin's had planted a time-bomb in my mind which now suddenly exploded into questions and ideas. Why were all our own children's books still rooted in the pre-1914 assumptions which serious adult literature had abandoned? In the boys' adventure story especially there had been no development since my own childhood. Such

Marian and Geoffrey in their first home, the basement flat in Lansdown Place, Bath, 1933

stories still implied that war was glorious, that the British were superior to foreigners, that coloured 'natives' were 'loyal' if they sided with the invading white man and 'treacherous' if they used their wits to counterbalance his overwhelming armaments. In historical tales the Cavaliers and the French aristocrats were always in the right, no matter what the teachers explained at school, and the lower orders, like the lesser breeds, figured only in one of two possible roles, as howling mobs or faithful retainers.

'Robin Hood', I wrote a few months later in a Co-operative Society magazine called *Dawn*, 'is about the only proletarian hero our children are permitted to admire.' My use of the word 'proletarian' reveals, incidentally, how slight was my acquaintance with Marxism. 'Yet even he', I continued indignantly, 'is not allowed to remain an ordinary working man! He has to be really Earl of Huntingdon ...'

It was in this spirit that I had approached a publishing firm whose sympathies were sufficiently indicated by its list, composed mainly of Marx, Engels, Lenin and contemporary Soviet novels with such alluring titles as *Cement*. Would the firm be interested in a Robin Hood story that would be revolutionary in more ways than one? The response was more than I had dreamed of. By return post the publishers informed me that they had been looking for someone to do this kind of book for a long time. Would I submit a synopsis and three chapters?

I set to work immediately. I had little notion in those days of what historical research was required. I had grown up in the Robin Hood country, nourished on the tradition. What more did I need to know? What, indeed? Some slight notion may be gained just from comparing the description of medieval Nottingham in that first story with the more accurate one I painstakingly built up in *The Red Towers of Granada*, thirty-two years later.

Bows against the Barons was, as Margaret Meek has fairly written, 'genuine black-and-white' and I would not quarrel now with the verdict in her Bodley Head Monograph: 'At this time Trease believed that it was his duty to be a propagandist of social and political realism in opposition to those writers who trafficked in improbability. We find his villains capitalist in utterance, and the heroes are the downtrodden proletariat of the thirties rather than twelfth-century peasants, but as an example of shaking up the mixture and telling a clear yarn it has still much to offer.'

The book was accepted on that sample material. Fifteen pounds advance on publication, and a straight ten per cent royalty ... I felt I had my foot on the ladder.

It was not on a rung I had expected. My becoming a children's writer was an accident, for it was in politics, not children, that I was then mainly interested. I wrote because there was something I wanted to say, a respectable motive when writing for adults but at that period suspect in a children's author, for we were suffering a reaction against the didactic pieties of the nursery bookshelf in the nineteenth century. I was too close to my own childhood to look back on it with sentimental nostalgia. I never have done since. Nor, while appreciating that children, like puppies and kittens, foals and fawns, possess certain unique attractions of freshness and vitality, have I ever shared the common English view that the young of any species is inherently more interesting and important than the mature. I was never concerned with children as a separate (and in many eyes enviable) race absorbed in a special and limited world of their own, so I could never have written stories for the youngest of all. The older they were, the more they appealed to me. I saw them as adults in the making, moving inexorably forward to a wider world that was, according to the way you looked at it, either their doom or their heritage. Being fundamentally an optimist, I saw it as a heritage, even though, like most inheritances, it brought its problems. I did not want to call to my readers, 'Stay in your magical childhood, you will never have it so good.' My impulse was to beckon them on and shout: 'There is a wider view from the next bend. Come along—it's dangerous, but it's worth it.'

It never occurred to me that I should study my readers' tastes and try to cater for them. With the arrogance of my own age I knew that what mattered was what I wanted to tell them,

Back cover of the paperback edition of Bows against the Barons*, 1934 (See the front of this edition for a reproduction of the front cover.)*

Stifled Children

Nearly all books written to amuse children take very good care to build up only that point of view which will be acceptable to their employers in later life. This means that parents who hold views inimical to the existing regime are hard put to it to find literature which will not stifle the minds of their children but which will not deprive them of the excitements they naturally demand.

We are glad to say that some distinguished and experienced friends think we are providing such material in **Comrades for the Charter** and **Bows Against the Barons** [Geoffrey Trease, each 1/-.] Thus, Miss V. A. HYETT, of King Alfred School, writes of **Comrades for the Charter**: "I regard it as a desirable counterblast to the accepted blood and thunder patriotism, and well calculated to arouse interest in the Chartist movement. . . . I shall put it in my School History Fiction Library and recommend it to children studying the period." Then, Professor LASCELLES ABERCROMBIE writes of the two Geoffrey Trease books that:— "the author is to be congratulated in having imposed such first-rate stories with so sound a tone. I have always held that the right social attitude should make for, not against, thrilling narrative in this kind of work, and the author has done admirably what I have long wanted to see done."

Mr. J. H. BADLEY, Head of Bedales School, writes:—"I have read **Comrades for the Charter** with much interest, and am putting it in our School Library. I hope that in publishing this and similar volumes you may find your venture justified—it is certainly good for children to have this side of the social problem brought home to them."

And Miss STORM JAMESON:—"I certainly think it very necessary that children should discover that knights and cavaliers were not the only adventurers in history, and be given as well the thrill of reading about heroes whose heroism they can begin imitating to-morrow. Both stories are exciting in themselves, and a vast improvement on the usual children's book."

These books are translated into German and Russian. A companion volume is **Eddie and the Gipsy**, Alex Wedding (2/6).

The new Trease is **Call to Arms** (2/6), based on the Chaco War—and what might have happened!

Martin's Annual (edited by Joan Beauchamp, 1/-) gives in the same kind of country all the brightness and attractiveness of its genre.

ALL PRICES NET

MARTIN LAWRENCE ml LIMITED
33 GREAT JAMES STREET W.C.1

not what they wanted to hear. Many years later I came across a remark of Arthur Ransome's which showed that, utterly different as our books had been, we had this in common: we both wrote to please ourselves without much regard for the preferences of our public. Clearly such an attitude would not had been tenable if sufficient children were not prepared to take what we offered. But our stories were acceptable, I would guess, not because we studied childish tastes and put in the right ingredients but because some of those tastes had survived, deep down, in our own natures and came out spontaneously in our writing. Books, if they are any good, can be enjoyed on more than one level, and when children single out their reasons for specially loving a story they often pick things that disconcert and disappoint the author, at least until he has learnt to accept the experience as normal.

Thus, at one level, *Bows against the Barons* was written because I wanted to expose even to children the falsity of the romantic Merrie England image. But when I sent my hero stealing shadowlike through the bracken, creeping disguised into the villain's castle, or escaping perilously through the nightmare labyrinth of caves and passages which (I knew) underlay my native Nottingham, I was reliving the fantasies of my own boyhood and enjoying the work on this level, as much as the conscious fulfilment of my social purpose. I was certainly not deliberately sugaring a political pill.

The book poured out fluently and effortlessly, two or three thousand words a day, straight on to the typewriter. The publisher seemed delighted with the result. It really looked as though I had the knack of writing for children. Barbara Nickalls introduced me to her friend, May Marshall, then assistant editor to G.J.H. Northcroft on the *Boy's Own Paper*. Published by the Religious Tract Society, this was not a fertile field for Left-wing propaganda, but I managed to work out an idea for a public-school story which, while superficially in the Talbot Baines Reed convention, concealed enough novelty and social content to satisfy my conscience. May Marshall wrote that Mr Northcroft liked the idea but never commissioned an unknown writer. She was sure, however, that I could safely go ahead.

In those opulent days the *B.O.P.* could buy a book-length story, cut it into two great slabs of twenty-five thousand words each, and publish it as a 'serial'. I wrote *The New House at Hardale*, setting the scene in Derbyshire and once more reliving, with appropriate adaptation, some of the real or imagined experiences of my own schooldays. I sent in the story and kept my fingers crossed. It would have reassured me a little if I had known then that the great Talbot Baines Reed, like myself, had been to a day school, the City of London, and had had to create the world of the dormitory and study at second hand. After an agony of suspense I received news that the story was accepted. A guinea a thousand words, and there were fifty thousand. *Fifty guineas!* We nearly went mad. Instead, we rushed out and spent the fifty odd shillings on a beautiful new half dinner-service.

Later, when we became friends, May Marshall confided the story behind the acceptance. When my typescript had arrived, Northcroft had at first refused even to glance at it. May had fought for me. 'But you *must*,' she insisted. 'You approved the idea.' She nagged him until he read it. When the first instalment appeared he had the nerve to print an editorial note. 'Geoffrey Trease', he announced, 'is a new author I am glad to have discovered.'

CHAPTER SIXTEEN

A Cottage in the Quantocks

OUR tide seemed to be turning. Though my Robin Hood story would not be published for some months the publishers had encouraged me to begin a second, which they suggested might deal with the Chartist movement. This time, conscious of my own ignorance, I did a good deal of research, carrying armfuls of books from the public library and studying the age-yellowed pages of the *Bath Chronicle* for 1839. The Newport Rising of that year provided the dramatic climax I needed for a children's book, and for the main setting I used the Black Mountains which had so powerfully caught my imagination a few years earlier. Despite my research, however, *Comrades for the Charter* (as its title indicates) carried more than a flavour of twentieth-century politics. It was the easier to fall into anachronism since I had, from the start, set my face against the 'ye olde varlet' type of diction which deterred so many children from reading historical stories. My Sherwood outlaws and now my Chartists conversed in modern English. In this respect I was consciously following Naomi Mitchison, whose novel *The Conquered* I had read at school. My characters, unfortunately, lapsed occasionally into the phraseology of a Communist meeting.

Bath is not the best place to be poor in. The elegant shops mocked us. It was hard to make friends: Lansdown Place was a 'good address' but basement-dwellers were not recognised. I introduced Marian to the very mild excitements of Labour Party meetings, and thereby we at least made the acquaintance of a delightful Quaker couple, a schoolmaster and his psychologist wife, who welcomed us to their book-crammed flat with its almost obligatory anti-Nazi refugee in the spare bedroom. Our only other entertainment was the gallery of the Theatre Royal, so uncomfortable and so cold that winter that we took a travelling rug and once even a hot-water bottle.

We could not for ever trespass on the hospitality of Marian's friends upstairs, and my modest progress now encouraged us to consider moving to a real place of our own. A cheaply rented country cottage seemed the best idea. It was the right thing for a struggling author. Years ago, Hogg had lent me Gissing's *Private Papers of Henry Ryecroft*, and the book, often re-read, had had an ineradicable influence. 'Let's find a cottage further west in Somerset,' I said, 'and we might serve teas to visitors to make a bit extra for the time being. You know you make jolly good scones and cakes.'

A study of the county newspaper revealed no likely cottages and an advertisement of our own produced only two answers, one at Wheddon Cross on Exmoor and the other at Over Stowey in the Quantock Hills. We decided that the best thing would be to pack our rucksacks, catch a train to Taunton, and make a wide sweep through the Brendons, Exmoor and the Quantocks, view the two cottages in question, and inquire for others in every village on the way.

It was fresh spring weather. There were primroses everywhere, but snow wisped down as we ate our picnic lunch on the first day, and that evening we were glad of the crackling fire kindled for us at the isolated Brendon farmhouse where we stopped for the night. Next morning, the Wheddon Cross cottage was depressingly impossible. The landlord was a shifty-looking clergyman who repelled Marian at sight. We tramped on over Dunkery Beacon and down through the woods overhanging Horner Water to spend our second night by the sea near Porlock. It was all picture-postcard country, unbelievably beautiful in the fresh greens of spring, with the pale blue wood-smoke curling up from humpy thatched cottages with white and pink walls. But none of those cottages was available for an embryo Henry Ryecroft. They mostly belonged to semi-feudal estates and outsiders were not wanted.

It was the same tale next morning in the little villages with their tithe-barns and packhorse bridges, smithies and water-splashes, that hemmed the skirts of Selworthy Beacon. We tramped doggedly eastwards now, asking everywhere, but by nightfall we had still drawn blank. We slept at West Quantoxhead, only a mile or two from Kilve where I had spent my first night on that eventful hitch-hike five years before. We had now walked about sixty miles in three days without finding a single cottage to let. The letter from Over Stowey represented our sole remaining hope. We decided to waste none of our last day on fruitless road-walking. After breakfast we struck up the seaward face of the Quantocks, intending to keep on the heights until it was time to descend upon the hamlet in its fold of the hills.

The Quantocks are on a similar scale to the Malverns in whose shadow we live now. The Somerset range is slightly longer, on average higher, much more wooded, and markedly more widely spread in lateral combes. In short, though the skyline track, with its long open prospects in both directions, gives you the illusion that you could not possibly become confused about your whereabouts, on the Quantocks it is quite easy to do so, and as soon as we slanted down into the woodlands we were lost.

We had met no one all the morning. Now, as we broke through the stunted oakwoods and came out on the stony red track known locally as 'the Coach Road', we suddenly heard hoofs and voices, and round the bend rode a tall young man and a pretty schoolgirl in a blazer. They set us on our way and we parted. Half-an-hour later, thanks to a providential muddling of 'Over Stowey' and 'Nether Stowey', we found ourselves in the latter, a much larger village with inns and shops. And almost the first thing we saw was a cottage to let.

Things moved then with incredible speed. For the owner was the village grocer, not fifty yards down the street. We viewed the cottage. It opened straight on to the narrow pavement, as most of the Nether Stowey houses did. It had massive walls, exposed beams and a homicidal staircase. Years later we heard that the title-deeds went back to Henry VIII's reign. There were two decent little rooms in front, a scullery and lavatory at the back, two and a bit bedrooms above, electricity throughout, mains water, but no bath and no hot-water system unless you counted an ancient copper. But we could hardly expect luxuries for eight shillings and sixpence a week, including rates.

Though courtesy demanded that we still trudge up the hill to Over Stowey, we both knew that this was the place for us. We went back to the grocer's shop and discussed details with his wife, a dear woman who was to mother us whenever she got the chance during the next two years. As we chatted, the pretty schoolgirl entered. We greeted her gaily, confessed to our muddling her directions. She smiled—I cannot say 'wanly' for the colour was mounting warmly in her cheeks. 'What were *you* doing, up on the Coach Road, Betty?' demanded the grocer's wife—who was now seen to be also Betty's mother, for the poor girl mumbled something and fled to the living premises at the back. Only then did we realise the game we had given away. But no lasting harm was done, and years later Betty was allowed to marry her forbidden riding companion.

Nether Stowey was T-shaped, the horizontal being the main coast road between Minehead and Bridgwater, while the upright was Castle Street, climbing inland to the castle mound and thence across the flank of the hills to Taunton. At 3 Castle Street, which we named Castle Cottage, we faced the vanished market cross, the place where the long green buses pulled in and the hounds met, and in many other ways the hub of village life.

It was a village of immense character. Just up the street towards Minehead stood Coleridge's cottage, a miniature museum, and in some respects Stowey was little altered from the days when Coleridge had lived there and written *The Ancient Mariner*, when the Wordsworths had come stalking over from the next village, and when Lamb had hopped brightly off the coach in front of our door, forgetting his overcoat when he returned to London. The same stream went burbling down Castle Street, the lock-up stood on the corner, the elegant gazebo surmounted the garden wall of Stowey Court, the little toll-house survived, though now it was the doctor's surgery, the hill ponies were still driven clattering down the road, and the gipsylike 'broom squires' plied their ancient trade in clothes-pegs, mushrooms, whortleberries and whatever else could be gathered free from the hills.

This was a land of long memories. On our first shopping visit to Bridgwater I went to the panelled restaurant where Mrs Shipster had taken me to lunch. I was told that she now lived at Brymore Lodge, halfway along our homeward road to Stowey. I wrote reminding her of our encounter, and a few days later we were invited to dinner. It was served with old-world elegance in that boxlike dwelling— she gave us guinea-fowl, stuffed with rosemary and marjoram, and afterwards displayed with childlike pride her bathing arrangements, a zinc tub suspended high

Marian and Geoffrey Trease, with a friend, outside their second home, the cottage in Nether Stowey

from her kitchen ceiling, which she could lower, raise and tilt with a Heath-Robinson system of ropes and pulleys. But what really delighted her was that she had regained a foothold, albeit tiny, on her ancestral lands. She was a descendant of 'King' Pym, whose birthplace was the great empty house up the drive. About 1800 a family feud had stung the then occupier to vow that no member of the other branch, hers, should ever set foot on the estate again. Mrs Shipster, by using her slender means to acquire the lodge and its ribbon of garden at the recent sale, felt that she had bested her jealous kinsman even though more than a century had gone by.

Out of compliment to her the local hounds regularly met in front of her gate. She never lost the air of a *grande dame*. I once saw her waiting for her bus in the humming centre of Bridgwater. Why should she stand? Broad-beamed, she sat on the flagstones at the base of Admiral Blake's statue, an open newspaper extended beneath her, inevitably *The Times*, unmoved by the stares and sniggers of the ill-bred. The bus pulled in, she rose majestically and sailed towards it, leaving the sheets of newspaper (I regret to record) to rise and flap and drift unregarded along the pavement. Few would have dared to rebuke King Pym's descendant for leaving litter.

She was charmed with the wife I had acquired since our previous meeting and approved our idea of serving teas to augment my earnings. She advised us sensibly on the fixing of prices in ratio to the cost of the food. She insisted on lending us a boxful of spare crockery, which we found very useful, and an ice-cream-making device, which defeated us.

In the event, our catering never contributed much to our income. Ten days after we hung up the sign I had painted we had the first response, a letter from the electricity company warning us that, since we now advertised ourselves as a 'hotel or guest-house', their phrase, we could no longer enjoy the benefit of the domestic tariff. But if our profits were insignificant in return for the cake-baking and washing-up and emergency dashes down the road for sixpennyworth of clotted cream from the farmer's wife, the human contacts were welcome.

One morning I was thrown into some excitement by a postcard from Suffolk. Could we provide supper, bed and breakfast for the writer and his schoolboy son at the start of their walking tour? It was signed 'H. I'A. Fausset'. It *must* be Hugh I'Anson Fausset, I assured Marian. Somehow the famous author must have heard of his struggling junior confrère … this was a significant encounter … we must make the most of it.

Everything was laid aside to prepare for our distinguished visitor. Steak, Marian decided, the best steak and hang the cost. She beat it until her arm ached. Early in the evening father and son arrived, as handsome and agreeable as anyone could have wished. As I conducted them upstairs Fausset looked round him and won our hearts by declaiming in a rich, organlike voice that rolled through the cottage: 'All the charms of elegance upon a basis of simplicity!' Then, slipping off his rucksack, he added, 'By the way, as to supper—we are both vegetarians. I trust that that will not make for any difficulty?'

Our olive oil saved the situation. He confessed he had not dared to hope for good olive oil. He had obtained our address merely by writing to the village post office. Frankly, he confessed, he had been prepared for brass bedknobs and texts on the wall. He sat up late talking to us and decided to stay for a second night. We enjoyed the talk and we enjoyed the unwanted steak, but the visit did nothing to further my literary career.

Neither my first nor my second book had set the Thames on fire. The headmaster of Bedales and some other progressive educationists welcomed them. Lascelles Abercrombie wrote that 'the author has done admirably what I have long wanted to see done', but I cannot imagine where he wrote it, unless in a letter to the publishers designed for quotation, since no medium existed for the serious critical discussion of new children's literature. Britain was smugly proud of her classics, a rich heritage unrivalled by any other nation, but there was an indifference to living authors and an assumption that nothing fresh of any interest was being produced in this field. I myself was quite unaware that Ransome's *Coot Club* and P.L. Travers' *Mary Poppins* were coming out at that same time. Admittedly, children's literature was at a low ebb. Most books were mediocre, the text frequently bought outright for a meagre sum and then printed in artificially bulky volumes to impress parents. Hidden in the mass were stories of originality, but it was nobody's job to look for them. In schools the classics reigned unchallenged. Teachers felt safe only with authors who had been a long time dead.

I was not helped by my publishers' reputation as specialists in Left-wing literature. I was even handicapped by the frontispiece to *Bows against the Barons*, for that first illustrator, in a praiseworthy desire to match the grim realism of the narrative, had produced a scarifying picture of a mutilated corpse dangling from a Sherwood oak. More than one parent told me how they had had to tear out the illustration before handing the book to their children. Others must have felt they could not buy. So, for one reason or another, the books made slow headway, even in circles where they would have been approved. George Orwell had never heard of them when he published his famous essay on boys' stories in 1940. In May that year he wrote to me that, since then, 'two people had written to me telling me of your *Bows against the Barons*, etc … There is no question that this matter of intelligent fiction for kids is very important and I believe the time

Frontispiece to the first edition of Bows against the Barons, *1934*

137

is approaching when it might be possible to do something about it … Did you by the by see in *Horizon* Frank Richards's reply to my article? I can't make up my mind to what extent it was a fake, but it certainly wasn't *altogether* a fake, and it's well-nigh incredible that such people are still walking about, let alone editing boys' papers.' Orwell's closing paragraph made me realise how precarious even his position must be—and this was in 1940: 'It makes me laugh to see you referring to me as "famous" and "successful". I wonder if you know what my books sell—usually about 2000. My best book, the one about the Spanish war, sold less than 1000 …'

I cannot recall the sales figures of my own first books, but at a threepenny royalty (they sold at half-a-crown) I doubt if either, in the five years before the war, equalled the fifty guineas earned by the *B.O.P.* serial. Today, with a few small revisions, the Robin Hood story has attained the respectability of a special school edition. Few teachers would have dared to read even their own copies to a class in 1934.

When the first book was commissioned on synopsis I gave up the hack work from the puff papers. For nearly a year I tried to do without it. I wrote the two boys' historical stories and the *B.O.P.* serial, three book-length tales, that is, of about fifty thousand words each. I wrote, and placed, a small book, *Walking in England*, which distilled my love of all the regions I had explored on various tours. I sold articles to the *Scottish Educational Journal* and to various religious publications, the *Baptist Times*, *Christian World*, and *Sunday at Home*, varying my pseudonym for each denomination. I wrote not only for the *Hiker and Camper*, but, using my imagination and adjusting my mileages, for *Cycling* and the motoring press, though I could not drive a car. Using yet another pseudonym, so as not to lose my Nonconformist markets, I even contributed articles on the lonelier and most wooded areas to a nudist magazine. All this was not as unprincipled as it sounds. I never wrote anything against my conscience. I merely packaged my material to suit the customer.

These were my pitiful 'successes'. God knows how many more ambitious efforts I dispatched to other editors in vain. Within the year I was driven back to the treadmill, to the weekly parcel of big buff envelopes, the contents of each to be processed into a bright publicity article for a few shillings. I was in a dilemma. If I wrote enough of such stuff to support us, I was left with little time or energy to attempt any real writing. The only solution was to dictate the copy at speed.

I advertised for a part-time secretary. One evening a tall girl knocked at the door, her boots and breeches explained by the motorcycle propped outside. She had come from the Polden Hills, beyond Bridgwater, where her father was a doctor. I explained the work, which could be taken home for typing, and the shamefully low pay per thousand words. She did not demur. Mastering my nerves, I went through the farce of testing her shorthand. When Joy Webster knew me better, she confessed that she had been as paralysed with fright as I was. She had walked up and down the village street for ten minutes before she could summon up enough courage to knock. 'I thought an author would have a beard,' she said.

'There's just one thing,' she told us shyly, the first time she came to work. 'I sometimes get backache—it's my spine—and I just *have* to lie flat for a few minutes … Oh, no, on the floor. The hard floor is best. So long as you understand.'

We could only hope, privately, that our neighbours would. On that busy corner every passing villager hugged our strip of pavement and seldom resisted the temptation of a glance through our windows, for we scorned net curtains as genteel.

I cannot remember whether backache ever did interrupt my dictation. Certainly Joy was a great help to me at that time of stress. After a complete loss of contact for thirty-five years I met her again, Joy Parsons now, married to the architect she had once brought to a party in the cottage, herself the author of a book on painting but better known as an artist. It was a comfort to learn that she too had been quite happy in our work together and had not felt herself exploited.

Perhaps our catering income would have built up into something more substantial the second summer, with returning customers and recommendations, but when that time came Marian and I were in Russia.

CHAPTER SEVENTEEN

Frozen Roubles

'YES, but have you ever *been* there?'

In those days every political argument seemed to revolve round Russia, the young progressive's Promised Land. One got tired of all one's eloquence being deflated by the same challenging question from sceptical opponents.

Suddenly I heard that *Bows against the Barons* was published in Moscow. As Russia had never subscribed to the international copyright convention my permission had not been asked and no payment would be sent me. But the money was there all right in frozen roubles. If Marian and I cared to go there for a long visit, my London publishers were confident that, with their special Communist contacts, they could get us visas, not as 'tourists', which would cut no ice in arguments when we returned, but as 'workers'. We could be found temporary jobs with my Moscow publishers, the Co-operative Publishing Society of Foreign Workers in the U.S.S.R. It had an Anglo-American section and innumerable other national departments, boasting as it did that it published in more of the world's different languages than any other organisation except the British and Foreign Bible Society.

Marian was willing. Whatever reserve she felt about my political enthusiasms, she backed me loyally and uncomplainingly in this as in all my other ventures, even when it involved her in the same undeserved suspicion that we were Bolsheviks living on 'Moscow gold', a fashionable phrase of the period which we found especially ironical since we could not obtain in England a penny of the Russian royalties I had legitimately earned. I myself never seriously considered joining the Communist Party, even in the 'Popular Front' days when its demands seemed mainly reasonable. Ingenuous I might be, but I noticed early what happened to individuals who left the Party on a sincere difference of opinion, and how they were transmogrified into 'Fascist hyaenas' overnight. It is fair to say that no one, either in England or in Russia, ever asked me to join. Left-wing idealists, I came to realise, were of more use outside, 'fellow travellers' in the original sense of the phrase which I believe Stalin coined that year, easily manipulated by the Party and expendable.

We had a vivacious young friend who, in narrating some particularly outrageous incident, would frequently preface her statements with the phrase, 'Believe *me*'. We arranged with her that we would adopt this as a simple code in letters from Russia to indicate that any subsequent passage should be read in a directly contrary sense. If we wrote, 'Believe me, it is all nonsense about food shortages,' she would draw the right conclusion. As things turned out, there was never any need to employ this device. The year 1935 was a brief golden interlude of economic and political relaxation. The austerities of the first Five-year Plan were over and the Stalinist purges still lay ahead. Fear of Hitler meant that Britain and France were to be wooed at all costs. Liberal or Labour—or even sympathetic Conservative—the English visitor was warmly welcomed as a potential ally against the Germans. It was perhaps easier then, than at any other date before or since, to get a favourable impression of Soviet society.

Soviet passenger vessels left London twice a week for Leningrad, offering a cheaper if slower journey than the train to Moscow via Poland. We planned to sail almost as soon as the Baltic was ice-free, so as to be there for May Day. We shut up our cottage two days beforehand and went up to stay with the Warbeys, who gathered all my old London friends for a farewell party in our honour. Alas, the usual visa trouble now began, which, I have noticed throughout the subsequent decades, clouds so many of such visits in either direction. My London publishers had not received our visas. It was puzzling, but would be sorted out. Everything would be all right. The Soviet attaché was cabling Moscow ... They had enlisted the aid of Harry Pollitt, then leader of the British Communist Party ... With people like that exerting themselves on our behalf we were sure to catch the next boat ...

We were in London a whole month, unable to go back to Somerset because we did not know from one hour to the next when the visas would arrive. Ashamed of imposing on the Warbeys any longer, we accepted an invitation to stay with Petey and Patience in Hampstead. After a week there, we went back to our original hosts. I began to write a story with a South American setting, *Call to Arms*, inspired by the recent revelations of the way private armament manufacturers exploited the petty quarrels of countries like Bolivia and Paraguay. Then at last one Thursday, when Marian had gone out for the day, the telephone rang. We could sail on Saturday afternoon. The visas had been discovered in Paris, where they had been waiting all the time. Moscow had assumed that people who seemed to be in such a hurry would travel the quickest way, via Paris, and they had helpfully sent the visas there for us to pick up. They had just not bothered to mention the fact to anyone in London.

We duly embarked in the *Sibir*, moored below London Bridge. When we had found our third-class cabin and looked round the saloons of that quite agreeable motor vessel, Marian suddenly remembered that good toilet soap was reputedly scarce in the Promised Land, and decided to go ashore again. No sooner had she vanished at a leisurely pace into the drab region behind the wharf than the ship burst into vociferous life. Visitors were ominously warned to quit the vessel. One gangway was trundled noisily away. I leant over the rail, frothing with apprehension. After a month of delay Marian had chosen this moment to disappear on a shopping errand! *Soap!* What should I do if they began to remove the last surviving gangway? I was beside myself with panic when with (I doubt not) bulging eyes I beheld the well-loved figure weaving its elegant unhurried way between the parked cars and bollards.

'Were you worried, darling? It's a long way to the shops.'

And it's a long way, I thought, to Leningrad.

She was absolutely right, of course. It was a full hour before we began to slide away from the wharf and saw Tower Bridge opening to let us through.

We were met at Leningrad by a young Englishman from the branch office of the Publishing Society there. In charm and appearance he was the traditional Public School type, tall, fair, and doubtless clean-limbed, whatever that implies. It was odd to see him wearing Soviet badges proclaiming his readiness in 'labour and defence'. He took us in a taxi to one of the half-finished, barrack-like apartment blocks on the Lesnoy Prospekt where we must stay for a few days until accommodation could be found for us in the acutely overcrowded capital. He showed us the food-store in the building, gave us a wad of roubles, and explained that we should not need ration-cards as rationing was about to finish. Then he pointed out the nearest tram-stop, told us how to reach his office, and warned us that we could not use our Russian money in the restaurants of tourist hotels. A tram pulled up, he leapt aboard, and we were on our own in Russia before we had eaten our first meal.

My memories of Leningrad are thus, not surprisingly, of coping with trivial problems rather than of sightseeing. The place was in any case a shabby fairyland compared with the Tsarist capital or the carefully restored city of today. It had been run down as part of the policy to magnify the importance of Moscow. The endless Nevsky was drab and faded.

Once only did we experience a revelation of the city's magic. We had been to a party in a tourist hotel, given by an English jazz band we had met on the boat. About three in the morning, elated with apple brandy, we set out on the long walk back to our room on the Lesnoy Prospekt. The trams had stopped running. Apart from the watchmen huddled in the doorways like bundles of rags, Leningrad was briefly asleep.

We were entering the midsummer period known as the White Nights, when the sun dips only for an hour or two into the Gulf of Finland, when real darkness never quite arrives, and when a mother-of-pearl half-light suffuses the city of rivers and canals, domes and spires and triumphal arches. As we trudged across one of those long bridges the sunrise began to flame behind the splendidly architectural skyline. If the sky became molten gold, the Neva racing under our feet became a river twinkling with a million diamonds. The poetry of that morning lived with me until, over thirty years later, I tried to express it in a story called *The White Nights of St Petersburg*.

We went to Moscow in style, with first-class sleepers in the famous Red Arrow express. True, our reservations, 18 and 19, gave us different partners in the two-berth compartments, but a courteous army officer insisted on changing places so that I could join Marian. When we glided into Moscow next morning, punctual to the second, a miniature reception committee from the publishing house awaited us.

This time we were accommodated in a corner of the genuine old Russia. Several old wooden houses stood in a dusty compound. Each held a number of families. Our first-floor room was sub-let to us by a couple of married students leaving town for the long vacation. As a safeguard against capitalistic exploitation, this arrangment had to be supervised by the house committee for the whole unit. Our address was Apartment 8, Kalyaevskaya Ulitsa 31. It was on the north of the city, beyond the outer boulevards, a moderate tram-ride from the publishing offices in Nikolskaya, just off Red Square.

We never saw much of our neighbours. We shared a kitchen with the other tenants of our particular flat, but we hesitated to intrude upon the kerchiefed women who perpetually monopolized the stove with their mysterious pottages. We preferred simple cooking on an electric ring in our own room, and a solid dinner most afternoons in the restaurant allotted to publishing staff. Their office day ran from ten till half-past four, with only a brief canteen break for the 'second breakfast' about twelve, when slices of cold ham and sausage, hard-boiled eggs, salads and fancy cakes were available with glasses of tea.

At Kalyaevskaya, apart from the kitchen, the only shared facility was—inescapably—the dark cupboardlike water closet built for climatic reasons in the very centre of the flat, an advantage we did not fully appreciate in Moscow's torrid June.

Our most forthcoming neighbours were the children who played in the compound, very attractive, once you got used to the reptilian effect of the little boys' shaven skulls. They would gather below and chant in English: 'Pliz—come—to de—vindo!' until we showed ourselves, bowing and smiling like a parody of King George V and Queen Mary at Buckingham Palace. Once they knocked shyly and offered a bunch of flowers.

It was I who saw most of them. When, on our second morning, we called at the office in the old walled quarter of the Kitai-Gorod, I was at once asked: 'Why should we waste your time on routine editorial jobs? You are an author. Go away and write us a book.' So immediately I was back to my familiar working pattern. I sat alone in the shabby room at Kalyaevskaya, tapping out the story I had begun in London.

Marian spent the day at the office in the Anglo-American section, which, though primarily concerned with disseminating translations of Marx and Lenin, was extending its scope to publish Dickens, Defoe, Jack London, and other approved authors in the original. Marian's chief task was to check the proofs of *The Pickwick Papers*, a Sisyphean labour, since as fast as the Russian printers corrected one error their unfamiliarity with the Western alphabet caused them to make two more. As a whole, the publishing house must have contained a fairly high proportion of tragic exiles and dedicated revolutionists—Germans, Austrians, Poles, Spaniards, Bulgarians, Indonesians, and a dozen other nationalities. The Anglo-American section was rather more light-hearted but not untinged by the general earnestness pervading Soviet life. The notice-board carried voluntary pledges of dead-lines which individuals set themselves for specific editorial jobs. Marian was momentarily shaken to see one such announcement pinned up with the terse promise to 'finish Trease by June 17'.

We must have been under some surveillance—that, I now realise, has been the Russian way since long before the Revolution—but it was not obvious. We roamed Moscow as freely as we would Paris today. We went to the first carnival in the Park of Rest and Culture, we saw the Bolshoi in a superb open-air production of *Carmen* under a midsummer full moon. But there was little attempt to impress us with show-pieces, though, on the assumption that a children's writer would be interested in children, we were taken to a Young Pioneer camp in the forest and treated to an impromptu concert by the boys and girls living in a modern block of flats. Much more of our time was spent anonymously strolling along the boulevards, visiting American friends, or shopping for the 'Kornfleks', the date-stamped (but pathetically pale-yolked) eggs, the dark bread, the bottles of milk, and the other food we consumed in our room.

I was invited to write my impressions for the English-language *Moscow Daily News*, and my old Promethean friend, Pat Sloan, appeared suddenly with the request that I should broadcast. It was emphasised that only objective description was wanted, no propaganda, above all, no adverse reflections upon the West. Once my copy was cut, and then only after consulting me, because I had written that children's play facilities in London parks were inferior to those in Moscow. 'Say only,' I was told, 'what you have seen here with your own eyes.'

One's own eyes can, of course, be deceived. Marian arrived one morning at her office to find her colleagues missing. Soon they trooped in together, late and laughing, and explained that they had been filming. The Soviet newsreel people wanted shots of some foreign delegations leaving Moscow but had learned to their dismay that the departure had taken place several days earlier. Someone then had the bright idea that a plentiful assortment of non-Slavonic faces could be found in our polyglot publishing house. The staff had therefore been asked to report at the railway station first thing in the morning. They were duly marshalled into plausible-looking 'national delegations' and packed into a train with all the usual business of bouquets, embraces, red banners and a brass band playing the 'Internationale'. The train glided out but stopped again at the end of the platform, just beyond camera-range, and the delegates went off to work. Marian was thankful that she had not been involved. The cynicism of the exercise came as a considerable shock.

My talks and articles brought in useful fees to supplement my book royalties and her salary. We needed a lot of roubles to maintain even our simple standard of life, for as temporary residents we missed many advantages and allowances. Our rent was high, we ate as well as we could, and we went to the theatre. If we fell ill—as we did, briefly but alarmingly—we had to pay the doctor when at last we secured one.

My Robin Hood story had sold several thousand copies in the English language—more than in England. A German translation followed. They printed 8600, which meant in Russia that they sold practically that number. A young man had got as far as translating the first chapter into Russian. With its description of serfdom in medieval England, it reminded him (he insisted) of the conditions his own grandfather had known. On the strength of this first chapter the book was accepted by OGIZ, the 'State Publishers of Children's Books'. They would print 100,000 copies. As these were sure to be sold, they would pay me at once the maximum sum permitted, 75 per cent. I should have left the country long before the final 25 per cent was due, so they gave me a letter to another organisation, the Literary Fund, which was empowered in the circumstances to give me the balance at once and reimburse itself later. It was no wonder that I contrasted such figures ruefully with my sales at home and decided that Soviet publishers at least were gentlemen, despite the tiresome restrictions which prevented their transmission of royalties abroad.

We wanted to see more of the country and we were given every encouragement. It was arranged that I should write a documentary travel story about two English children in the Soviet Union. The formula was like that of the *Young Traveller* series, launched in Britain a decade later, to which I myself was to contribute several volumes. I would tour for some time—Moscow thought it odd that I insisted on taking my wife—and the book would be written in some quiet holiday-home on the Black Sea.

Quite apart from the official reluctance to let any foreigner loose in Russia, such a trip obviously demanded some companion to interpret interviews (for our Russian was fragmentary) and to battle for railway-tickets, seat-reservations and hotel-rooms, almost everywhere in short supply. It was suggested that we took with us a girl from the publishing house, who would gladly make it her month's holiday if we paid her expenses. Pauline Greneblum was a rather prim Russian Jewess, who wore pince-nez and a steeply tilted beret, and was equally fluent in English, French and German. Only rarely did she confuse her languages. 'If we cross here,' she warned us as we were about to step off the kerb with scarcely a vehicle in sight, 'the policeman will siffle at us.' In the monastery catacombs at Kiev she explained that the electric light had been put in since the Revolution. 'Before that the monks had their scandles.' Pauline watched over us like a nanny. Doubtless she had her instructions. But she never pushed Soviet propaganda down our throats.

We began with a twenty-four-hour train-journey to Kiev, third class, sleeping on wooden benches in a richly proletarian atmosphere of garlic and other odours. We travelled second class only on longer stretches. Though I had amassed a large sum from my various advances, we were going to need it all. I had no expense allowance and only one important privilege: our sheaf of introductions included a general letter to the Intourist hotels, authorising us to use them and pay in roubles.

We loved Kiev. The city retained a hint of Western elegance, the people looked smarter and gayer. Our week there was well filled. One morning Pauline swept us off to meet the Ukrainian Writers' Union. We sat round a flower-decked table and I was welcomed in no less flowery terms by men of letters old enough to be my father or grandfather. What could I do but bask in such unaccustomed, if unmerited, recognition? Photographs were taken. As we left, one bearded Ukrainian with a charmingly impulsive gesture snatched the flowers from their vase, wrapped the dripping stems in a newspaper, and presented them to Marian. Without pausing for breath, Pauline whirled us away to another part of the city for harangues of welcome by the Ukrainian teachers. The programme was comically similar. Marian even collected a second damp bouquet.

'We shall lunch', Pauline promised us, 'at a wonderful sanatorium for tubercular children. In the forest.'

We drove there. It was dusty over those dirt roads in an open car. The Director and his colleagues welcomed us. Eloquently. We were conducted through the spacious grounds from one dormitory hut to another, saluted by shrill and smiling little patients. Marian and I were dying on our feet. At each fresh building we murmured to each other, 'This *must* be where we eat', but always it was another dormitory. The Director was justly proud of the modern and efficient plumbing, and could not pass a lavatory without demonstrating that the cistern responded to the pull of the chain. '*Prekrasny!*' we gasped politely, 'Splendid!' or, when that grew monotonous, '*Ochin khorasho!*' signifying, 'very all right'. We made up a private little song afterwards, with the refrain:

Ubornaya, ubornaya,
Prekrasnaya ubornaya!

meaning, 'Lavatories, lavatories, luvverly lavatories'. At long last we reached the dining-room and our well-earned meal. After more complimentary speeches we were escorted to our car. I had shaken the final hand when a shy-looking little man rushed up with a bouquet twice the size of those we had already been given. I stood up in the car, about to launch into yet another speech of thanks. Marian pulled me down. 'It's the same flowers,' she hissed. 'He's only been looking after them for me.'

From Kiev we flew to Kharkov, both too horribly air-sick in that small plane to appreciate the landscape beneath us with its pattern of vast cornfields and blazing yellow hectares of sunflowers. After a day or two Pauline managed to get second-class berths for the long train-journey across the Don to the northern foothills of the Caucasus. Arrived at Ordzhonikidze, we found the hotel full, for a mountain storm had washed away a bridge and all traffic was suspended over the Georgian Military Highway. Pauline used all her blandishments upon the manager. 'Author?' he echoed contemptuously. 'We have too many authors! My own

Kiev, 1935. An informal reception given by the Ukrainian Writers' Union
Geoffrey and Marian Trease seated, left and centre; the Russian interpreter, Pauline
Greneblum, standing behind Marian Trease

brother is an author.' To make matters worse our arrival had coincided with that of a whole party of English lady sociologists with a suave Polish émigré from Bloomsbury as their courier. At last by superhuman efforts Pauline secured us accommodation. A few minutes later she rushed in to us almost in tears. 'Dr O.', she said, naming the Pole, 'says he must share my room. He says he will respect me, but I am afraid.' Luckily there were three beds in our room, so she spent the next two nights with us.

The Military Highway reopened as soon as sappers could improvise a bridge, and we crossed the Caucasus to Tiflis, a long day's bus-ride through wild scenery, the highest pass being nearly eight thousand feet above sea-level. We liked Tiflis, with its clattering two-horse carriages and its swaggering moustachioed Georgians with their sheepskin caps and silver-handled daggers and slanting rows of cartridges across their chests. We celebrated our wedding anniversary in an underground restaurant, eating *shashlik* and drinking red Georgian wine. In letters to my mother I had played down the discomforts and given an enthusiastic account of all the wonders we were seeing. She merely replied, with her innate distrust of unfamiliar experiences, 'Poor Marian, what she has had to go through!'

At Batum we had an experience we had certainly not expected in the Soviet Union: we went round a tea-farm. We walked through bamboo plantations and saw groves of orange-trees. Then we embarked in a steamer and sailed for two or three days along the Black Sea coast, that incomparable mountainous coast which Jason must have seen when he sought the Golden Fleece. We called at Sukhum, Sochi, and various other ports until at last we landed at a Crimean seaside town we had then never even heard of, Yalta. Here we were to have a week or two at a hotel on the front, followed by the month booked for us at a holiday-home.

Yalta had a Mediterranean climate which upset all my preconceived ideas acquired from reading about the Crimean War. A wall of dove-grey precipices sheltered the place from the north. Below them was a humpy coastal strip, lush with vineyards, orchards and tobacco-fields. The beaches were littered with monumental Russian sun-bathers. I found the complete absence of commercial exploitation as impressive as the scenery.

We went to the old Tsarist palace at Livadia, where Stalin, Roosevelt and Churchill were one day to hold their historic conference, and we took a motor-launch excursion to the architecturally fantastic villa at Alupka, a mixture of English Elizabethan and Alhambra Moorish. We spent a bibulous afternoon at some famous wine-cellars and a bug-disturbed night at Artek, the show-piece among all the Young Pioneer camps. It was the one occasion when we encountered bugs in strength. We had to climb through the window of our hut and spend most of the night on a chilly verandah overlooking the sea. Waiting for dawn, we let our fancy roam over England and her superior comforts, especially bacon and eggs and marmalade. When it was light enough to read we had nothing but my tiny copy of *A Shropshire Lad*, in those circumstances unbearably nostalgic.

Otherwise, our visit to Artek was enjoyable enough, especially a picturesque open-air entertainment put on by boys and girls of the various Soviet nationalities. On our return to England I suggested an article on the camp to the editor of the *Boy's Own Paper*. He havered, and I feared that once more political prejudice had won the day. But no. 'There's just one thing,' he said awkwardly, 'could you say as little as possible about half the campers being girls?'

An expected remittance from Moscow had not arrived and at this point of the journey we were desperate for funds. With great difficulty we convinced Pauline that we could now manage by ourselves until the date when we moved into the holiday-home, and she returned to Moscow. I had a canary-yellow polo-necked sweater, much admired by the Russians. I sold it surreptitiously to an Intourist guide. We developed the habit of lingering in the hotel lounge before mealtimes and dropping into conversation with English or American tourists. It was not only that we ached to talk with compatriots and hear uncensored news from the West. There always came a moment when they said, 'Are you coming into the dining-room?' and *we* said we couldn't afford to, and they made the invariable response—they had spare coupons for meals they had never taken, so would we do them a favour by using a couple and not breaking off such an interesting conversation?

Somehow we survived until it was time to enter the holiday-home, a little way up the cypress-dotted hillside above Tchekhov's villa. All guests were subjected to a searching medical examination on arrival and the doctors seemed greatly concerned about my thinness until they finally wrote me down as an 'asthenic type'. But our hungry days were over. The holiday-home provided a solid if unexciting diet, which we were able to vary with meals in the town as soon as my money came through from Moscow.

The life in general there proved equally solid and unexciting. As the special Writers' Rest Home, elsewhere in the Crimea, was fully booked, we had been sent to an establishment for Ukrainian Young Communists, and being neither Ukrainian nor Communist, but merely young, we found ourselves isolated and dull. The day opened with physical exercises, undemanding and rather comic, performed in the sun-baked garden to a tinkling piano. After lunch there was a compulsory 'dead hour' when I dared not break the silence with the patter of my typewriter. After dusk fell, the electric light was too weak for comfortable reading, and there were several power failures every week, usually at the most exciting moment of the film-show provided in the garden on alternate evenings. We were sometimes reduced to playing innocent card-games together, but after a puritanical Young Communist had rushed up to us in the lounge and, if we understood his vehement harangue, denounced our bourgeois degeneracy, we dared not do so in public again. Perhaps we were resented as a married couple with a room to ourselves. Most husbands and wives had to take their holidays separately.

September passed. I wrote my travel story, *Red Comet*, read the one English novel I could find, *Oliver Twist*, and worried about the impending Abyssinian war. Marian spent long days on the beach, acquiring a wonderful tan, and renewed her efforts to master Russian grammar. Then, more than readily, we drove along the dramatic coast road to Sevastopol and climbed into the train for the two-day journey north to Moscow. We felt we were already virtually on the way home.

There were, of course, hitches. There were no problems about my book, we had ample roubles for our last days in Russia, our exit-visas were forthcoming, and with winter about to clamp down on the Baltic sailings there were plenty of berths vacant. But once more the Soviet hunger for foreign currency asserted itself. All the roubles I had earned would not buy two third-class passages in a Russian vessel. We had to cable England for sterling.

We sailed home in the *Sibir* in late October after five months in the Soviet Union. In no subsequent conversation, to the best of my recollection, did anyone ask if we had 'ever been there'. Our relatives and more conservative friends preserved an embarrassed silence, much as though we had been in prison. At Nether Stowey, we heard long afterwards, an irate county lady went to our landlord and demanded that he evict us from the cottage. To his credit, as a shopkeeper who preferred to offend no one, he refused.

Front board and map endpaper from Red Comet *(published in Moscow, 1936)*

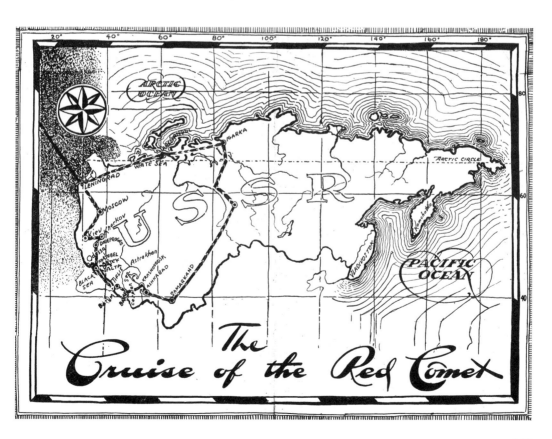

CHAPTER EIGHTEEN

Politics and Plays

SOMETIMES one does the right thing for what is shown later to be an absurdly wrong reason.

Despite our petty tribulations in Russia we came back more optimistic about the world in general and our own future. We had seen the sunny side of life there, concentrating on the children, who seemed happy, well nourished and appreciative of the arts. I had received some badly needed personal encouragement. A writer cannot endure endless disappointment without a break. That break had been given me. There was even at the back of my mind a thought not utterly fantastic in 1935 that, if the worst came to the worst, we could always return to this land which, with all its shortcomings, at least valued authors and gave them a livelihood. Luckily we never had to put this idea to the test.

So, however illusory our assessment of the future, we determined to delay no longer but to have a child. The cottage was unsuitable, opening on to a busy road and lacking both bathroom and garden. Much as we loved the Quantocks, if we had to move it seemed better to live nearer London and its supposed literary opportunities. The Oxford area attracted me, for its general memories were wholly happy. We thought in terms of another cottage, with more modern conveniences, perhaps in the Cotswolds. My brother Bill, as soon as he heard, recommended us to buy. True, we had no money, but Mother would give us a second mortgage, up to the full price, and I need never pay off the principal since it would one day be part of my inheritance. We accepted the offer gratefully, as well we might, wishing only that the possibility had been mentioned earlier, so that we could have postponed our parenthood a few months and chosen a new home at leisure.

As it was, we had to meet Bill and the family solicitor one cold spring week-end in Oxford, drive rapidly round a number of houses and bungalows, and make a snap decision on a still uncompleted building which appeared a sound investment rather than an inspiring background for a struggling man of letters. Our child was due in September, so we did not want our search prolonged. By June we were able to move in, which was quite late enough for all the curtain-hanging, floor-staining and other jobs that had to be done.

'Abingdon' conjures up pleasant mental images of ancient Thames-mirrored walls, Wren's elegant market-house on its arches, the cobbled courtyard and wistaria of the Crown and Thistle, the Abbey gateway, the gables and protruding upper storeys, the tall Georgian frontages with their fanlights and wrought iron. But our new home was a mile and a half from all this, for Abingdon was a bad example of the ribbon-development which defaced England in the nineteen thirties. Long tentacles of speculative building wriggled outwards along half-a-dozen country roads. Our house came almost last in a single line that petered out among the honey-golden cornfields towards Radley. We had a pleasant outlook towards the College on its low green hill and to the wooded heights of Nuneham Courtenay beyond the unseen river, but we and our neighbours must have created regrettable red-brick excrescences on a prospect unchanged since Matthew Arnold's time. Mercifully, we had a fringe of fir-trees and sycamores just inside our front fence, partly veiling us and compensating a little for the house's lack of character, and there was no building on the opposite side of the road. We called the place Green Garth, for the garden was a segment of grass field, most of it so little disturbed by the builders that we could leave it thankfully as lawn. At the back, where this was impossible, I planted some fruit-trees. I remember so vividly digging the holes in the shallow, gravelly ground. Those were the first months of the Spanish Civil War, in which my generation felt such an agonising involvement. We were conscious of the wider conflict impending if the democracies did not wake up. I dashed off a few lines of verse which, though I no longer deluded myself that I was cut out for a poet, relieved my feelings and may still be of interest in so far as they caught my mood in 1936:

Marian, Jocelyn and Geoffrey Trease in the back garden of Green Garth, Abingdon, 1937

> I must be swift, and plant my apple-tree
>   Where the builders have made their wilderness
> Of sand and broken brick. Or I'll not see
>   The imagined garden putting on the dress
> Whose lines and tints I dreamed, and the young tree
>   Spreading its silver arms in loveliness.
> I must be swift. And you—be swift for me.
>   Lift soon your misty blossoms to caress
> The stooping clouds, before War's devilry
>   Makes here a second shattered wilderness.

Our daughter Jocelyn was born in late September at the local cottage hospital somewhat alarmingly named the Warren. Our wanderings were now necessarily over. We settled down

151

to much the same suburban domesticity as our neighbours, except that I did not depart each morning to Pressed Steel or Morris Motors but could be glimpsed through our front bow-window, rattling away on my typewriter, or across the fields at the back, pensively strolling along the footpaths. Our neighbours were civil, but writers puzzled them. As before, we found ourselves isolated, Marian especially, being tied by a baby, though it was I who felt the greater need for society. A writer suffocates in a social vacuum. Yet when he settles in a strange place he has none of the ready-made contacts that other men take for granted. He meets no colleagues, staff, clients, pupils or patients. He may pass a week with no outside conversation but the barber's.

The accepted antidote for such isolation is to join organisations. I joined two. I read in the local paper that an attempt was being made to revive the Abingdon Labour Party. I learned also that the town possessed, in the Guild of Abbey Players, one of the best amateur dramatic societies in the country, which had just won the British Drama League trophy at the Old Vic. The Labour Party was so short of talent that I quickly found myself chairman of the branch, the Guild so rich that I was lucky to obtain the shortest speaking role in *Richard of Bordeaux*. The contrast between these two activities underlines the two levels on which the thoughtful person was compelled to live in those years. In some moods one felt so sure that war was coming that it seemed frivolous to waste energy on anything but political agitation. At other moments one faced problems more trivial but also more immediate. The gas-bill must be paid until the world itself went up with a bang. And, if the bang was coming, was there not all the more reason to enjoy the innocent transitory pleasures while one could—a visit from old friends, a good meal, a night at the theatre in Oxford, a walk on Boar's Hill, or the daily after-breakfast excursion with Jocelyn in her push-chair to see the ducks on the pond by Radley church?

Those two or three years in the Labour Party, my sole experience of working in a political association of any hue, gave me some valuable and amusing insights into the democratic system. Sitting on the divisional executive I saw a little behind the scenes in the adoption of a parliamentary candidate and the appointment of a salaried agent. Writers seldom make good committee members, but a stint of such service, with its constant accidental revelations of human nature, can be quite good for the writer himself.

The constituency was in those days a forlorn hope for Labour and I doubt if Transport House worried much about us. Had we mattered, headquarters would scarcely have allowed me to be branch chairman of the biggest town in the division, for I was quite without experience or accurate knowledge of the party line on most issues. Where I did know it, I frequently disagreed, and never let my official status deter me from voicing the most unorthodox opinions. Labour Party Socialism I regarded as analogous to Church of England Christianity, with room in it for every individual's interpretation. Even Bill Warbey winced at my cheerful indiscretions when he visited us and saw me in action, and, as his subsequent parliamentary career showed, he was never himself an exemplar of party discipline.

I recall meetings in Abingdon's hideous Corn Exchange and on the gracious cobbled market-square outside. I recall a summer's evening in Wantage, mounting my soap-box under the indifferent gaze of King Alfred's statue: my fellow-speaker, that day, was Elizabeth

Pakenham. But more of my memories are of addressing children and dogs on otherwise deserted village-greens. Conditions in some parts of Berkshire were still semi-feudal. 'Oh, there's plenty listening all right,' we were assured by our solitary local contact. 'See all them open windows? They're listening—but they're scared of being seen listening to a Labour man.' This was mildly encouraging, but a terrible strain on the voice. Even in Abingdon itself one shopkeeper explained why his donation must be anonymous. 'If you're a Liberal you lose some Conservative customers but you do get the Liberals, and t'other way round. If you're Labour you offend 'em both, and your own party go to the Co-op!'

In one corner of the constituency, however, we had the sincere and influential support of a peer. He employed a very smooth butler who shared his views but had been heard to say darkly, 'His lordship has still a great deal to learn about Socialism.' Once, when entertaining a Labour M.P. who was to address a meeting in the village hall, the peer conferred anxiously with the butler. It would be too early to serve dinner before the meeting, too late afterwards … 'I fancy, my lord, that something in the nature of a high tea is indicated.' 'And just what *is* a high tea?' The butler's version of this meal was something I myself enjoyed on a later occasion when I was the speaker. Half-a-dozen of us sat spaced along the two sides of a long table, separated by what seemed like yards of polished wood, so that conversation was difficult and each place-setting required its individual jam-dish as well as its pepper and salt. Scrambled eggs were offered reverently by a liveried footman, and the tea could not have been poured more ceremoniously if it had been château-bottled.

Our struggles were not always waged in such an urbane atmosphere. At this period two of Labour's future cabinet ministers, Sir Stafford Cripps and Aneurin Bevan, had been cast into the wilderness for advocating a united front against Fascism. One evening a fiery colleague of mine on the divisional executive drove over to see me. He was organising a meeting in Wantage to be addressed by Bevan, then in deep disgrace at Transport House. Would I be the other speaker? I agreed cheerfully, and had the stimulating, if testing experience of sharing a platform with, probably, the foremost Socialist orator of his generation. This political indiscretion put the cat among the local party pigeons. On the following Saturday my colleague and I were carpeted by the rest of the divisional executive. Waiting downstairs in the Abingdon office, I felt like an undergraduate summoned to a critical don rag. Pitiably innocent of party rules and procedure, I only now began to realise the enormity of my offence. When we were at last called in, I was nerved for expulsion.

The pleasures of martyrdom, however, were denied me. I had left our joint defence to my capable colleague who sailed zestfully into action against the solemn-faced comrades ranged along the table. By what authority, he demanded, had this extraordinary meeting been convened to sit in judgement upon us? The divisional chairman answered that the decision had been agreed at a hastily summoned gathering of the principal officers, who felt that our unconstitutional behaviour must be dealt with firmly and at once. Who was asked to this gathering, my fellow-rebel persisted? The party agent glibly reeled off the names. Chairman, vice-chairman, and so on … As he finished, my colleague pounced like a terrier. 'There are *two* vice-chairmen. Wasn't the other invited?' There was a moment's awkward hesitation. 'No.' 'Why not?' The answer sounds too good to be true, but it was really made:

'Because we knew perfectly well he wouldn't agree!' My colleague was not the man to miss an opening like that. In five minutes he had the court-martial standing on its head and the chairman almost tearfully offering his own resignation.

Such parochial triumphs brought no comfort at a time when Hitler's power was spreading unopposed through central Europe. We went on, speaking to tiny and apathetic audiences, achieving nothing. The policy we were advocating, which caused us to be regarded at best as pitiable cranks, at worst as unpatriotic menaces, was the one to which Churchill unhesitatingly committed the nation three or four years later, a whole-hearted alliance with Russia against the Nazis.

For me the personal lesson of this period was that an author does not make a good politician. His urge is to use words to express the truth as he sees it, as fully and frankly as he can. A politician, to succeed, must use words far more often to say as little as possible, safeguarding himself with ambiguity. I learned also that I could never be at ease treading a party line, even the wavy indeterminate line of a democratic mass organisation. No party could ever be right on every issue, and when it was wrong I should never be good at keeping my mouth shut. I began to dislike propaganda and develop a passion for objectivity. This development was completed during the year I later spent in the Army Educational Corps, but it was in progress, radically affecting my work as a writer, long before the war began.

That work had continued diligently but without conspicuous success. I perhaps showed lack of enterprise in not writing a book on our Russian trip, but too many people had done so, often on the basis of much shorter visits, and I had vowed before going that I would resist the temptation. I did make some capital out of my experiences by writing articles and lecturing, but financially this did not amount to much.

I did no more copy for the puff papers after our return from Russia and only one book for my original publishers, whose Left-wing imprint set a hopeless handicap on any children's story aimed at the general market. We agreed amicably that I should do better to seek my fortune elsewhere. The trouble was that most of the established publishers who handled juvenile books had a far less generous attitude to their writers.

Thus, I approached one ancient and much-respected house with the synopsis of a new kind of children's mystery story—it was new then—in which there should be no melodramatic sensation but only the kind of incident that boys and girls might conceivably encounter on a real holiday. I was encouraged to go ahead, but when I delivered the manuscript I was shattered by the answer that, though it was entirely satisfactory, the firm had decided after all not to proceed with the idea. I pointed out the injustice of this, and received the rather grudging reply that, after consulting its travellers, the firm was prepared to publish my story after all, but on one condition: it must be the start of a series, there must be a companion volume for simultaneous publication, and I must deliver this within six weeks or the offer lapsed. If the publishers had imagined that this was a certain and dignified way to get out of the situation by setting me impossible conditions, they were disappointed. I needed the money, I could not waste the labour that had gone into the first book. I set to work instantly and without a day's break. I was subject to streaming head-colds and high temperatures that occasionally put me out of action for a week at a time. It was late winter and I was terrified lest some such affliction should upset all my calculations, so I conceived, planned and wrote that second book in nineteen days. The contract for the pair was niggardly, but I had to take what terms I could get. One concession which my struggle wrung from the publishers may indicate the general scale of their generosity: '… and £10 (Ten Pounds) on a further edition of 10,000 copies of the book being sold at the full or a reduced price.'

I was more fortunate in other quarters. Basil Blackwell had just started a series called 'Tales of Action' with the aim of combining excitement and literary quality. L.A.G. Strong, C. Day Lewis, and Rex Warner were contributors. Here was my chance. I had outgrown my initial desire to correct the old Henty bias with a partisan counterbalance on the Left, but I believed that there were many things that could be said usefully in children's fiction and yet still acceptably to an open-minded publisher. I found my theme in the first ventures of the East India Company. The true story of William Hawkins, his voyage and journey inland to Agra, offered all the adventures I needed, and at the same time it unanswerably supported the statement I wished to make: that the English had first gone to India neither to build an empire nor to preach Christianity, but to trade at a fantastic rate of profit. I did my research, far more than ever before, in the Union library in Oxford. The book, *In the Land of the Mogul*, came out in 1938, and the London *Evening News* paid it the compliment of printing a column-length extract.

That year it almost seemed that my work was beginning to move. Membership of the dramatic society had revived my boyhood itch to write for the theatre. A short play was needed for a club evening. I obliged with a one-acter, exotically set on a Pacific island twenty years in the future, with a quartet of castaways learning abruptly of the social changes that had taken place in the outside world during their long isolation. The title, *After the Tempest*, was at once an echo of Shakespeare, my heroine being a modern Miranda with no experience of civilisation, and an allusion to the man-made catastrophe which was supposed to have turned that civilisation upside down. Forecasts that the hereditary peerage had been abolished and the public schools made co-educational struck my fellow-members as exquisitely absurd, and they resolved to make my play their entry for the Welwyn Festival, an important six-day contest which they had never managed to win. There was a preference for fresh material, indeed an extra prize for new plays, and they felt that my 'fantastic comedy' might improve their chances.

I was fortunate in my producer, A.K. Boyd, a Radley College master who had written a standard book on production and thoroughly knew his job. Of the five players two subsequently became professionals. But the competition was keen: twenty-four societies were participating throughout the week, seven with a new play. Our team, because of their long cross-country drive, were allotted a place on the Saturday. The suspense was thus relatively brief. Within a few minutes of the curtain's falling on the fourth and final play in the evening's programme, it rose again to reveal the beaming adjudicator, Miles Malleson, ready to deliver his verdict. We sat tensely through the obligatory but agonising preliminaries and the detailed criticisms of the four productions we had just seen. At last he announced the awards. Abingdon took not only the main trophy but the prize for the best new play. In a delirious dream we went out into the summer night and crossed to the big hotel for the dance with which the Festival traditionally ended. Between whirls, people came up and said nice things. A pleasant couple talked about film possibilities. Their names, which meant nothing to me at the time, were Sydney and Muriel Box. Malleson wagged a jovially reproving finger and told me I had thrown away a marvellous idea by using it for a one-act play. I said that I thought one act was as much as the joke would stand. 'Next time you get an idea like that,' he said, 'if you can't see how to make three acts of it, just get on to me!' As we drove back to Berkshire at three o'clock in the morning I felt an unaccustomed sensation of triumph. Nor did anti-climax immediately set in. Monday brought a summons from the B.B.C. and a day or two later we went up to Alexandra Palace for the cast to televise a scene on the somewhat rudimentary service then in existence. Later, the play was accepted for publication in J.W. Marriott's annual volume, *The Best One-Act Plays of 1938*.

This taste of success encouraged my theatrical aspirations.

Unity Theatre had been recently established in a converted chapel near King's Cross, had made a great hit with Clifford Odets' *Waiting for Lefty*, and wanted new British plays of 'social significance'. It was a club theatre, playing six nights a week including Sunday, and the productions were of a high standard. Unity had the backing of many professionals with Left sympathies. They included Miles Malleson himself, André van Gyseghem, Tyrone Guthrie, Sean O'Casey, Lewis Casson and Paul Robeson, who had offered to act in the anonymous company himself if a suitable play could be found.

With Robeson in mind I wrote and submitted a full-length script entitled *Colony*. Again I chose an imaginary island as my setting, but this time the treatment was realistic. The drama arose from a strike of West Indian sugar-workers, but I was trying to draw attention to the whole problem of colonialism, irrespective of continent or flag. My approach, I was told with apparent approval, was reminiscent of Galsworthy. Whether the compliment was deserved or not, it sufficiently indicates the trend of my writing towards a calmer balance. In the end I did not get Robeson for my negro strike-leader, but I was promised a production of my play.

It was to be directed by Bert Marshall, who had studied in the Russian theatres and was a keen exponent of the Stanislavsky method. I was impressed and bewildered by the thoroughness with which he threw himself into the preliminary work of the production. As novice playwrights go, I was treated with unusual gentleness. There were the inevitable rewritings, the passages that had to be cut or shortened or built up, but many an established dramatist must have suffered far more heartaches. Bert knew what he wanted and could explain it to me, and, so long as I knew, I was willing and usually able to do it. Otherwise, he paid me the compliment of assuming that I knew best what the play was about, and never forgetting that it was my play that was being put on. Sometimes my wishes were almost embarrassingly deferred to, and I was consulted on nuances in my own script that had never occurred to me. I was thankful that I lived sixty miles away and was not expected to run up and down continually. Once I recall answering him with a heartfelt cry, 'For God's sake treat me as a dead classic and do as *you* think!'

Herbert Marshall (director of Colony*) and his wife with Marian and Jocelyn Trease at Green Garth, 1939*

The play was cast with some difficulty, since most of the black characters were to be played by coloured people, harder to assemble in the London of 1939 than they would be now. The strike-leader was Robert Adams, a professional actor from British Guiana, who had just been in the film of *King Solomon's Mines*. Other parts were taken by an American negro, a Nigerian, and a mulatto girl. To the dismay of the white idealists in the theatre it was found that the black members of the cast did not necessarily coalesce into fraternity. The American, I was warned in a pained whisper, seemed to think himself a cut above the West African. But everyone settled down eventually into a happy family, welded together by Bert's dynamic direction. The Governor's lady was played by the wife of a very famous dance-band leader, and her main worry was lest her off-stage identity should leak out, with undesirable political repercussions for her husband.

Once he had assembled his cast, Bert subjected them to the full and merciless Stanislavsky treatment. I still have a copy of the questionnaire they had to complete after the first reading. 'What parts of the play stood out most clearly? With whom did you sympathise and by whom were you particularly moved? How would you generalise about the characters, e.g. petty bourgeois, heroism of progressive people, etc? What in your opinion did the author want to say and what did he actually say? Do they agree or differ?' Having answered these and half a dozen other questions, each player was ordered to 'make a close analysis of the character in writing', which was to include his 'social background, and development *to* position in the play, *during*, and *afterwards*'. I could not help feeling that, as author, I was getting off lightly. I had spasms of guilt that there was so much here that I had not myself worked out. I learnt a lot, without being called upon to admit it, and I privately resolved in all humility to do better next time.

None of this homework could be done in five minutes, but then, on the Stanislavsky scale, who thought in terms of minutes or even weeks? It was nothing for a production to be gestated months or even years. I was promised, however, that I should not have to be patient for ever. Unity was then running a political pantomime. When it came off, a North Country play would follow. I could hope to see the curtain rise on *Colony* round about Easter.

It did not. *The Babes in the Wood* proved unexpectedly—but most deservedly—popular. It was satire as the word was understood in those days, verbally brilliant, ingenious and gay even when it was most savage. The 'babes' personified Austria, just seized by the Nazis, and Czechoslovakia, about to be. The make-up of the two robbers, Hit and Muss, left no doubt as to their identity. The Wicked Uncle, with his rolled umbrella or his fishing-rod and deerstalker cap, was just as unmistakably Chamberlain. But, since Unity was a club theatre, neither Downing Street nor the Foreign Office nor the dictators could apply pressure to stop the show. People flocked to see it. You had to, whatever your political affiliations. It was so funny, everyone was talking about it, you could not keep away. And, what with the low annual subscription of one shilling and the block membership open to all kinds of organisation, there was only one real problem, to get a seat. The advance bookings poured in. It seemed as though *The Babes* would run for ever.

I tried to be philosophical and fill my mind with other things. In any case I could not afford to slacken in my work. I decided to try my hand at a novel again, and, as I had got nowhere with my early, over-autobiographical efforts, to make it at all costs funny. I was at the time much influenced by the early extravaganzas of Evelyn Waugh, and I was surprised, but not unflattered, when Orwell described me a little later as 'that creature we have long been needing, a "light" Left-wing writer, rebellious but human, a sort of P.G. Wodehouse after a course of Marx'. For, at that time, I had read almost as little of Wodehouse as I had of Marx. In both cases, clearly, the influence had been indirect.

My novel was a disrespectful satire on royalty, still topical after the recent abdication, but once again I did what I had so often enjoyed doing in my childhood stories—I invented a country, not a third tropical island but a Baltic state I named 'Bothnia' and slipped in between Finland and Sweden. It made a change, too, from the Balkans and the Ruritanian landscape. I wrote the novel at high speed and in high spirits, titled it *Such Divinity*, and sent it off to Evelyn Waugh's own publishers, Chapman & Hall, who accepted it. It was all rather intoxicating. Everything seemed to be going right for me. Now I was a novelist as well.

I was basking in a wayward personal sunbeam while all the world was growing dark around me—a fact of which I could not fail to be agonisingly conscious. Would my novel ever reach publication-day, would *Colony* go on, or would the whole future splinter under Hitler's fist? It is easy now, with hindsight, to smile at the way we still scuttled about on our own affairs in 1939 like so many ants. How could we delude ourselves with little personal ambitions, especially those of us who were shouting loudest about the imminent danger of war? Yet war was *not* inevitable. The argument still rages, between those who had inside knowledge at the time, as to whether there would have been a war if Hitler's bluff had been called. And would there have been one if the alliance with Russia, so painfully achieved in 1941, had been more enthusiastically sought in the early summer of 1939? Whether or not it could have been achieved, and had had the desired effect, we clung to the hope until the black day in mid-August when the Nazi–Soviet pact was announced.

It must be remembered too that most of us expected the war, if it *did* come, to be an instant holocaust, something like what eventually happened to Dresden, not the six years of dull dogged endurance which it turned out to be. So—there would be continuing peace or annihilation, probably by poison gas. One or the other. It was ironical, twenty years later, to be told by a new rising generation that we could not possibly imagine what it felt like to live in the shadow of the Bomb.

Like so many of my contemporaries, I went on living at two levels, public and private, as I had done throughout the past three years—through the Abyssinian and the Spanish wars and the unchecked advances of Germany and Japan. On some days I despaired. On others I hoped. In any case life, for the moment, went on. And if the moment was a happy one, why not grasp it with enhanced appreciation?

That phenomenal Christmas entertainment, the Unity pantomime, came off at last in May. The next play was likely to run for a couple of months. The curtain might rise on my long-delayed *Colony* before July was out. Bert Marshall's patiently matured production was coming to life. Rehearsals were going well. He had designed a splendid set. All the action took place on the seaward terrace of Government House. This gave him scope to use a variety of acting areas, with plenty of steps, and a wide choice of natural routes for exits and entrances.

At last we got a firm date: 25 July. My novel came out a week or two earlier. It was treated generously by the critics. Howard Spring in the *Evening Standard* found it 'most entertaining; and, if this be a first novel, most promising', and James Agate in the *Daily Express* called it 'a nice bit of fun'. The *Sunday Times* also spoke of its 'wicked fun' and recommended it as 'a pungent bit of satire'. Seán O'Faoláin called me 'a bright young novelist' and even the Olympian *Times Literary Supplement* had 'nothing but praise for the speed and ingenuity'. I am conscious of some embarrassment in thus rummaging among my age-yellowed press-cuttings—it makes one a sitting target for wicked fun and pungent satire oneself—but I can think of no other way of conveying in a few lines either an objective view of the book which mattered so much to me at the time or the exaggerated hopes which its reception encouraged.

Of the first night of *Colony* I have, surprisingly, no very significant memories. Nervous and excited I must have been, but I felt no compulsion to pace the drab streets around King's Cross while the play's fate was being decided. Instead I sat in the back row with Marian, buttressed by old friends and new, and thoroughly enjoyed a performance to which, I was well aware, I had made only one of many contributions. It seemed to go well. People laughed where, more or less, I had meant them to. The dramatic episodes seemed to grip, I could tell from the silences and tensions of the auditorium. And it *was* a splendid set they had given my play, gay with coloured umbrellas and tropical foliage, and lending itself to imaginative lighting as full sunshine changed to evening and then a night enlivened by a naval bombardment. I felt none of the disappointment that dramatists traditionally suffer when their fancies are made flesh.

You know when a play goes well. You can tell when your neighbours and the people back-stage are merely being kind. My brother George had come up from Nottingham, my Oxford friend Bob Leaney from his Sussex vicarage, other friends from my Bloomsbury period and even my schooldays, and newer ones from the Abingdon dramatic society. A lot of my past life was concentrated in that back row of the stalls. It was a memorable occasion. I wish I could remember it more clearly.

In the days that followed, the press criticisms brought no disillusionment. The eulogies of the extreme Left were, of course, predictable but there was warmth in unexpected quarters, and once more the best record of the affair, and my own deducible reactions, is provided by a few short quotations. The professional theatre weekly, the *Era*, described the play as 'a pleasant surprise … a piece of really effective theatre written by a young man who obviously has a political cause at heart; but who, nevertheless, is concerned with creating real characters'. The *Queen* said that there was 'no ranting' and spoke of 'impressive thoughtfulness and lucidity, and a good deal of humour'. Lionel Hale gave us two columns in the *News Chronicle*—he was dead against that kind of propaganda in the theatre, but he very fairly testified that the play was 'most ably written' and had 'a continuous excitement' and that Bert's set was 'a little miracle of intelligent compression'. The *New Statesman* said: '*Colony* has the wit that makes good entertainment and the understatement of convincing propaganda, and should certainly be visited by anyone who deplores the silliness but admires the competence of the ordinary West End success.' One of the most agreeable remarks came from a specialist journal in which one would not normally seek quotable dramatic criticism. The *Accountant* concluded a eulogistic paragraph: 'I should like to see *Colony* receive the wider publicity of a West End presentation.'

I do not know whether that sentence was a shot in the dark or truly inspired. At all events, Unity was already planning to expand its activities and mount fully professional productions in the West End. The Kingsway Theatre was taken. Now, thanks to the favourable reception of *Colony*, it was decided to go ahead and make my play the first of a season. It passed the Lord Chamberlain without difficulty and, while the original production continued to play to good houses, plans went forward to open publicly at the Kingsway in September.

If my mind had not been full of more pressing matters I might have paused for a little personal stocktaking on that 11 August, which was at once my thirtieth birthday and the sixth anniversary both of my marriage and of my taking the plunge as a freelance writer. At all events I had not been idle in those six years. To start, so to speak, from the bottom end of the list, I had written one rejected novel, one children's book ditto, a mass of unsold articles and stories, and an equally formidable mass of 'editorial publicity'. On the other hand my accepted work, discounting these puffs, comprised the new novel, a dozen children's books, *Walking in England*, my one-act play, and some scores of journalistic contributions, a few of them in quite well-known magazines and newspapers.

Turning to the financial side, I might have been less pleased with the outcome of six years' work. So far the receipts from those fourteen books, the journalism, the puff articles, the plays—and the B.B.C. fee for that moment of glory on television—totalled £812 13s 5d, making an average yearly income of £135 8s 11d. Still (I should probably have consoled myself) it was well above the basic thirty-odd shillings a week then earned by a farm labourer. Anyhow the lean years were behind me. I was 'a bright young novelist'. In another month or so I should be a West End playwright.

Before me now as I write is the preliminary agreement I signed with Unity Theatre (West End) Ltd. The date on it is 30 August 1939. Forty-eight hours later, Hitler attacked Poland.

It was a long time before any bombs dropped on England, though we all expected them. The London theatres closed at once. When in due course they were allowed to reopen, it was obvious that a controversial play like *Colony* could not be put on while Britain was at war. Six years later, when the war was over, it was equally obvious that the play was out of date. The colonies themselves were on their way out.

In 1939 I did not foresee this ironical ending. Nor had I any inclination, at that time, to sit about bewailing my bad luck. There was some understandable uncertainty whether any of us would be alive in 1940, still less in 1945. We were nerved for the poison gas and the *blitzkrieg*.

The enemy bombers did not appear. The evacuees did, with nits in their hair which they distributed liberally. I listened to endless official announcements and instructions on the radio, my ears cocked for a mobilisation order that never came. For, on the slender qualification of the War Office Certificate 'A', which I had taken at school, I had some months earlier volunteered for the lowliest of the various officer reserve categories that had been instituted since the Czech catastrophe.

So the first alarms died away, the theatres reopened in a blacked-out London but without my play, and we entered the notorious winter of the 'phoney war' with almost no perceptible action in any field. Poland was down and out, Britain and France had not budged, and there was much talk of a negotiated peace with Hitler. It was a strange, unreal season. One felt numb with anti-climax. Life was in suspense, no plans possible. It was like queueing up in a dim corridor before a blank door with no notion of when it would open or what, if anything, lay beyond.

One might as well do something. I sat down to my typewriter and began another novel, *Only Natural*, drawing on my bitter-sweet experiences of life in Abingdon but transferring that stolid Berkshire town to a more attractive setting, the thinly disguised Quantock Hills. This was the novel Orwell specially liked, calling it 'a lovely picture of English provincial life, with all its hypocrisy, its charm and its absurdities'. Frank Swinnerton found it 'kind and tolerant comedy'. Candid friends told me it was maturer than its predecessor. I knew myself that it was less crude and that I was straining less for laughs. I hoped that, if the world went on, I might be able to write a good deal more in that vein.

Still the unreal non-war continued. His Majesty seemed in no pressing need of my services. I started a new children's adventure story, set in Elizabethan times and entitled *Cue for Treason*. It was laid partly in Cumberland, partly in the London theatres. All my frustrated passion for the theatre welled up in it and mingled with my strong affection for the Lakeland scene. As I drew near to finishing it in April, the war flared suddenly to life with the invasion of Norway and Denmark. When I signed the contract all was uncertainty and confusion again, and I wondered whether the story would ever appear in print. In fact it did, though within a week or two of its publication all warehouse stocks were obliterated by Nazi bombs. Most publishers suffered similarly. *Only Natural*, though published by a different firm, was also blown not to glory but to oblivion, and today I have no copy on my own shelf.

One was sometimes tempted to ask oneself, 'What's the use?' But I knew that I had to go on writing. All my life I had had to write. Even a world war could not stop the itch.

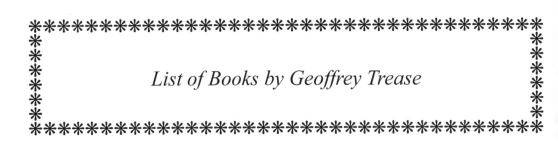

List of Books by Geoffrey Trease

NOVELS
> *Such Divinity*, 1939
> *Only Natural*, 1940
> *Snared Nightingale*, 1957
> *So Wild the Heart*, 1959

TRAVEL
> *Walking in England*, 1935

HISTORY
> *The Italian Story*, 1963
> *The Grand Tour*, 1967
> *Matthew Todd's Journal* (editor), 1968
> *Nottingham, a Biography*, 1970
> *The Condottieri*, 1970

CRITICISM
> *Tales Out of School: a Survey of
>   Children's Fiction*, 1949; revised
>   edition, 1964

PLAYS
> *After the Tempest* (in *Best One-Act Plays
>   of 1938*)
> *Colony* (unpublished, produced at
>   Unity Theatre, 1939)
> *Time Out of Mind* (unpublished,
>   produced by the Repertory Players at
>   the Comedy Theatre, 1967)

For Young Readers

JUNIOR NOVELS
> *Bows against the Barons*, 1934;
>   revised edition, 1966
> *The New House at Hardale*,
>   serialised 1934, book 1953
> *Comrades for the Charter*, 1935
> *The Call to Arms*, 1935
> *Missing from Home*, 1937
> *Mystery on the Moors*, 1937
> *The Christmas Holiday Mystery*, 1937
> *Detectives of the Dales*, 1938
> *In the Land of the Mogul*, 1938
> *Cue for Treason*, 1940
> *Running Deer*, 1941
> *The Grey Adventurer*, 1942
> *Black Night, Red Morning*, 1944
> *Trumpets in the West*, 1947
> *The Hills of Varna*, 1948
> *Silver Guard*, 1948
> *No Boats on Bannermere*, 1949
> *The Secret Fiord*, 1949
> *Under Black Banner*, 1950
> *Black Banner Players*, 1952
> *The Crown of Violet*, 1952
> *The Barons' Hostage*, 1952
> *The Silken Secret*, 1953
> *Black Banner Abroad*, 1954
> *Word to Caesar*, 1956
> *The Gates of Bannerdale*, 1956
> *Mist over Athelney*, 1958
> *The Maythorn Story*, 1960
> *Thunder of Valmy*, 1960

Change at Maythorn, 1962
Follow My Black Plume, 1963
A Thousand for Sicily, 1964
The Red Towers of Granada, 1966
The White Nights of St Petersburg, 1967

CHILDREN'S STORIES
The Mystery of Moorside Farm, 1949
The Fair Flower of Danger, 1955
The Dutch Are Coming, 1965
Bent Is the Bow, 1965
The Runaway Serf, 1968
A Masque for the Queen, 1970
A Ship to Rome, 1971

TRAVEL
Red Comet, 1936
The Young Traveller in India and Pakistan, 1949
The Young Traveller in England and Wales, 1953
The Young Traveller in Greece, 1956

HISTORY AND BIOGRAPHY
Fortune My Foe, 1949
The Seven Queens of England, 1953
Seven Kings of England, 1955
Edward Elgar: Maker of Music, 1959
Wolfgang Mozart, 1961
Seven Stages, 1964
This Is Your Century, 1965; revised edition, 1969
Seven Sovereign Queens, 1968
Byron, a Poet Dangerous to Know, 1969

CRITICISM
Enjoying Books, 1951
The Young Writer, 1961

PLAYS
The Dragon Who Was Different, 1938
The Shadow of Spain, 1953

About the Author

Margaret Meek, *Geoffrey Trease*, a Bodley Head Monograph, 1960

Girls Gone By Publishers

Girls Gone By Publishers republish some of the most popular children's fiction from the 20th century, concentrating on those titles which are most sought after and difficult to find on the second-hand market. Our aim is to make them available at affordable prices, and to make ownership possible not only for existing collectors but also for new collectors so that the books continue to survive. We also publish some new titles which fit into this genre.

Authors on the GGBP fiction list include Angela Brazil, Margaret Biggs, Elinor Brent-Dyer, Dorita Fairlie Bruce, Christine Chaundler, Gwendoline Courtney, Winifred Darch, Monica Edwards, Josephine Elder, Antonia Forest, Lorna Hill, Clare Mallory, Helen McClelland, Dorothea Moore, Violet Needham, Elsie Jeanette Oxenham, Malcolm Saville, Evelyn Smith and Geoffrey Trease.

We also have a growing range of non-fiction titles, either more general works about the genre or books about particular authors. Our non-fiction authors include Mary Cadogan, James Mackenzie, Brian Parks, Stella Waring and Sheila Ray. These books are in a larger format than our fiction titles, and most of them are lavishly illustrated in colour as well as black and white.

For details of availability and when to order (please do not order books until they are actually listed) see our website—www.ggbp.co.uk—or write for a catalogue to Clarissa Cridland or Ann Mackie-Hunter, GGBP, 4 Rock Terrace, Coleford, Bath, BA3 5NF, UK.